SECRET
PARIS
AN UNUSUAL GUIDE

Jacques Garance and Maud Ratton

PHOTOGRAPHS
Stéphanie Rivoal

D0813725

JONGLEZ PUBLISHING

We have taken great pleasure in drawing up *Secret Paris* and hope that through its guidance you will, like us, continue to discover unusual, hidden or little-known aspects of the city.

This practical guide is the result of over five years' work: all the places mentioned are accessible and clearly indicated on the plans at the beginning of each *arrondissement*.

Descriptions of certain places are accompanied by thematic sections highlighting historical details or anecdotes as an aid to understanding the city in all its complexity.

Secret Paris also draws attention to the multitude of details found in places that we may pass every day without noticing. These are an invitation to look more closely at the urban landscape and, more generally, a means of seeing our own city with the curiosity and attention that we often display while travelling elsewhere …

Comments on this guidebook and its contents, as well as information on places we may not have mentioned, are more than welcome and will enrich future editions.

Don't hesitate to contact us:
  E-mail: info@jonglezpublishing.com
  Jonglez Publishing, 25 rue du Maréchal Foch
  78000 Versailles, France

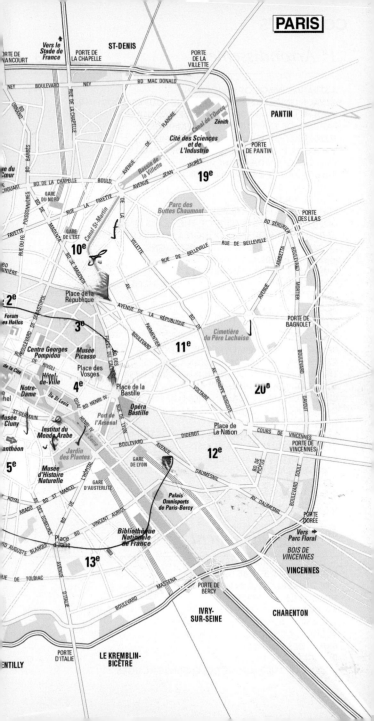

CONTENTS

1st Arrondissement

2nd Arrondissement

3rd Arrondissement

4th *Arrondissement*

5th *Arrondissement*

CONTENTS

6th *Arrondissement*

7th *Arrondissement*

8th Arrondissement

9th Arrondissement

CONTENTS

10ᵗʰ *Arrondissement*

11ᵗʰ *Arrondissement*

12ᵗʰ *Arrondissement*

13th *Arrondissement*

14th *Arrondissement*

15th *Arrondissement*

CONTENTS

16th Arrondissement

17th Arrondissement

18th *Arrondissement*   MM

19th *Arrondissement*

20th *Arrondissement*

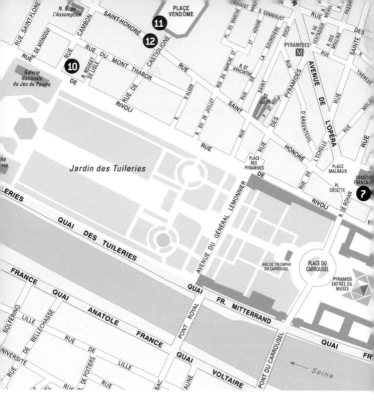

1st *Arrondissement*

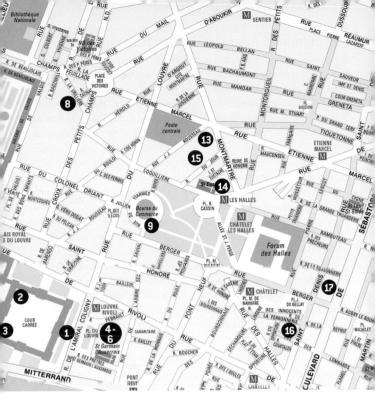

Real human hearts in Louvre paintings?

An amazing story recounted in 1950 by Y. Ranc in an article published in *Paris Presse* was circulating at the beginning of the 20th century: once, for certain artists, the human heart possessed an extraordinary quality that other animal hearts did not – it alone secreted an organic substance, known as *mumie*, which when mixed with oil made a unique glaze for paintings. Until the 18th century, it was difficult to get hold of this unusual raw material: corpses came from the Orient and the price of extracting and conserving the *mumie* under satisfactory conditions was high. Since the 17th century in France it had become customary to deposit the hearts of members of the royal family, including that of Anne of Austria, in the chapel of Val-de-Grâce. With the Revolution, the sansculottes dispersed the royal assets, among which were the embalmed hearts. They soon found buyers from the artists' fraternity. The painter Drolling, notably, found himself owner of the heart of Anne of Austria, that of Marie-Thérèse and even that of the duchess of Montpensier. His painting *Intérieur de Cuisine* in the Louvre thus still retains today traces of the ground-up royal organs on the canvas. Although this hypothesis makes an interesting anecdote, it has not been borne out by scientific analysis of the works so in the end may only be a legend.

Why does the axis of the Louvre oratory pass through the centre of Cour Carrée?

At the beginning of the 17th century, Louis XIII realised that the Louvre, then under construction, had no chapel. It occurred to him to use the church that Jacques Lemercier was building for the Oratorians. In the end, though, the church and the Louvre palace were never united. Under Napoleon the chapel became a Protestant temple, but its name (Temple de l'Oratoire) and orientation is a reminder of its historic links with the Louvre.

The Louvre: out of alignment with the Champs-Élysées

Although the perspective from the Louvre to the Champs-Élysées, to the Grande Arche de La Défense, as far as Cergy-Pontoise, is well known, it is in fact not quite straight: the Louvre, parallel to the Seine, is actually several degrees out of alignment with the axis of the Champs-Élysées. To find the perfect alignment you need to stand a few metres from the pyramid near Louis XIV's statue. This, a copy of a work by Bernini, was commissioned in 1988 during the refurbishment of the Grand Louvre and placed in alignment with the Champs-Élysées. Logical enough as the initiator of this perspective was none other than Louis XIV himself.

A STRANGE IMAGE OF NAPOLEON ①

Napoleon disguised as Louis XIV!

Musée du Louvre – Colonnade de Perrault

The colonnade facing the place du Louvre, designed by Claude Perrault and begun under Louis XIV, bears a curious detail.

Although during his reign Napoleon had had his image sculpted near the centre of the colonnade, at the Restoration of the monarchy (1814/1815–30), an attempt was made to disguise that awkward heritage by adding a wig to make the bust look more like Louis XIV.

Just below, the letter L stands for Louis XVIII (see monograms on Louvre façades, page 20), which in 1815 replaced the N of Napoleon I. But below the medallions carrying the letter can be seen some bees, one of the principal symbols of the First Empire: was it out of laziness or subversion that the sculptor neglected to obliterate them?

Traces of Napoleon in Paris

Although a major figure in the history of France and Europe, Napoleon Bonaparte is little celebrated in the capital city of a country that he would profoundly transform. Rue Napoléon was renamed rue de la Paix in 1814, Pont Napoléon became Pont National in 1870 and avenue Napoléon became avenue de l'Opéra in 1873. Avenue Joséphine also became avenue Marceau and avenue du Roi-de-Rome, avenue Kléber. Here nevertheless is a suggested walk that picks up traces of the emperor in Paris, other than the eponymous **rue Bonaparte**. In place de l'Étoile, commemorating the Republic's victory over the German Empire in 1918, the **Arc de Triomphe** (architect Chalgrin 1806, completed in 1836), is a high point of the Napoleonic capital. The left face of the arch, giving onto the Champs-Élysées, represents the apotheosis of 1810 (the year of the reunion of Rome with the Empire) with the French Emperor as a semi-naked Graeco-Roman hero (Cortot, 1836). On the other side of the arch, towards Neuilly, avenue de la **Grande-Armée** recalls the vast concentration of troops at Boulogne planning to invade England, the gymnastics of their about-turn to the east, and victory at **Austerlitz** (2 December 1805). Place de l'Étoile is ringed by rue de **Presbourg** (1805 treaty with Austria) and rue de **Tilsitt** (1807 peace with Russia and Prussia). From the Étoile towards the Seine, avenue d'**Iéna** (victory over Prussia, 1805) leads to the bridge of the same name (1807). Imperial eagles (Barye, 19th century) grace the bridge. Avenue de **Wagram** and avenue de **Friedland** also celebrate Napoleonic victories.

Towards place de la Concorde, the Champs-Élysées becomes "**La Voie Triomphale**" that leads to **Invalides**, on the other side of the river. This refuge and hospital established by Louis XIV for his army veterans houses Napoleon's tomb in the Église du Dôme, by Jules Hardouin-Mansart.

From Concorde, on the other side of the bridge you can see the Palais-Bourbon (colonnade by Poyet, 1806), today the home of the Chambre des Députés – under Napoleon it was the **Corps Législatif**. It squares up some distance away with the Église de la **Madeleine** (Vignon, 1810, completed 1824), originally seen as a "Temple de la Gloire" by Napoleon whose decision it was that the two buildings with their similar colonnades would face one another. From Concorde, **rue de Rivoli** (Bonaparte's victory in Italy, 1797) the construction of which was planned and begun in 1802, runs east, together with rue de **Castiglione** (victory 1796, opened 1802) and rue de **Mont-Thabor** (victory 1796, opened 1803), before opening out onto rue and place des **Pyramides** (first victory of the Egyptian campaign, 1798). Rue de Castiglione opens onto place Vendôme, where stands the **Vendôme**

column, perhaps the best known of the Napoleonic memorials in Paris. Originally Napoleon wanted it surmounted by a statue of Charlemagne, but he was persuaded to place his own image there instead. The bronze plaques affixed to the column, inspired by Trajan's Column in Rome, were cast from cannons taken from the Russians and the Austrians. The **railings** separating rue de Rivoli from the **Jardin des Tuileries** were designed and built during the Empire, with the intention of offering Parisians a view of an ancient park that had long been open but hidden behind walls and gates on the north side. From **place des Pyramides**, still heading east, rue de Rivoli runs parallel to the **north wing of the Palais du Louvre**, planned since the 17th century by the royal architects but only built by Percier and Fontaine in accordance with the wishes of the emperor, and partly only after the fall of the Empire, as far as the gateways that now let motorists cross through the Louvre towards the Seine. In the palace courtyard at this level stands the **Arc de Triomphe du Carrousel**, built by the same architects in one year (1806–07) to celebrate victory at Austerlitz (1805) and the Presbourg peace. The eight statues surmounting this monument, inspired by the arch of Septimius Severus in Rome, are faithful reproductions of soldiers in the uniform of the imperial army. The **Palais du Louvre, west wing completed under Napoleon III** is rich in "N" monograms, as much as for this monarch as for his uncle, who was the model for two sculpted busts (see below). A little further to the east, in the centre of place du Châtelet, the **Palmier fountain** dating from 1808 celebrates the victories of the emperor and the immortality of his glory (statue by Boizot). A fair distance from here, not far from

today's Périphérique, are the **boulevards "des Maréchaux"** that surround Paris, so named between 1860 and 1870 in honour of Napoleon I's generals. They are all represented, with the exception of Grouchy and Marmont, whose weakness, even treachery, Bonaparte refused to forgive. Duroc is not there either: although killed in action he was only "palace marshal", i.e. in command of the imperial palaces. The "Egyptomania" of the consular and imperial age is covered separately (see page 47).

ROYAL MONOGRAMS HIDDEN IN THE LOUVRE COURTYARD

Secrets of the Cour Carrée

Cour Carrée du Louvre

The Louvre in general, and the Cour Carrée in particular, conceal some fascinating details that will impress your partner, or new-found friend, in Paris! Here's how: sit down peacefully on the fountain in the courtyard, preferably in the evening when the twilight and the superb lighting make it one of the most magical places in the city. On each wing of the courtyard are inscribed the ciphers of the sovereigns who had them built.

On the pyramid side, left of the Pavillon de l'Horloge: Henri II (H and H interwoven with a double C for Catherine de Médicis, which could quite easily be confused with a double D in homage to Diane de Poitiers, his mistress).

On the river side to the right: K (signifying Karolus) for Charles IX, H for Henri III, HDB (Henri de Bourbon) for Henri IV and finally HG for Henri IV and Gabrielle d'Estrées, his mistress.

On the Pavillon de l'Horloge to the right: L and LA for Louis XIII and his wife Anne of Austria.

On the other wings, built by Louis XIV, you can read LMT (Louis and Marie-Thérèse, the queen) and LB (Louis de Bourbon.)

Outside the courtyard, these monograms are found at regular intervals on the façades and have the same significance.

NEARBY

Evidence of the site of Charles V's donjon ③

In the Cour Carrée, gratings and a circle traced on the paving mark the outlines of the former donjon of Charles V. Visit the Sully aisle to see the base of this donjon and the Salle des Maquettes, open only at weekends, which retraces the different stages in the construction of the Louvre.

RAT BALL
OF SAINT-GERMAIN-L'AUXERROIS

An enigmatic ball

2, place du Louvre
Tel.: 01 42 60 13 96
www.saintgermainauxerrois.cef.fr/
Open Monday to Saturday 8am–7pm, Sunday 9am–8pm

Just opposite the Louvre, on the façade of Saint-Germain-l'Auxerrois church, under the central gargoyle, is a very enigmatic *boule aux rats*. This, unlike other rat balls in France (see box) is not surmounted by a cross and the rats, eyed by a devilish-looking cat, seem to be running out of the ball rather than being swallowed up by it. Even today explanations for this vary … Might it signify that the church is the sole remedy for the ills of the world, represented by the rats and the sphere?

The history of Saint-Germain-l'Auxerrois, the parish of the kings of France, goes back to the 7th century. Sacked by the Normans, entirely rebuilt from the 12th to the 16th centuries, the only vestige of that time is the 12th century Romanesque tower, a superb door, the choir and the 13th century chapel of the Virgin. Inside the church are magnificent 15th century windows, a wooden sculpture of Saint Germain and a stone one of Saint Vincent, as well as a beautiful carved wood altarpiece.

The four rat balls in France

There are four rat balls in France: other than the above, there is one at the Cathedral of Saint-Siffrein at Carpentras (see *Secret Provence* in this series of guides), another at Le Mans cathedral and the fourth at the church of Saint-Jacques de Meulan in the Yvelines *département*.

Ashes for artists

A discreet plaque, fixed to the sixth pillar on the right in the church, bears an inscription that reads: "In this church, in accordance with the wishes of Willette carried out by Pierre Regnault, the artists of Paris in solidarity with their comrades from around the world have come here since Ash Wednesday of the year 1926 to receive the ashes and pray for those among them who must die within the year." This is the testament of the painter and illustrator Adolphe Willette (1857–1929). The vow is still respected today and the prayer is generally read by a well-known artist.

TOWN HALL OF THE 1ST ARRONDISSEMENT

Town hall or church?

4, place du Louvre
Tel.: 01 44 50 75 01
Open Monday to Friday 8.30am–5pm, Thursday until 7.30pm and Saturday
9am–12.30pm

Strolling by Saint-Germain-l'Auxerrois you cannot fail to notice the 1st *arrondissement* town hall, harmoniously blending in with the church.

Built in 1858 on the orders of Baron Haussmann who wanted it to echo the neighbouring church without replicating its shape and details, this magnificent Renaissance Hôtel de Ville is the work of Jacques Ignace Hittorff (1792–1867), the architect of the Gare du Nord.

NEARBY

Carillon, 1st arrondissement Town Hall

Bell ringing: 10am, 12pm, 2pm, 4pm, 6pm and 8pm
Extra bell ringing Sundays at 12.45pm
Concert Wednesdays 1.30pm–2pm

Between the town hall and the church is a belfry that is impossible to dissociate from the two buildings. Despite what you may think, this is not the church belltower but belongs to the town hall. Built in 1858 to plans by Théodore Ballu, 38 m high with four unequal storeys (the lower two square in plan, the upper two octagonal), this belltower has one of the most perfect and complete carillons in France. Consisting of 38 bells in three octaves, it dates from 1862 and is the oldest in Paris. It has been entirely restored since 1975. Also visible from rue de l'Arbre-Sec.

The bloody bells of Saint-Germain-l'Auxerrois

This church is also associated with a bloody episode in the history of France. Its bell, donated by François I in 1527, was rung to announce the beginning of the Massacre of Saint Bartholomew's Day (massacre of Protestants by Roman Catholics in Paris on 24 August 1572).

VISIT THE COMEDIE-FRANÇAISE ⑦

Lift the curtain on the Comédie-Française:
Delacroix, Renoir ...

1, place Colette – Métro: Palais-Royal-Musée-du-Louvre
www.comediefrancaise.fr
Individuals: prebooked guided tours (online) every Saturday and Sunday at
11am (Children after 10 only, the visit lasts 1.30pm)
Admission: full rate €12/ concessions €8
Groups: guided tours Saturday and Sunday, leaving between 9.30am and 10.30am
Maximum 30 persons over 12 • Admission : 250 euros for an adult group,
130 for a school group. • Further information and booking: 01 44 58 13 16
frederique.brunner@comedie-francaise.org

L ittle known by most Parisians, the Comédie-Française open its doors
each week end for a visit that is an excellent way of reaching the private areas of this theatrical institution: the guided tour includes the public
sections accessible to spectators during shows (lobby, main stairway, public
foyer, galleries and auditorium), but also the private sections. Thus you will
see the Salle du Comité, Foyer des Artistes and Foyer La Grange, which has
several unusual artworks on display. At the entrance, Talma,* immortalised
by David d'Angers, welcomes visitors who are then directed to the stairway
leading to the administrative offices where busts of Molière, Corneille and
Racine are enthroned, polished by the superstitious hands of the actors. On
the various floors, each of which bears the name of an artist, are a number of
masterpieces: a portrait of Molière by Mignard, another of Talma by Delacroix and, in the Salle du Comité, a Renoir. A gallery of busts represents the
great 18th-century authors next to a corridor covered in Lucien Jonas sketches. The ceiling of the intermission gallery (visible during performances) is
decorated with Guillaume Dubuffe paintings lorded over by a marble sculpture of Voltaire by Houdon. The main attraction in the Société des Coméd-
iens-Français collection (of which only 20% is on show) is nevertheless the
armchair that Molière borrowed from his ailing uncle. The story goes that
he died seated there in 1673 while playing Argan. In homage to the "actors'
patron", the Salle Richelieu built by Victor Luis between 1786 and 1790 is
commonly referred to as the *Maison de Molière.*

*A great figure of French theatre, he set the fashion for costumes, as formerly the actors played in their street clo-
thes. He was Napoleon's favourite actor, which is why the Comédie-Française found a home in place Colette.

GALERIE DORÉE OF THE BANQUE ⑧ DE FRANCE

A rare example of Regency style

2, rue Radziwill
Métro: Bourse
Prebooked tours only on Saturday mornings at 10.30am
Individuals: visits organised by Centre des Monuments Nationaux
(around five a year) • Programme at www.banque-france.fr (Organisation/
History/Gallery photos) or www.monum.fr (News/Visiting conferences/
Programme) – Direct registration at the Centre, terms indicated
Groups: write to PHAR – 19-2205- Banque de France, 75049 Paris Cedex 01

The organised tour offers the rare privilege of admiring the magnificent gilded gallery of the Hôtel de Toulouse, headquarters of the Bank of France. The building as we see it today is the result of a number of improvements and the annexation of several houses adjoining the original main structure. Models displayed at the entrance to the Galerie Dorée give an accurate idea of the work carried out over the years. In 1635, Louis Phélipeaux, lord of La Vrillière, acquired a small plot left vacant by Richelieu. He decided to build, under the direction of François Mansart, a *hôtel particulier* in which one of the rooms, the Grande Galerie, covered in white stucco and of imposing dimensions (40 m long by 6.5 m wide) would serve as an exhibition space for his ex-

ceptional collection of Italian paintings. In 1713, the Count of Toulouse acquired the mansion, which was naturally renamed Hôtel de Toulouse. The new owner, none other than the illegitimate son of Louis XIV and Madame de Montespan, appealed to Robert de Cotte, the king's chief architect, to refurbish the building as a princely residence. In pure Regency style, gold dominated the Grande Galerie and its decoration was updated to illustrate the hunting and marine themes dear to the heart of the Count of Toulouse. In 1793, after the Revolution, this property was declared national heritage and the artworks were distributed among several museums (a Veronese and a Poussin can be seen at the Louvre). The Galerie Dorée was used at the time for paper storage for the Imprimerie Nationale, which had taken over the place. The Bank of France bought the mansion in 1808. In 1870, the gallery building required total restoration: the vault frescoes were thus copied and the Regency woodwork reintegrated into the design. Today the effect is perfect and the gallery, lit by its huge windows, is resplendent in its gilding

Tenir le haut du pavé

The expression "keep to the highest point on the pavement" (to consider oneself superior) dates from the time when pavements were still rare: in the middle of the street ran a stream of dirty water. High on the pavement, where the better-off walked, there was no sewage.

COLONNE MÉDICIS

Predictions of the astrologer ...

Rue de Viarmes
Métro: Louvre-Rivoli or Les Halles

Voüe de l'Hostel de Soissons bati par Catherine de Médicis, et conduit par Ioan Bullant Architecte du Roy.

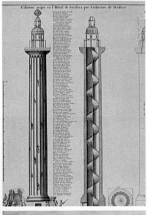

There is a mysterious column, not very noticeable although it is 28 m high, not far from Les Halles, just in front of the Bourse du Commerce [Stock Exchange].

Its history is intriguing: the Queen of France Catherine de Médicis, who was fascinated by astrology, had it built around 1575 by her architect, Jean Bullant, a few years after the construction of her magnificent residence, the Hôtel de la Reine.

The fluted tower, crowned by a platform reached by a spiral staircase with 147 steps, was once covered with a glass roof, but all that is left now is the iron frame. It was connected to the queen's apartments. This column, which is not mentioned in the plans for the construction of the mansion, some believe has a commemorative function: the intertwined ciphers of King Henri II and Catherine de Médicis (H and C) are believed to be a tribute to the king killed in circumstances predicted by Nostradamus.

Many feel that it is in fact a result of the queen's obsession with astrology. After Nostradamus had made his prophecies and left for Provence, Catherine de Médicis is reported to have ordered the column built to serve

as an observatory and a place for the experiments of Cosimo Ruggieri, her astronomer, sorcerer and childhood friend. Nothing if not mysterious, Ruggieri was among other things the author of the famous prediction of the death of his benefactor. The four corners of the column's capital are oriented with the four points of the compass. The preservation of this column, after the palace was destroyed in 1748 and the construction of the current Bourse du Commerce, is almost a miracle.

Where and when was Molière really born?

The plaques at 31, rue du Pont Neuf and 98 rue Saint Honoré contradict each other. The first states that Molière was born there in 1620, and the second that he was in fact born on 15 January 1622 at the other address! Experts seem to support the second claim.
The Molière Fountain, at 37, rue Richelieu, was the first statue in Paris to honour someone other than a king.

CERCLE SUÉDOIS

An explosive club

242, rue de Rivoli
Métro: Concorde
Tel.: 01 42 60 76 67
www.cercle-suedois.com
Open to the public the second and last Wednesdays of the month 6pm–9pm

A short distance from place de la Concorde, the very discreet and chic Swedish Club, founded in 1891, has a historic room. It was here that Alfred Nobel, the inventor of dynamite, wrote his explosive testament on 27 November 1895, founding the famous Nobel Prize. The desk is still there and may be seen twice a month on Wednesday evenings.

Also on these evenings you can have a drink in the Club's very beautiful salons, which look out on the Jardin des Tuileries (see *Secret Bars and Restaurants in Paris* in this series of guides). The ambiance of a bygone age is a delight for connoisseurs and for those who appreciate a rather old-fashioned setting. On the walls are many paintings by Swedish artists, including Zorn, Grünewald, Dardel and recently Lennart Jirlow.

NEARBY

Standard metre: 13, place Vendôme ⑪

Along with the standard metre on a plaque in the Rue de Vaugirard, the standard metre in place Vendôme, to the left of the Ministry of Justice, allowed the French to familiarise themselves with the new unit of measurement adopted during the Revolution (see page 118). In contrast to that displayed in rue de Vaugirard, this standard metre is not in its original place: it was moved here in 1848.

Commemorative plaque of the Texas Embassy ⑫

At the corner of rue de Castiglione and place Vendôme, an inscription marks the site of the embassy that Texas, yes Texas, opened in Paris in the nineteenth century. It is often forgotten that after gaining independence from Mexico in 1836 Texas was an independent republic until 1845, when it was annexed to the United States.

Balconies in place Vendôme in tribute to Louis XIV

On both sides of the column, the balconies of place Vendôme are a tribute to the glory of Louis XIV. They are decorated with an allegory of the sun surrounded by gilded leaves, which clearly make reference to the sovereign known as the Sun King. Earlier, this square was named place des Conquêtes or place Louis-le-Grand, also in honour of Louis XIV and had at its centre an equestrian statue of the king sculpted by Girardon. Inaugurated in 1699, it was demolished during the Revolution.

NEARBY

Ceramic tiles of the Cochon à l'Oreille *restaurant*

15, rue Montmartre • Tel.: 01 42 36 07 56 • Open from 6 until midnight every day except Sunday • Lunch from €15 • Traditional French cuisine

Superb decoration with ceramic tiles from 1914 on the theme of Les Halles (the former central market), which was a short distance away (see *Secret Bars and Restaurants in Paris* in this series of guides).

Medallion of the Crypte Sainte-Agnès ⑭

1, rue Montmartre

A medallion in the form of a fish marks the entrance to Saint Agnes' crypt, recalling a certain Jean Allais, who made a fortune from selling fish in this neighbourhood in the 13th century and had a church built, of which only this crypt remains. It is open for exhibitions: ask at Saint-Eustache church.

Origin of the semicircular niches on the Pont Neuf

Completed in 1604, the Pont Neuf is one of the oldest bridges in Paris. When it was built, it had three unique characteristics: it had footpaths (which did not come into general use until the 19th century), it was decorated with 384 *mascarons* (grotesque masks on the cornices), and it did not have houses built on the roadway, with the exception of the shops that were installed in the *demi-lunes* that still exist today.

NEARBY

Musée du barreau de Paris

Hôtel de la Porte. 25, rue du Jour
Tel.: 01 44 32 47 48 • Free entry only for groups on weekdays by appointment with the curator at 01 47 83 50 03

In the very beautiful mansion, Hôtel de la Porte, the small museum of the Paris Bar Council is not well known yet it has a very rich collection of exhibits evoking the history of the people and trials that have marked the course of justice since the 17th century.

Murder of Henri IV by Ravaillac ⑯

11, rue de la Ferronnerie

A plaque on the ground with a *fleur de lys* marks the spot where Henri IV was murdered in 1610 by Ravaillac.

The elephant at 3, rue de la Cossonnerie

The upper part of this façade is decorated with a beautiful elephant's head, probably inspired by Indian Muslim art (see page 107).

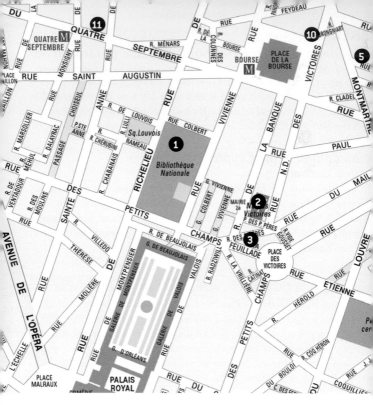

2ⁿᵈ Arrondissement

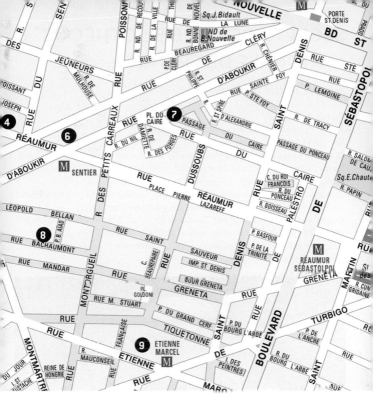

SECRETS OF THE BIBLIOTHÈQUE NATIONALE DE FRANCE ①

Secrets of the library

58, rue de Richelieu
Métro: Pyramides, Bourse or Quatre-Septembre
Tel.: 01 53 79 53 79 • www.bnf.fr
Temporary exhibitions: open from Tuesday to Saturday 10am–7pm and
Sunday 12pm–7pm. Closed Monday and public holidays
Annual closure beginning of September
Musée des Monnaies, Médailles et Antiques open Monday to Friday 1pm–5.45pm,
Saturday 1pm–4.45pm, Sunday 12pm–6pm, admission free
Guided tours for individuals: first Tuesday of the month 2.30pm, prebooking only
01 53 79 87 93 / 86 87 • Duration: around 1h30 • Admission: € 6.80
Access to reading rooms not allowed without accreditation (available from the
library website: www.bnf.fr)

Although the temporary exhibitions put on by the Bibliothèque Nationale and the Musée des Monnaies, Médailles et Antiques are well known to Parisians, less well known is a fascinating guided tour on the first Tuesday of each month that covers some of the rooms normally reserved for researchers or those with accreditation.

The famous Labrouste reading room, normally inaccessible, is impressive with its sixteen slim cast-iron pillars 10 m high supporting nine cupolas of translucent enamelled tiles. At the back of the room, an enormous glazed bay leads to the central stacks. Although empty since the printed material was transferred to the Bibliothèque François-Mitterrand, the place is still redolent with the smell of books.

When the reading room was opened in 1868, an ingenious system of pneumatic shuttles (which can still be seen) let readers request and receive works from the stacks. In the Regency-style Salon d'Honneur stands the original plaster model for Houdon's statue of Voltaire on which the marble statue in the Comédie-Française Salle d'Entracte (see page 23) was based. The philosopher's heart rests in the base of the statue.

Strangely, the Salle Ovale is off bounds, even during the guided tour, but you can admire its gigantic proportions (18 m high under a vast glass roof) from the outside. The tour ends at the Musée des Monnaies which houses a number of presti-gious items such as Dagobert's throne and the treasure of the Sainte-Chapelle.

Short covered walk for rainy days

The lack of pavements until the 19th century was the main reason for the vogue for covered passageways from the Revolution to the Second Empire: when it rained the streets quickly became a sea of mud. The construction of passages dealt with this problem: you could stroll around and keep dry.

Astute Parisians can still take advantage of them today if they forget their umbrellas. From the Louvre you can get to rue de Provence and rue Cadet via Palais-Royal, rue des Colonnes (covered) and the passages of Panoramas, Jouffroy and Verdeau, almost completely sheltered from the rain. The passage des Panoramas, No. 47, is home to Maison Stern (printer and engraver), a very attractive shop unchanged since 1830.

EX-VOTOS OF NOTRE-DAME-DES-VICTOIRES

Over 37,000 ex-votos cover the basilica walls and ceilings

Place des Petits-Pères • 6, rue Notre-Dame-des-Victoires
Métro: Bourse
Tel.: 01 42 60 90 47
Open daily 7.30am–7.30pm and Sundays 8.30am–8pm • Mass weekdays
8.30am, 12.15pm and 7pm, Saturdays 11am and 6.30pm, Sundays 9.30am,
11am and 6.30pm

Rather unexpectedly, the Notre-Dame-des-Victoires has a unique collection of over 37,000 ex-votos fixed here, there and everywhere. The prevailing atmosphere of contemplation and the expressions of gratitude of these thousands of marble plaques cannot fail to impress and move visitors, even non-believers. So take the time to examine these testimonials, some of which are particularly poignant.

Founded in 1629 by Louis XIII at the request of the Augustin brotherhood known as the "Petits Pères" (Little Fathers), the basilica was named Notre-Dame-des-Victoires in thanksgiving for the royal troops defeat of the Huguenots at La Rochelle. The king attributed this victory to prayer and the intervention of the Holy Virgin. As soon as the church was built a statue of the Virgin erected in the convent chapel evoked great devotion from worshippers.

In 1836, when the parish was becoming less popular with pilgrims, its priest, Abbé Desegenettes, twice heard the following command: "Consecrate your parish to the Very Holy and Immaculate Heart of Mary." He rapidly set up an association of prayers in honour of the Coeur Immaculé de la Très Sainte Vierge, which had the effect of greatly increasing the number of faithful and newly converted. Through his actions the abbot turned his church into an "immense hymn of love" of which the ex-votos now in the basilica bear ardent witness.

NEARBY

Trompe-l'œil *just beside place des Petits-Pères*   ③

Just beside place des Petits-Pères, the street windows of the bank building are only *trompe-l'œil*.

RUE RÉAUMUR FAÇADES

First prize in façades competition 1897/1898

116, 118, 124, 126 and 134, rue Réaumur
Métro: Bourse or Sentier

A succession of lofty and prestigious buildings constructed for the large textile manufacturers and printers at the beginning of the 20th century, rue Réaumur was opened up 1895–96 between rues Saint-Denis and Notre-Dame-des-Victoires.

Inaugurated in 1897 by Félix Faure, this street displays a profusion of very decorative façades that reflect the new planning regulations at the end of the 19th century (extended roofs, bow windows allowed). The architects mainly used a metal framework hidden behind stone frontages, into which they inserted vast glazed bays that let in the natural light needed for the activities of the locality. Several façades won prizes at the annual architectural competition launched in 1897/1898.

Note especially No. 116 (built by Walwein, for which he received the gold medal in 1897), No. 118 (built by Montarnal in the Art Nouveau spirit and an award-winner in 1900), and No. 126 and 134. The industrial building at No. 124, however, deserves special attention: built in 1905, it is different from the other designs of architect Georges Chedanne. The façade shows the all-metal framework of the building (note the steel beams supporting the metal bow windows), which does not detract in the slightest from the Art Nouveau delicacy of the ensemble.

NEARBY

Café Croissant: assassination of Jaurès ⑤

146, rue Montmartre
Tel.: 01 42 33 35 04
Open every day except Sunday 7am until 2am in the morning

As the frontage indicates, Café Croissant is a historic place: it was right here in the café that Jean Jaurès was assassinated on 31 July 1914. Inside there is a mosaic, a small statue of the hero and some contemporary press cuttings describing the event. The table at which he liked to linger has also been preserved.  The staff will be pleased to show you the rather sombre stain, still there after all these years, on the pale wood of the table – from the blood he lost in the attack. He had risen before collapsing a few metres away, where the mosaic is now.

The city walls of Charles V (1356–1420) and the Fossés jaunes (1543–1640)

After the defeat by the English at Poitiers in 1356 and the fear of an attack on Paris, Étienne Marcel, provost of the merchants, vowed to improve the city's defences. The artillery that was coming into use in the 14th century changed the deal: it was too costly to build a wall 30 m high (the height cannon balls could reach). The alternative was to build wide fortifications. Those of Charles V, including the ditches, extended over 87 m and had an embankment 30 m wide at the base and 3 m high, on top of which was built a wall 6 m high and 2 m thick. A century later, from 1529, François I decided to construct a wall with bastions. To the east and south, they were placed alongside Charles V's wall using, where possible, the *voiries*, i.e. the mass of all kinds of rubbish dumped outside the walls by the residents over 150 to 200 years. The dump was higher than the walls, compromising the defensive system. To the west, a new fortified wall, known as the *Fossés jaunes* because of the yellow earth, was built from the present place de la Concorde (east side) to Porte Saint-Denis. The new ramparts enclosed 300,000 citizens within 1,000 hectares. Other than the traces that can be seen in around the Sentier district (see opposite), some vestiges of these two walls are still visible:

– A section of wall (scarp and counterscarp) of Charles V's fortifications under place du Carrousel at the Louvre.
– Bastion No. 1 of the Tuileries: part of the bastion can be seen in the basement of the Musée de l'Orangerie (*Fossés jaunes*).
– A section of counterscarp at Bastille métro station, in the direction of Bobigny, line No. 5 (platform and access corridor).

NB: two other vestiges are not accessible to the public: in the basement of No. 39, rue Cambon and in the cellars of the Bibliothèque de l'Arsenal.

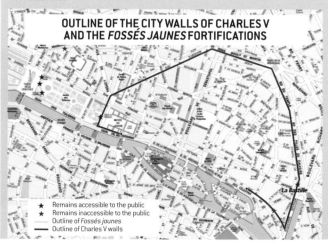

OUTLINE OF THE CITY WALLS OF CHARLES V AND THE *FOSSÉS JAUNES* FORTIFICATIONS

★ Remains accessible to the public
★ Remains inaccessible to the public
— Outline of *Fossés jaunes*
— Outline of Charles V walls

La Bastille

DIFFERENCES IN LEVEL OF THE LAND AROUND SENTIER

(6)

Remains of Charles V's fortifications

Passage Sainte-Foy
Rues de Cléry and d'Aboukir
Grands Boulevards
Métro: Sentier

Some topographical details of the Sentier district are very interesting evidence of the existence of the fourth and fifth Parisian fortifications between the 14th and 17th centuries: the walls built by Charles V and those known as *Fossés jaunes* (yellow ditches). Both used earth ramparts and ditches, which resulted in some incredibly uneven ground and differences in level.

From rue Sainte-Foy, passage Sainte-Foy leads to 263 rue Saint-Denis via a steep flight of steps which compensates for the difference in level between rue Sainte-Foy and rue Saint-Denis. More than just ordinary rough ground, this is evidence of the rampart on which Charles V's wall was built.

The route of **rues de Cléry and d'Aboukir** are also clear markers: the more elevated rue de Cléry was built on the outer side of the ramparts whereas rue d'Aboukir follows the ditch built in front.

All the Grands Boulevards, notably boulevards Saint-Martin, Saint-Denis, Bonne-Nouvelle and Poissonnière, were also built on the ramparts and the roadway frequently climbs and descends for no apparent reason, while neighbouring streets remain at the same lower level. The road is simply crossing the former bastions of the walls of Charles V and the Fossés jaunes: boulevard Bonne-Nouvelle crosses bastion No. 6. Just after Porte Saint-Denis the road climbs, with the left-hand pavement overhanging. Boulevard Saint-Martin, on the other hand, cuts through bastion No. 7, with pavements overhanging the roadway by almost 3 m. The steps in passage du Pont-aux-Biches give access to the rampart 7 m higher up. And rue René-Boulanger follows closely the path of the outer wall of the bastion. The recesses and projections of the **façades of Nos. 42–48, boulevard du Temple**, are the exact shape of bastion No. 8. A little further on, boulevard Beaumarchais, built on the rampart itself, forces rues des Tournelles and Saint-Gilles to climb steeply in the last few metres before they join it. On the other side of the road, steps have had to be constructed to descend to rue Amelot.

Scarp: inner wall of a fortification with ditch.
Counterscarp: outer wall of a fortification with ditch.

Egyptian revival in Paris

2, place du Caire
Métro: Sentier

*P*assage du Caire, the oldest of the Parisian alleyways (1798) as well as the longest and certainly one of the most animated, was inspired by the great souk of the Egyptian capital. Built on the site of the Filles-Dieu convent, it is said that some of the paving comes from the tombstones of the nuns. Apart from its name it bears no relation to the splendour and riches of Egypt, having been deliberately designed to attract more down-market traders. It does however open onto place du Caire, where the façade of No. 2 is covered with hieroglyphs and decorated with columns with lotus capitals and three heads of the goddess Hathor. The influence of the capitals of the Egyptian temple of Dandarah is very clear.

Probably constructed by the architect Berthier, the building dates from 1828 and the sculptures are by Gabriel-Joseph Garraud.

Over and above its exoticism, the structure has another unusual feature: look closely at the hieroglyphs on the recessed frieze and you will notice the caricature of a certain Auguste Bouginier. A pupil of Gros, in the midst of the Romantic period he was considered a late neoclassical. "Gifted with as much nose as spirit", Bouginier thus saw himself decked out with a nose of impressive size that has remained to this day. This nose is the last witness of a joke which would show him on a great number of walls around the city. Victor Hugo himself mentioned Bouginier's nose in *Les Misérables*.

La cour des miracles

Place du Caire was one of the twelve "*cours des miracles*" of 19ᵗʰ century Paris. A meeting place for all manner of crooks and outlaws, it was also the platform for a number of fake beggars who came here to practise their art. At the end of the day, work finished, they divested themselves of their accessories (crutches, false wooden legs, fake stumps) and went home. For those who dared venture into this notorious neighbourhood in the evening, the spectacle was stupefying: the blind suddenly regaining their sight and the deaf turning at the sound of their name called by one of their comrades. The nickname "miracle courtyard" soon stuck.

Origins of the bonne nouvelle district

The *cour des miracles* of place du Caire existed since the 13ᵗʰ century. In the 17ᵗʰ century, Louis XIV's chief of police, Nicolas de la Reynie, cleaned it up for the first time. On hearing the good news (*bonne nouvelle*), the residents so named their neighbourhood.

Vestiges of Egypt in Paris

Contrary to received wisdom, the Parisian infatuation with Egypt dates from before Bonaparte's expedition. From the mid-18th century, young artists sent to Rome were marked by Egypt: at the time researchers were looking for the Etruscan origins of Roman art. Pope Benedict XIV had opened an Egyptian museum at the Capitoline and an Egyptian room had been installed at the Villa Borghese in Rome. The young French artists thus came back home loaded with engravings by Piranesi, who had set himself up as promoter of this style. During the Revolution, with the help of the Freemasons, the Republic identified with the immoderation, cult of the dead and mysteries of Egyptian art. Bonaparte's Egyptian expedition of 1798 only followed a fashion already well established. The Napoleonic era nevertheless had enormous influence. Some streets were renamed and a number of monuments commemorate events of the expedition.

Other than the Louvre pyramid and its museum collections, the **Concorde obelisk** is the most famous souvenir. Donated by Mehmet Ali, in 1831, its twin was left in Luxor: it also was offered to France but the second half of the gift was officially declined until 1994 ...

Near **place du Caire, rue d'Aboukir, rue du Nil, rue de Damiette and rue d'Alexandrie** also owe their names to Egypt. Two fountains can also be attributed to this fashion. The famous **Fontaine du Fellah**, rue de Sèvres (near Vaneau métro) symbolises an Egyptian farmer (*fellah*). Built between 1806 and 1809, the statue was damaged and replaced by a copy in 1844. The **Fontaine du Palmier**, place du Châtelet, has a capital in the form of a palm tree surrounded by four sphinxes. There is also the Egyptian retro bathroom of **Hôtel de Bourrienne** (see page 213), the **west façade of Cour Carrée** which includes a fantastical representation of the goddess Isis, **Hôtel de Beauharnais** (now the German embassy) at 78 rue de Lille, the **Temple du Droit Humain** (see page 255), the **Louxor cinema** (junction of boulevards Magenta and de La Chapelle), **pillars with palm-tree capitals on avenue Ledru-Rollin** under the former railway line and an **Egyptian tabernacle in Saint-Roch church**. In all there are over a hundred sphinxes scattered around the city and a couple of dozen Egyptian-inspired tombs in Père-Lachaise cemetery, the country often being associated with eternity.

Finally, there are still two Egyptian mummies in a cave under the Bastille (see page 221).

Are there any maisons closes *left?*

On 13 April 1946, the famous "bawdy houses" (*bordels*) were made illegal throughout France. Thousands of prostitutes found themselves literally in the street. Although the 195 Parisian brothels were closed, some traces still remain of a time that is missed by some, in particular the important role they played in social order.

The most common relic is the street numbering: to be easily spotted the brothels feature plaques with a larger number than usual, or the shape of the windows and certain ornamental details may also give a clue to interested parties.

Thus you can still seek out these plaques that reveal the former use of an establishment ... such as **36, rue Saint-Sulpice** with its unequivocally large numbering. Men in cassocks, plentiful in the neighbourhood, were among the clients of a certain Miss Betty, and at **15, rue Saint-Sulpice**, where the name of the tenant Alys is still on the tiled floor and the mosaic of the former brothel's hammam on the second floor (now private). In the 9ᵗʰ *arrondissement*, 9, **rue Navarin** – Chez Christiane – was appreciated by fans of sadomasochism. The fine neo-Gothic façade has not changed. At **122, rue de Provence**, the well-known One Two Two has kept the façade only, and **50, rue Saint-Georges** – Chez Marguerite – has kept in two staircases a wood-painting showing the capture of a Sabine woman, naked, and a sculpture of women draped in the long tunics of antiquity. Le Chabanais, at **12, rue Chabanais** in the 2ⁿᵈ *arrondissement*, still has its two lifts which spared visitors embarrassing meetings: one could go up while the other went down ... The whorehouse at **32, rue Blondel** is probably the one with the finest vestiges (unfortunately very difficult to see, as the current trade in rue Blondel is not very much different from what it used to be ... Finally, at **6, rue des Moulins** (1ˢᵗ *arrondissement*), female cherubs have survived.

STAINED-GLASS WINDOW OF THE SOCIÉTÉ IMMOBILIÈRE DE LA CHARCUTERIE FRANÇAISE

Aesthetic charcuterie

10, rue Bachaumont
Métro: Sentier

Currently occupied by private societies and lawyers' offices, the building at 10 rue Bachaumont was built by Jules Michel for the Company of French Pork Butchers. Access is unfortunately controlled by an entryphone but through the glazed entrance to the building you can glimpse its superb hallway with walls covered in old signs from butchers' shops serving as commemorative plaques to the society's contributors, as well as paintings and a beautiful stained-glass window dedicated to the profession. If you're lucky the door might open unexpectedly and you can have a quick look inside to admire the bust of a former president of the corporation by Alfred Boucher. But be discreet as this is private property.

NEARBY

La tour de Jean Sans Peur   ⑨

20, rue Étienne-Marcel
Open daily 1.30pm–6pm
www.tourjeansanspeur.com
tjsp@wanadoo.fr
Tel.: 01 40 26 20 28

The only Parisian example of medieval military architecture (the Hôtels de Sens and de Cluny are not military and the Conciergerie and Tour du Vertbois have been largely rebuilt), the tower leans against part of Philippe Auguste's wall (see page 81). It was built to allow Jean sans Peur, Duke of Bourgogne, who had just assassinated Louis d'Orléans, brother of King Charles VI, to sleep securely, safe from possible reprisals. In 1477, on the death of Charles le Téméraire, son of Philippe le Bon and grandson of Jean sans Peur, Louis XI reunited Bourgogne with the kingdom of France.

Parisian records

Shortest street: rue des Degrés, 2nd arr. (5.75 m), is actually a flight of fourteen steps (with no entrances to buildings or houses)
Longest street: rue de Vaugirard, 6th–7th arr. (4,360 m)
Widest avenue: avenue Foch, 16th arr. (120 m)
Narrowest street: rue de Venise, 4th arr. (2 m), followed by rue du Chat-qui-Pêche, 5th arr. (2.50 m)
Highest point: Montmartre (129.75 m – rue Saint-Rustique, 13th arr.) and not in the 20th arr. as many claim (128 m)
Narrowest house: 39, rue du Château-d'Eau, 10th arr. (1.2 m).

NEARBY

Stained-glass window: 21, rue Notre-Dame-Des-Victoires ⑩

21, rue Notre-Dame-des-Victoires
Métro: Bourse

A very fine but forgotten stained-glass window embellishes the façade of 21, rue Notre-Dame-des-Victoires. Listed as a historic property since 1994, the window was specially commissioned at the end of the 19th century from master glassmaker Eugène Grasset and painter Félix Gaudin to decorate the debating chamber of the new wing of the Paris Chamber of Commerce at 2, place de la Bourse. Entitled *Le Travail, par l'Industrie et le Commerce, enrichit l'Humanité* (Work, through Industry and Trade, enriches Humanity), it represents Work personified as a man holding a hammer, accompanied by two women, Industry and Trade. The upper part of the window shows the river port of Ivry, built on the initiative of the Chamber of Commerce. This stained glass, originally shown at the Universal Exhibition of May 1900 in the Chamber of Commerce's pavilion, was definitively installed in the building at place de la Bourse in November 1900.

A better view can be had in the evening when the window is lit from inside, as in broad daylight the details are almost impossible to make out.

Eiffel window, former headquarters of Crédit Lyonnais ⑪

18, rue du Quatre-Septembre

The former headquarters of Crédit Lyonnais bank, gutted by fire in May 1996, has been entirely rebuilt, preserving only the Eiffel cupola and the façades, listed as historic monuments. Although the building is not open to the public, you can still admire the magnificent window by Gustave Eiffel from the hallway of No. 18, rue du Quatre Septembre, which is accessible.

Geography of the Opéra-Comique

The Opéra Comique was built between 1781 and 1783 for the Comédie Italienne, a theatre company of Italian actors who staged Italian plays. To avoid confusion with the theatre later known as Théâtre de Boulevard, thought too common, a second auditorium was built at Boulevards, which explains its rather curious orientation today: several metres from boulevard des Italiens (named after the theatre), but at an opposing angle. Rossini, who directed the theatre between 1824 and 1826, gave his name to a street nearby. The surrounding place Boieldieu (French composer of the first quarter of the 19th century) and rues Marivaux (famous dramatist), Grétry (Belgian composer) and Favart (family of French playwrights) also have links with the Opéra-Comique.

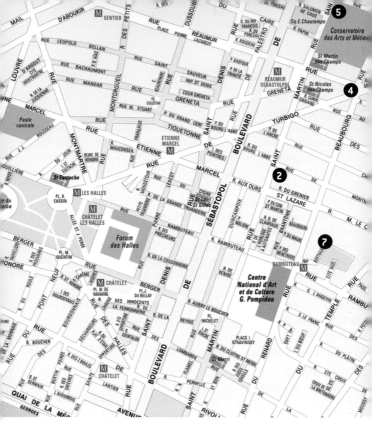

3rd Arrondissement

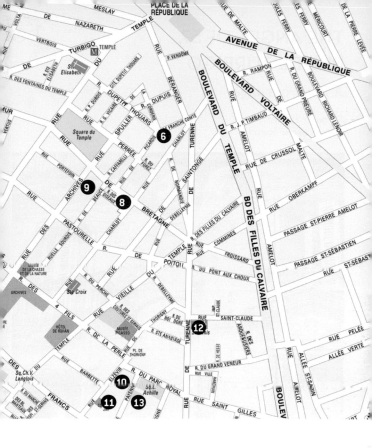

THE ANGEL OF 57, RUE DE TURBIGO

A wondrous angel

57, rue de Turbigo
Métro: Étienne-Marcel

This beautiful façade features an imposing angel whose outspread wings seem to welcome visitors and protect the residents. Unfortunately neither historians nor those who live in the building have managed to discover the origins of this celestial being, which appeared in a short film by Agnès Varda in the 1980s.

NEARBY

The oldest house in Paris? ②

51, rue de Montmorency

The house at 51, rue de Montmorency is thought to be the oldest in Paris. Built in 1407, the house of the "Grand-Pignon" (Big Gable, which no longer exists) belonged to the enigmatic Nicolas Flamel (1330–1418). Although there is no doubt that this enlightened spirit, a university jurist, really lived, his life is shrouded in mystery. Legend has it that he possessed the philosopher's stone that allowed lead to be transformed into gold.

To give thanks for his discoveries, the alchemist was responsible for a number of good works, such as the pious foundation at 51, rue de Montmorency. The rents paid on the ground-floor shops allowed him to offer the really destitute free accommodation on the upper floors, on the sole condition that they recited *Our Father* and *Hail Mary* each day so that the dead might rest in peace. This request, in old French, is still legible on the front of the house: "*Nous homes et femes laboureurs demourans ou porche de ceste maison qui fut faite en l'an de grâce mil quatre cens et sept somes tenus chascun en droit soy dire tous les jours une paternostre et un ave maria en priant Dieu que sa grâce face pardon au povres pescheurs trespasses. Amen.*" You can also see the founder's initials, N and F.

House at 3, rue Volta ③

Long considered the oldest house in Paris (some postcards still make this claim), the house at 3, rue Volta in fact dates from 1644, as discovered in 1979 following in-depth research.

ARTS-ET-MÉTIERS MÉTRO STATION ④

A station worthy of Jules Verne

© RATP/Marguerite Bruno

Arts-et-Métiers is probably the most remarkable métro station in the Paris network. Being on a branch line, No. 11, the station is little used by Parisians.

Refurbished in October 1994 for the bicentenary of the Conservatoire National des Arts et Métiers [CNAM, National Conservatory of Arts and Crafts], located just above, the station was planned and executed by François Schuiten, the celebrated Belgian illustrator and author of *La Fièvre d'Urbicande* (strip cartoon album in the series *Cités obscures*). The station is completely covered with copper sheeting and features a series of portholes, giving the impression of being in a submarine.

NEARBY

The amazing acoustic of Cnam ⑤
270–292, rue Saint-Martin

The room used by French scientist Antoine-Laurent Lavoisier for his experiments has incredible acoustic qualities. Two people facing opposite walls and with their backs to one another can easily converse without anyone in the centre of the room hearing a word. It is said that the room was used in this way by the monks of the former abbey in order to hear confession from those with contagious diseases.

Vestiges of the Templars in Paris ⑥

Unexpectedly perhaps, there are several relics of the Temple where Louis XVI was imprisoned: panels from the coach-house door of 1, rue Saint-Claude were recuperated for the door of the Grand Master of the Temple's stronghold. At 73, rue Charlot (entry also via 32, rue de Picardie) part of a tower built around 1240 survives (now private and inaccessible). It used to stand at the east corner of the walls around the Templars' enclosure.

Musée des poupées ⑦
Impasse Berthaud (22, rue Beaubourg)
Tel.: 01 42 72 73 11 • www.museedelapoupeeparis.com
Open 10am–6pm, except Mondays

Concealed in an alley behind Beaubourg, this little museum displays over 500 dolls, the oldest of which dates from the 19ᵗʰ century.

Abortive plans for a "Place de France"

Rues de Normandie, de Bretagne, de Poitou and de Saintonge are all named after French provinces. They recall a project of Henri IV for a semi-circular place de France, from which streets bearing the names of the various regions would radiate.

POTAGER DES OISEAUX

Birds of good omen

Entrance via 39, rue de Bretagne or rue de Beauce
Métro: Filles-du-Calvaire
Open Saturday and Sunday 10am–1pm or, during the week, when a gardener is present
http://potagerdesoiseaux.blogspot.com/
Association responsible for the gardens: potager_des_oiseaux@yahoo.fr

O n the site of a former stable, just beside Enfants-Rouges market, an attractive vegetable garden was opened in September 2004 in response to city residents' keen interest in growing their own food. A relaxed and congenial place run along the lines of "shared gardens" (see page 353), Potager des Oiseaux's 120 m² consists of ten rectangles divided into three plots, run by the association "Jardiniers du IIIᵉ". There are some sixty members who come along to garden, chat, drink coffee, pass on helpful hints – in short, mutual encouragement. You can have a look round and pick up some advice on the way to shop at the market next door. Better still, acquire a key and some tools and get your hands dirty, by joining (e-mail the address above).

NEARBY

Legend of the Marché des Enfants-Rouges

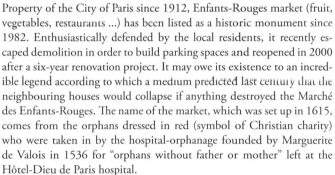

9, rue de Beauce
Open Tuesday to Thursday 8.30am–1pm and 4pm–7.30pm, Friday and Saturday 8.30am–1pm and 4pm–8pm, Sunday 8.30am–2pm

Property of the City of Paris since 1912, Enfants-Rouges market (fruit, vegetables, restaurants ...) has been listed as a historic monument since 1982. Enthusiastically defended by the local residents, it recently escaped demolition in order to build parking spaces and reopened in 2000 after a six-year renovation project. It may owe its existence to an incredible legend according to which a medium predicted last century that the neighbouring houses would collapse if anything destroyed the Marché des Enfants-Rouges. The name of the market, which was set up in 1615, comes from the orphans dressed in red (symbol of Christian charity) who were taken in by the hospital-orphanage founded by Marguerite de Valois in 1536 for "orphans without father or mother" left at the Hôtel-Dieu de Paris hospital.

The word *potager* (kitchen or vegetable garden) comes from "plants for the pot" that grow there, such as onions, cabbages and turnips.

Rue des coutures-Saint-Gervais

Rue des Coutures-Saint-Gervais is in no way a reference to a sartorial tradition but to one of the great challenges posed by Parisian geography: that of transforming the marshy land of the appropriately named Marais district into ground suitable for cultivation: the *coutures*.

Positivism

Although the social theorist Saint-Simon had already used the term "positivism", it was the philosopher Auguste Comte (1798–1857), secretary of the movement for six years, who made it widely known. Comte's positivist doctrine is linked to confidence in the progress of humanity through science and to belief in the benefits of scientific rationality as opposed to metaphysics. The word comes from references to "positive" or "exact" sciences such as mathematics, physics, etc.

In 1845, Auguste Comte fell hopelessly in love with Clotilde de Vaux and his scientific positivism took a religious form that was intended to reconcile the principles of scientific rationality with human love.

Positivism, little heard of today, had enormous influence in the 19th century, particularly in South America: notably being behind the motto "Order and Progress" (*Ordem e Progresso*) on the Brazilian flag.

TEMPLE OF HUMANITY

Love, order and progress

5, rue Payenne
Métro: Saint-Paul
www.chapelle-humanite.fr
contact@chapelle-humanite.fr
Opening hours and days discretionary, information at 01 44 78 01 97

A listed historic monument, the Chapelle de l'Humanité is the only Positivist temple in Europe. It was inaugurated on a misunderstanding: the Positivist Church of Mexico which bought the place in 1903 believed it to be the house of Clotilde de Vaux (see opposite). In fact, she had probably died at No. 7. No. 5 was a private mansion that François Mansart had had built for himself and in which he died in 1666.

Today, the first floor houses a "Chapel of Humanity", a faithful reproduction on a smaller scale of Auguste Comte's plan. It comprises fourteen pointed arches corresponding to the thirteen months of the calendar as redefined by Comte, the fourteenth arch being dedicated to Héloïse, who was held in high regard by the philosopher. The allegory on the altar represents *Humanity Holding the Future in its Arms* by Eduardo de Sá. There is also a bust of Auguste Comte by Antoine Etex.

The street frontage has been transformed by the architect Gustave Goy: you can see there a statue of Clotilde de Vaux as "virgin mother" and a bust of Auguste Comte with the inscription: *L'amour pour principe et l'ordre pour base, le progrès pour but* (Love as a principle and order as the basis, progress as the goal).

Auguste Comte's house in the 6ᵗʰ *arrondissement* can also be visited (see page 129).

HÔTEL DE MARLE

A Swedish experience

Centre culturel suédois
11, rue Payenne
Métro: Saint-Paul
Tel.: 01 44 78 80 20
Open every day except Monday 12pm–6pm (Café Suédois also open Tuesday evenings until 9pm)

© Centre culturel suédois

The superb Hôtel de Marle was built in the mid-16ᵗʰ century and then converted for Hector Marle, a parliamentary adviser. The building, bought in 1969 by Sweden, now houses the Swedish Cultural Centre – the only one that the country maintains abroad.

A variety of exhibitions and events provide the opportunity to admire the first-rate renovation and pure lines of the Renaissance architecture. When the weather allows you can also take advantage of the lovely garden adjoining the mansion, glimpsed through the gate of 8 rue Elzévir. Finally, Café Suédois on the ground floor offers, at rather attractive prices, typical home-made specialities and on fine days sets out tables in the handsome paved courtyard (see *Secret Bars and Restaurants in Paris* in this series of guides).

NEARBY
Delacroix' Pietà

Saint-Denys-du-Saint-Sacrement church
68 bis, rue de Turenne
Open daily 8.30am–7pm (closed 12pm–4.30pm during school holidays)
Few Parisians know that a major work by Delacroix is housed in Saint-Denys-du-Sacrement church. Many experts consider *Pietà*, painted between 1840 and 1844, to be one of the artist's masterpieces.
Besides those held by Paris museums, the churches of Saint-Paul-Saint-Louis (4ᵗʰ *arrondissement*) and Saint-Sulpice (6ᵗʰ *arrondissement*) also possess Delacroix paintings.

The electronic nightingale of Georges-Caïn Square

Square Georges-Caïn
8–14, rue Payenne
Resting on one of the benches in the delightful Georges-Caïn square, you might hear a nightingale sing. In fact the sound comes from a work by Éric Samakh in which birdsong is produced when there is enough wind. The square is also home to a few surprising relics: a ceiling rose from the Hôtel de Ville destroyed by the insurrectionary Communards in 1871, columns and a pediment from the Château des Tuileries, a sculpture from the Château de Saint-Germain-en-Laye and a statue from the Parc de Saint-Cloud.

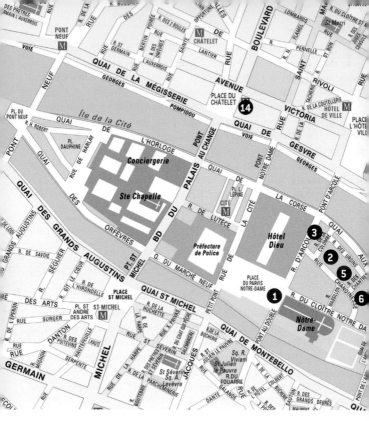

4ᵗʰ Arrondissement

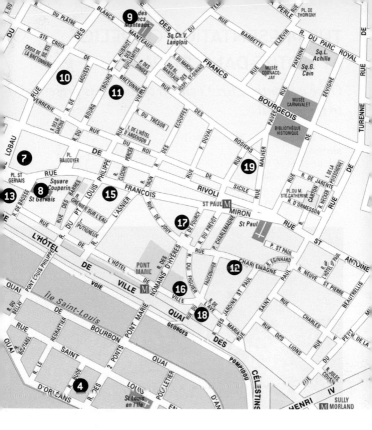

THE PRESENTATION OF RELICS AT NOTRE-DAME DE PARIS

Once a month, Christ's crown of thorns is presented to the faithful

Notre-Dame de Paris - Place du Parvis
Métro: Cité
Tel.: 01 42 34 56 10
www.notredamedeparis.fr
Every first Friday of the month and Fridays during Lent, 3pm–4pm, and Good Friday 10am–5pm

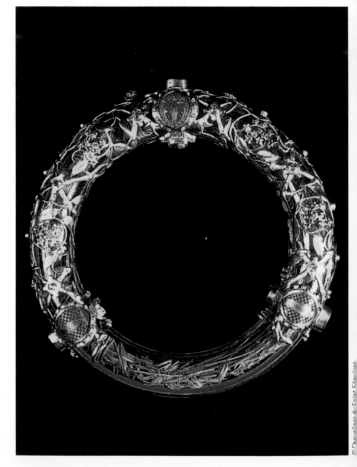

© Chevaliers du Saint-Sépulcre

Oddly enough, the immense majority of Parisians are totally unaware that Christ's crown of thorns, considered to be Christianity's second most important relic after the Holy Shroud of Turin, is presented in Notre-Dame cathedral once a month for veneration by the faithful. Contrary to common belief, the nearby Saint-Chapelle no longer has any relics: the other objects related to Christ's Passion (a nail and a fragment of the Cross itself) are also at Notre-Dame.

The first Friday of each month, in an atmosphere of profound devotion, the Knights of the Holy Sepulchre perform the duty of displaying the sacred crown to the crowd of worshippers. If most of those gathered are tourists who are blithely indifferent to the occasion, the fervour of the few Parisians present is impressive: when their turn comes to kiss the relic, it is by no means rare to see tears of emotion roll down their cheeks. The first reference to this holy relic dates from the year 409, when Saint Paulinus of Nola mentions it as one of the relics at the Mount Zion basilica in Jerusalem. Transferred to Byzantium to preserve them from being pillaged by the forces of the Persian Empire, the relics were then sold to the Venetians in 1238 by the Latin emperor of Constantinople, Baldwin II, who was experiencing financial difficulties. The French king Saint Louis (1126–1270) purchased them in 1239 and ordered the construction of a suitable chapel in Paris to house them: the Saint-Chapelle (some of the stained-glass windows in the chapel depict this event). After the Revolution, however, the relics were entrusted to the canons of the Notre-Dame chapter. In the 19th century, two reliquaries were built to house the crown of thorns, one commissioned by Napoleon I and the other by Napoleon III. They now lie empty, but are on display in the cathedral treasury (open to the public daily, 9am–6pm, except Sunday mornings). The authenticity of the relics is of course difficult to prove, although on the one occasion when the reliquary in which they now reside was actually opened, in 1940, it was observed that while the leaves were dried up, the ring of braided rushes was still green!

Was the devil a locksmith?

The Sainte-Anne portal in Notre-Dame cathedral possesses such perfect iron fittings that legend has it the Devil himself had a hand in their creation. The craftsman, Biscornet, was an apprentice locksmith said to have seen the demon in a dream, instructing him to carry out this masterpiece in the course of the night.

THE MOCK MEDIEVAL HOUSE OF FERNAND POUILLON

An architectural forgery

1, rue des Ursins

Few Parisians will have noticed that this medieval-looking house in fact dates from the 1960s. It owes its existence to the talent of the French architect Fernand Pouillon who successfully incorporated many elements from the past into this modern dwelling. The architect lived here himself for nearly a year.

Fernand Pouillon: a convict architect decorated with the Legion of Honour

Born in 1912 at Cancon (Lot-et-Garonne), Fernand Pouillon studied architecture at Marseille. Although his first buildings in Marseille and Aix date from before the Second World War, he remains best known for the reconstruction of the Vieux-Port of Marseille, ravaged by the Nazi occupation. The scandal surrounding the bankruptcy of the property company, "Le Comptoir du Logement" led to him being sent to prison, from which he later escaped. After a period spent hiding in Italy, he then presented himself of his own accord at his trial and was sentenced to three years. During his imprisonment he wrote two books, the most famous being *Les Pierres sauvages* (The Wild Stones). He later worked on major urban projects in Algeria (including the 200 columns of "Climat de France") and was awarded the Legion of Honour by President François Mitterrand. He died in 1986 at his château de Belcastel in the Aveyron region.

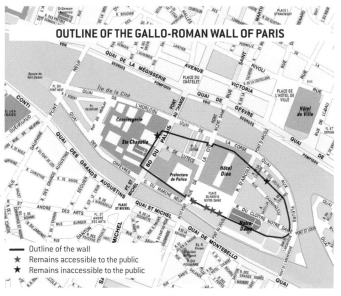

NEARBY

Traces of the first wall surround.
at 6, rue de la Colombe

An inscription on the pavement outside No. 6,
the discovery of the remains of the foundations
wall, as witnessed by a trail of paving stones 2.7
street at this point. The wall protecting the Gallo-
built in the first half of the 4th century AD, as a de   _arbarian
invaders. Measuring 1,500 m in length, it encircled .ost of the island of
Lutèce. The island was later enlarged (encompassing several smaller islands
nearby), raised with landfill (from 3 m to 7 m in places), and surrounded
with embankments, to become the Île de la Cité we know today. This first
defensive ring had a thickness of 2.50 m and a height of 7–8 m, with a
walkway on top, protected by crenellations.

Other vestiges of the first wall surrounding Paris

At place du Parvis-Notre-Dame, other vestiges of the wall (65 m in
all) were uncovered between 1967 and 1970 during construction
of the underground car park. They can be seen in the archaeological
crypt. In the Palais de Justice, more remains have been found, but
are off-limits to the general public.

OUTLINE OF THE GALLO-ROMAN WALL OF PARIS

— Outline of the wall
★ Remains accessible to the public
★ Remains inaccessible to the public

...KIEWICZ, CHOPIN
...EGAS MUSEUMS

...ull immersion in Polish artistic life

6, quai d'Orléans
Métro: Pont-Marie ou Maubert-Mutualité
Guided tours Thursdays at 2pm, 3pm, 4pm and 5pm, and Saturdays at 9am,
10am, 11am and 12pm
Tel.: 01 55 42 83 83

The Bibliothèque Polonaise has been housed since 1853 in the heart of île Saint-Louis in a handsome listed 17th-century building that belongs to the Société Historique et Littéraire Polonaise. Founded in 1832 by Polish immigrants fleeing from the brutal repression of an insurrection against the Russian occupiers of their country, this society had as its aim "gathering into one body and disseminating writings and documents related to the history of Poland, its present and future, with the goal of fostering and consolidating world sympathy to the Polish cause".

The library today possesses over 200,000 works and publications, including some rare items such as the personal letters of Frédéric Chopin, the minutes of the Polish Diet in the 18th century, a very precious 16th-century edition of Ptolemy's Map of Slavic Lands, and the three original editions (printed in Basel, Nuremburg and Amsterdam) of Copernicus' *De revolutionibus orbium coelestium* (On the Revolution of the Celestial Spheres – 1534). In a deliciously romantic atmosphere, three small museums have also been installed in this building. On the first floor, in a small salon, personal souvenirs, portraits, and engravings of Frédéric Chopin have been gathered together. On the second floor is a museum devoted to Adam-Mickiewicz, the great Polish romantic poet, born in 1798 in what is now Lithuania, occupying three rooms full of personal objects, manuscripts of his poems, and documents relating to his activities as a publicist and politician, as well as portraits and sculptures of Mickiewicz carried out by artists of his day. The visit ends on the top floor with the Boleslas-Biegas museum, presenting the work of this Polish painter and sculptor who lived at the end of the 19th century and beginning of the 20th, along with several paintings and sculptures by other contemporary Polish artists.

NEARBY

The tombstones at 26, rue Chanoinesse ⑤

In the courtyard at No. 26, rue Chanoinesse, some slabs covering the ground bear Gothic-looking inscriptions. These slabs are in fact tombstones from a religious establishment once located on the île de la Cité.

9 and 11, quai aux Fleurs: the memory of Héloïse ⑥ *and Abelard*

At No. 9, quai aux Fleurs, a plaque evokes the memory of Héloïse and Abelard, the celebrated star-crossed lovers, whose story somewhat resembles that of Romeo and Juliet in Verona. The buildings at Nos. 9 and 11 also feature stone medallions depicting the couple on their façades.

THE ELM TREE ON THE PARVIS OF SAINT-GERVAIS-SAINT-PROTAIS

At night, the women in the neighbourhood secretly took pieces of its bark

Place Saint-Gervais
Métro: Hôtel-de-Ville

f the elm tree in front of the Saint-Gervais-Saint-Protais church is not particularly eye-catching, it does have an astonishing history. Cut down during the French Revolution, the original elm that stood in this spot symbolised several things: from the beginning of the Christian era it was considered sacred due to its red sap, like the blood of the martyrs; it was also the place where justice was rendered after Mass, beneath its branches. In addition, people gathered here to drink and dance on feast days, and business deals were concluded. It is said, moreover, that women living in the neighbourhood used to come secretly in the night to take away pieces of the tree's bark, useful against fevers… Rather than the existing tree, which only dates from the beginning of the 20th century, it is the multiple references scattered throughout the neighbourhood to this famous older elm that help to keep the tradition alive. Wrought ironwork representing the elm and dating from the beginning of the 18th century can thus be seen on the balconies of the houses at Nos. 2 to 14 in rue François-Miron, while four choir stalls in the Saint-Gervais-Saint-Protais church also bear its image

NEARBY

Stalls at Saint-Gervais-Saint-Protais Church ⑧

Place Saint-Gervais
Masses held Tuesday to Saturday at 6.30pm, and Sunday at 11am (all services are accompanied by singing of the Fraternités Monastiques de Jérusalem)
http://jerusalem.cef.fr/paris-saint-gervais

Begun under François I and completed under Henri II, the misericords (seats) in the choir stalls are the only ones of their kind in Paris. They are decorated with symbols and marvellous little scenes of everyday life: three entwined lunar crescents (the emblem of Henri II), a scribe at his desk, an architect measuring stones, a cooper, grape harvesters, people quarrelling, others at prayer, a cobbler surrounded by shoes, a pig filling its belly, etc. One also sees the symbol of the elm that sits on the parvis in front of the church.

Front steps of Saint-Gervais-Saint-Protais Church: last traces of the second wall surrounding Paris

Measuring 1,700 m in length, the wall built in the 11th century enclosed three natural *monceaux* (hillocks), safe from river floods, on which the churches of Saint-Germain-l'Auxerrois, Saint-Merry, and Saint-Gervais were located. The front steps of the Saint-Gervais-Saint-Protais church and the route of rue des Barres are the only physical signs today of this wall's existence, and more specifically, of height variation formed by the monceau Saint-Gervais.

MONT-DE-PIÉTÉ

A visit to "my auntie"

Crédit Municipal de Paris
55, rue des Francs-Bourgeois
Métro: Rambuteau
Tel.: 01 44 61 63 63
Open Monday to Friday 8.30am–5.30pm

Renamed Crédit Municipal in 1918 and given full banking status in 1984, the Mont-de-Piété (the city pawnshop) is the oldest financial institution in France. Created by Louis XVI and Jean-Charles-Pierre Lenoir, the lieutenant general of the Paris police, two centuries after the first *mont-de-piété* was inaugurated in Italy, it was installed in 1778 in its present location.

Its first mission was to mitigate the effects of poverty by offering the poorest inhabitants a chance to escape the clutches of private moneylenders. Falling victim to its own success, the establishment closed in 1789 then reopened under Napoleon in 1804, marking the start of a remarkable growth and the extension of its activities to all levels of society. The Mont-de-Piété has accumulated its full share of picturesque anecdotes, such as the woman who pawned her mattress every morning to buy potatoes and resell them for a profit, or that of the Prince de Joinville, son of King Louis-Philippe himself, who once deposited his gold watch there in order to honour a gambling debt, while pretending that he'd forgotten it at "his auntie's" (an expression which gave rise to the place's nickname).

Even today, with average loans of €680 and 600 clients each day, the Crédit Municipal continues to serve all classes as there is no limit on the amount or the repayment period of its lending; the Mont-de-Piété's 40,000 m² of floor space holds over 80,000 objects whose value is estimated at 95 million euros. Of these objects, 80% are jewellery. The days when mattresses were pawned are not so long gone, however, as in 1946 there were still 50,000 of them on its accounts! (On this subject, see the poignant film, Bicycle Thieves.)

A visit to this place allows you to attend an auction, because the Crédit Municipal also has its sale rooms. As you leave by way of the courtyard, be sure to see the remains of the city walls built by Philippe Auguste: the 8 m high tower and the traces visible on the ground date from the end of the 12ᵗʰ century (see page 81).

The origin of "La Poubelle"

The French "*poubelle*" (rubbish bin) owes its name to the prefect of the Seine department, Eugène Poubelle, who in 1884 decreed the use of zinc bins to collect rubbish throughout Paris. Previously, rubbish had been deposited in more or less anarchic fashion in front of buildings and the streets often smelled very bad. Some people attached flowers to their buttonholes to mask this unpleasantness.

CLOÎTRE DES BILLETTES

A bleeding host

22–26, rue des Archives
Métro: Hôtel-de-Ville
Open during the frequent exhibitions, whose schedule can be found in Parisian entertainment listings magazines

Endowed with four galleries flanked by flamboyant vaults, the small cloître des Billettes is the only medieval cloister that remains in Paris. Dating from 1427, it belonged to the former monastery housing the "Frères hospitaliers de la charité de Notre-Dame", also known as the "Billettes" (little beads) in reference to the heraldic figures that adorned their habits. The adjoining church, rebuilt several times, dates from 1756 and from 1812 has been used by members of the Evangelical faith, while the monastic buildings were converted into a school at the end of the 19th century, and the cloister, property of the Paris city hall, was preserved and twice restored in the late 19th and 20th centuries.

If the general atmosphere that emanates from this timeless place is rather peaceful, its history is another matter altogether. In 1290, on Easter Sunday, a Jewish moneylender named Jonathas is said to have demanded of some poor woman that she bring him a consecrated host as repayment for her debt. Seizing this host, the man is supposed to have stabbed it several times with a knife, whereupon it began to bleed abundantly. He then threw it into a fire from which it emerged undamaged, flying across the room. Finally, the moneylender plunged the host into a pot of boiling water which was then changed into blood, while the host itself rose unto the air, now bearing the face of Christ! Jonathas is said to have been burnt alive for his misdeed... Once this story spread, the house of Jonathas quickly became a place of pilgrimage, and in 1294, a bourgeois citizen was granted authorisation to erect a chapel on this very spot where "God was boiled". In 1299, King Philippe le Bel installed the Frères de la Charité de Notre-Dame here to perform church services.

NEARBY
Mariage Frères *Tea Museum*   ⑪
30, rue du Bourg-Tibourg
Open daily 10.30am–7.30pm
The famous *Mariage Frères* tea shop installed a small museum devoted to the subject of tea on the first floor of the building it originally occupied, recounting the history of the beverage and displaying objects related to its consumption, including an amusing "moustache cup".
Legend has it that the Bodhidharma, a famous Indian religious sage, tore out his eyelids and lashes so that he could keep his eyes constantly open in order not to fall asleep during meditation. He then let them fall to the ground where they took root and became the first green tea plants.

REMAINS OF PHILIPPE AUGUSTE'S WALL ⑫

Bearing witness to Philippe Auguste

Rue des Jardins-Saint-Paul

REMAINS OF PHILIPPE AUGUSTE'S WALL OPEN TO THE PUBLIC

—— Outline of Philippe Auguste's wall
★ Remains accessible to the public

The sports field of the Charlemagne school enjoys a unrivalled view of the chevet of Saint-Paul church and a particularly well-conserved section of Philippe Auguste's wall (80 metres long) uncovered after the Second World War between two of its defensive towers. The Martigny tower, to the north, was torn open during the widening of rue Charlemagne, which crosses the wall where the former city gate of Saint-Paul once stood.

Philippe Auguste's defences (1190–1215)

An ambitious undertaking, the third wall in chronological order to encircle Paris was intended to encompass not only all of the city's existing dwellings, but also its surrounding fields, meadows, and orchards in order to ensure food supplies in case of siege.

Its dimensions were considerable for the period, protecting an area of 250 hectares by ringing it with a wall measuring 5,400 metres in length (2,800 metres on the Right Bank and 2,600 metres on the Left Bank). This wall had a height of 8 to 10 metres, with a thickness of 3 metres at its base and 2.30 metres at the top, including a walkway protected by crenellations. It had 65 defensive towers and 4 bigger towers located near the Seine river. There was no moat planned for it. Eventually, the city began to outgrow this wall, with various constructions being built against its inner or outer sides. Due to this fact, although much of the wall remains, it is rarely visible from the street. Places with public access, where the wall is clearly visible, include:

Right Bank

11, rue du Louvre, opposite the Bourse du Commerce

16, rue Étienne-Marcel : beside the Jean sans Peur Tower

57–59, rue des Francs-Bourgeois: the Crédit Municipal tower

Rue des Jardins-Saint-Paul: the wall and two towers are well preserved

Left Bank

30 bis, rue du Cardinal-Lemoine (see page 98)

Rue Clovis

4, cour du Commerce-Saint-André: a tower in a shop

27, rue Mazarine: remains in an underground car park (see page 133)

13, passage Dauphine: a tower in a language school

There are also plaques (but no actual remains) recalling the existence of the wall at No. 113, rue Saint-Denis, No. 172, rue Saint-Jacques, No. 9, rue Mouffetard, and No. 44, rue Dauphine.

A dozen other remnants of Philippe Auguste's wall exist, but are located in private properties and inaccessible to the general public.

Maison des Compagnons du Devoir

1, place Saint-Gervais – Métro: Hôtel-de-Ville or Pont-Marie
Tel.: 01 48 87 38 69 • www.compagnons-du-devoir.com
compagnonsparis@compagnons-du-devoir.com
Open Monday to Friday 9am–12pm and 1.30pm–5pm

Little known, and sometimes mistakenly linked with a religious sect or a secret society, the guilds have existed for over ten centuries (see page 348). The Association des Compagnons du Devoir is one of four guild associations in Paris and today groups together 21 different trades (masons, furniture makers, transport, food, leather) within 95 maisons des Compagnons. As with the other associations (see pages 29, 125, and 348), the main point of interest when visiting this place is the presence of a guild member; it is highly recommended to ask him questions in order to gain a better appreciation of this still very lively universe.

NEARBY

Sarah Bernhardt's dressing room

Théâtre de la Ville. 16, quai de Gesvres
Can be visited during intervals by members of the audience

Sarah Bernhardt's dressing room at the Théâtre de la Ville is sadly a mere replica, the real dressing room of the artist (1844–1923) having been destroyed in 1968 when the theatre was renovated. Some of the original items were nevertheless salvaged: you can still see a settee with the head of a sphinx, her famous bathtub, and various personal objects.

Maison d'Ourscamp ⑮

44–46, rue Francois-Miron
Open Monday to Saturday 11am–6pm, Sundays 2pm–7pm

In its basement, the Association du Paris Historique houses one of the most beautiful Gothic cellars in the capital. Dating from the 12th century, this cellar owes its survival to local residents, who used it as a storage space and filled it right up to the chapiters, thus preserving them. At Nos. 11 and 13, rue François Miron, two 15th-century houses have kept their gables and frame walls, although the latter actually date from their renovation in the 1960s.

Vestiges of the Hôtel de Ville

Various remnants of the Hôtel de Ville are now scattered throughout the capital: in addition to that in the Jardins du Trocadéro (see page 315), one can find others in Monceau park (near the naumachia, or small lake), in square Léopold-Achille (4th arr.), and in Georges-Caïn square (see page 65).

The origin of "La Grève"

"Faire la grève" (to go on strike) is an expression derived from the former place de la Grève in Paris, now called place de l'Hôtel-de-Ville. This square, located by the Seine, was one of the principal landing places for boats during the Middle Ages (a *"grève"* is a gravel or sand beach, by the sea or a body of water). Men seeking employment were readily hired here for loading and unloading vessels. In the course of time, workers dissatisfied with their wages and labour conditions tended to gather at place de la Grève to express their grievances.

"King of the French" rather than "King of France"

Hôtel de Sens – Bibliothèque Forney
1, rue du Figuier

Y ou need a particularly keen eye to spot the cannonball embedded at a height of several metres in the wall of the Hôtel de Sens. This cannonball, as the date inscribed on the wall indicates, was fired during the riots of 27, 28, and 29 July 1830 (known as the "Trois Glorieuses" or the July Revolution).

The liberal members of the French parliament, a majority of whom were monarchists, took charge of the popular insurrection, saving the monarchy at the price of a change of dynasty. King Charles X was forced to abdicate in favour of the House of Orléans, the junior branch of the Bourbon family. The French gave themselves a new king in the person of Louis-Philippe I, crowned "King of the French" and no longer "King of France". The July Monarchy (1830–1848) was proclaimed on 9 August 1830.

NEARBY

Japanese garden of the Maison Européenne de la Photographie ⑰

5–7, rue de Fourcy

Just before the entrance to the house on the left, the Niwa garden, laid out according to the Zen tradition, was created by Keijchi Tahara, a Japanese artist who has lived in Paris since the 1970s. Another, even bigger Japanese garden, is in the grounds of UNESCO (see page 145).

Square de l'Ave Maria, the square of the year 2000 ⑱

The work of Christophe Grunenwald, this square, entirely redesigned for the passage of the year 2000, is full of symbols. By going from one plot to another, the stroller is supposed to trace out the figure 2000 with the movement of his or her body.

Remains of the Bastille prison

For three years, a team of 800 men laboured to demolish the Bastille prison, a measure decided on 16 July 1789. The stones were used in the construction of the Pont de la Concorde, but also for building houses in the immediate neighbourhood. Some clever people sold the locks as paperweights and a certain Palloy made a fortune sculpting and selling stones in the shape of the Bastille. In the surrounding area, there remain a few vestiges: at the beginning of rue Saint-Antoine, a mark on the ground indicates the prison's former location, which you can also see on a map displayed at No. 3, place de la Bastille. Lastly, in square Henri-Galli, at the end of boulevard Henri-IV, are gathered the remains of one of the prison's towers, uncovered during construction of the métro.

SYNAGOGUE IN RUE PAVÉE

A rare Art Nouveau synagogue

10, rue Pavée
Métro: Saint-Paul
Tel.: 01 42 77 81 51 or 01 48 87 21 54
Open to visitors daily except Saturday, 10.30am–5pm by reservation

The only Art Nouveau building in the Marais neighbourhood and the last religious monument to be built here, the synagogue in rue Pavée is a curious sight. Its tall curved façade designed by Hector Guimard (see page 303) stands out from the nearby buildings. It remains one of the rare institutional and architectural traces of the immigrants who settled in this part of Paris. On Saturday mornings, on Sabbath day, when one sees the orthodox Jews in traditional costume with side curls and kippas, quietly filing into the building for the ritual reading of the Torah, it is easy to believe that you have been transported back to the beginning of the last century.

It was in 1913, as a response to the influx of Ashkenazi Jewish refugees from Central Europe since the end of the 19th century, that the Russo-Polish association, Agoudas Hakehilos, decided on the construction of a new synagogue on a narrow plot of land located in rue Pavée.

The choice of Hector Guimard as architect might seem surprising. It is hard to imagine the Parisian master of Art Nouveau joining forces with Orthodox Russian Jews, but it was in fact emblematic of their affirmation of a specifically French Yiddish culture.

It was also Hector Gumard who designed the furnishings (lights, chandeliers, wall lamps, benches), as well as the stylised vegetal décor and ironwork railings.

The building itself is made of hollow conglomerate over a concrete frame. The harmony between the rigour of a construction in reinforced concrete and the elegance of the façade's curves and counter-curves is complete.

The synagogue, which did not cost the wider Parisian community anything, was inaugurated on 17 June 1914. No representatives of the official French Jewish institutions attended, preferring to ignore this initiative on the part of immigrant Jews which they neither hindered nor assisted.

The synagogue in rue Pavée, along with all its liturgical elements, was listed as a historic building on 4 July 1989.

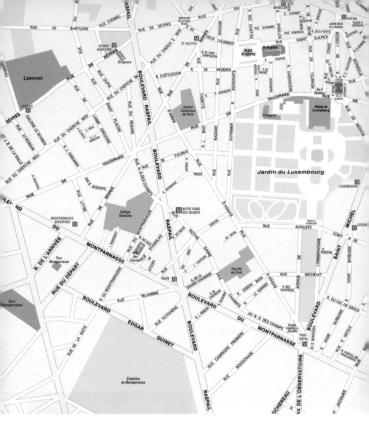

5th *Arrondissement*

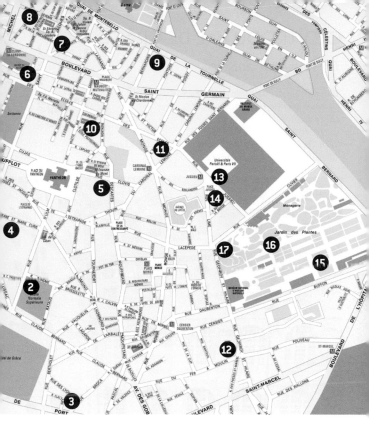

CLOÎTRE DU VAL-DE-GRÂCE

The forgotten cloister

Musée du Service de Santé des Armées
1, place Alphonse-Laveran
RER: Port-Royal
Tel.: 01 40 51 51 92
Open Tuesday, Wednesday, Saturday and Sunday 12pm–5pm
Admission: €4.60, concessions €2.30

A visit to the museum of the French army's health service is a very good excuse to admire the little known but magnificent cloister of the former abbey of Val-de-Grâce, built between 1624 and 1669.

The church itself was the result of a vow made by Queen Anne of Austria, in thanks for having given birth to a son after twenty-three years of marriage, in 1638. On 1 April 1645, the future King Louis IV therefore laid the first stone for a building whose construction was prolonged until the end of the 1660s. Mansart, then Le Mercier, and finally, Le Muet, assisted by Le Duc, all contributed to the design of the church, which is decorated with numerous statues, as well as four paintings by Philippe de Champaigne. The abbey was transformed into a military hospital in 1793 and is still the property of the French Army.

The museum itself is intended to help the visitor understand the multiple relationships between medicine and the military, but its chief point of interest is its location, beneath the vaults of one of the upper galleries overlooking the beautiful cloister. Note the superposition of the two galleries that compose it.

NEARBY

Garden of the École Normale Supérieure ②

45, rue d'Ulm
Open daily during class hours
A very pleasant garden graced with a small ornamental pond.

Musée des éclairages anciens – Lumière de l'œil ③

4, rue Flatters
Métro: Gobelins
Tel./fax: 01 47 07 63 47
E-mail : lumiara@aol.com • http://lumiara.perso.neuf.fr/lumiara/
Open Tuesday to Friday 2pm–7pm and Saturday 11am–5pm
For nearly twenty-five years, Monsieur Ara has been restoring and selling antique lamps. Crammed into a tiny room, one finds gas, paraffin, and electric lamps, along with glass lamp chimneys, wicks, mantles, pearly fringes, and other accessories waiting to find a buyer. In the rear of the shop is a little museum displaying lamps using paraffin, oil, petrol, alcohol and gas from all around the world, the oldest dating back to the 17th century. It is the only collection of its kind in France, as its proud owner will tell you. All of these lamps are in working order.

MUSÉE CURIE

The glory days of radium

11, rue Pierre-et-Marie-Curie
Métro: Place Monge or Cardinal-Lemoine. RER: Luxembourg
Tel.: 01 42 34 67 50 (practical advice) • www.curie.fr • E-mail : musee@curie.fr
Open Tuesday to Friday 2pm–6pm, Wednesday until 7pm (except holidays)
Guided tours Fridays at 3pm in French and at 4pm in English
Annual closure: the month of August and the last week of December
Admission free (but donations to the Institut Curie accepted)
Group visits: obligatory reservation for groups of 10+
Contact (reservations and information): Marité Amrani at 01 42 34 67 49
E-mail : visites.musee@curie.fr

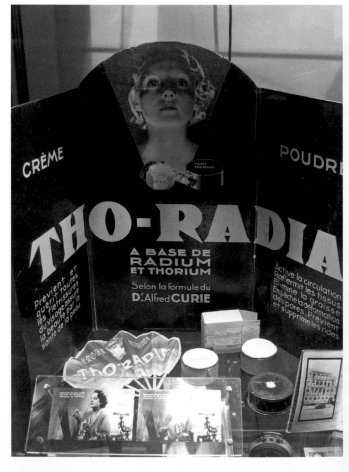

Located on the ground floor of the Curie pavilion, the intriguing Curie museum occupies the former laboratory and office of Marie Curie. This "Radium Institute" was built between 1911 and 1914 by the University of Paris and the Institut Pasteur after the discovery of polonium* and radium by Pierre and Marie Curie. The guided tour is strongly recommended for its numerous fascinating anecdotes. In the entry hall, glass display cases present the first instruments for measuring radioactivity as well as a history of radium. Visitors thus pass from the serious scientific research to the fanciful notions of the general public which, for example, even went as far as attributing radium with cosmetic virtues, as claimed by a Miss France at the time!

The second room is none other than Marie Curie's office, left in the state it was found upon her death in 1958 by her son-in-law, Frédéric Joliot: there are some personal items belonging to Marie and her daughter, Irène Joliot-Curie. As for the laboratory, it had a relatively high level of radioactivity and required decontamination before it could be opened to the public in 1992. The rear door opens onto the garden leading to the Institut Pasteur, specialising in medical and biological research. Conceived by Marie Curie, the principal purpose of this garden is to allow researchers from both institutes to meet informally.

The family with five Nobel Prizes

Of Polish origin, Marie Sklodowska-Curie was in 1903 the first woman to present a thesis in physics (she received the highest grade). The same year, she was also the first woman to receive the Nobel Prize in physics, together with her husband Pierre Curie and Henri Becquerel, for their discovery of radioactive elements. In 1911, after the death of Pierre, she was awarded, on her own, the Nobel Prize in chemistry for her work on radium. She remains to this day the only woman to have received two Nobel Prizes. Then, in 1935, her daughter Irène and son-in-law Frédéric Joliot obtained a Nobel Prize in chemistry for their research on artificial radioactivity (for more on this subject, see our guide, *Banlieue de Paris insolite et secrète*).

* The name given to this element by Marie Sklodowska-Curie in tribute to her native Poland.

THE JUBE
OF SAINT-ÉTIENNE-DU-MONT

The last jube

30, rue Descartes • Place Sainte-Geneviève
Métro: Cardinal-Lemoine
www.saintetiennedumont.fr

The Saint-Étienne-du-Mont church, whose construction was begun in 1517 by François I and only completed in 1627 (which explains the rather fanciful mixture of Gothic and Franco-Italian styles making this a unique monument) possesses the last jube that can be seen in Paris. An architectural marvel sculpted by the artist Biart le père, the jube is formed by a single arch with a span of 9 metres traversing the choir accessed by two spiral staircases in openwork stone. This piece of art, unmatched in its lightness despite the richness of its sculpted ornamentation (ivy, angels, palm trees, foliated patterns, interlacings, mascarons and worshippers), has by some miracle escaped destruction, the parishioners themselves having requested its demolition in 1735! The church also possesses some very fine stained-glass windows at the rear of the sacristy illustrating scenes from the Bible, as well as the relics of Saint Genevieve, the patron saint of Paris. Pascal and Racine are both buried here, behind the choir.

What is a Jube?

The jube is a transversal gallery separating the choir from the nave of a church, from where the Holy Scriptures would be read. Most of them vanished with the introduction of pulpits. The word stems from the Latin expression *Jube, Domine, Bendicere* (command, Lord, to bless).

NEARBY ⑥

The right foot of Montaigne's statue

The statue of Montaigne, opposite the Sorbonne on the side facing rue des Écoles, in Paul-Painlevé square, has a curious feature: its right foot, like Juliet's breast in Verona, or the sexual organ of Victor Noir in Père-Lachaise cemetery, seems to have been polished by numerous hands rubbing it over the years. Replacing a stone statue of the same Montaigne, this bronze statue dates from 1933. The story goes that any wish pronounced while caressing the writer's foot and saying "Salut Montaigne" will be granted. It seems that the origin of this practice was merely a student superstition.

Traces in Paris of the pilgrimage to Santiago de Compostela

One of the four French pilgrimage routes leading to the shrine of Saint James in Santiago de Compostela has its point of departure in Paris, at the former Saint-Jacque-de-la-Boucherie church, of which the last vestige is Saint-Jacques tower. The pilgrims then left the city by way of rue Saint-Jacques, rue du Faubourg-Saint-Jacques, and rue de la Tombe-Issoire. The present-day Musée de Cluny was on this route and it is therefore not surprising to see numerous scallops carved on the façade. The Saint Jacques-du-Haut-Pas church, in rue Saint-Jacques, also owes its existence to the pilgrimage.

Why was the statue of August Comte moved?

A few years ago, the statue of August Comte in place de la Sorbonne was moved and turned 90°. Although the official reason given was to facilitate the view of the Sorbonne from boulevard Saint-Michel, it seems that the controversial character of Comte's doctrine of scientific positivism was the real cause (see page 63).

Salvador Dali's sundial

27, rue Saint-Jacques

Created and engraved in 1968 by Salvador Dalí for friends of his who owned a shop at the corner of this building, an astonishing sundial adorns the wall of No. 27, rue Saint-Jacques. The engraving represents the head of a woman whose scalp resembles a Saint James scallop in allusion to the street and to Santiago de Compostela.

Rues des Fossés...

Rues des Fossés-Saint-Bernard, des Fossés-Saint-Jacques, des Fossés-Saint-Marcel: all these streets were originally built outside the wall of Philippe Auguste. In 1346, after the French defeat in the battle of Crécy against the English, as the Hundred Years War was getting started, it was deemed prudent to strengthen the wall's defences: "*fossés*" (trenches) were therefore dug in front of it. These later gave their names to various streets in the neighbourhood. the premises.

Charnier Saint-Séverin ⑧
Rue des Prêtres-Saint-Séverin

On the right-hand side of the Saint-Séverin church, a pretty garden is curiously surrounded by a Gothic-style gallery housing small alcoves, which make it look like a cloister. This place, at first sight charming, bears the name of "charnier Saint-Séverin": it is the vestige of a medieval charnel house first opened in the 15th century. Its galleries and niches were meant to receive the remains of Parisian dignitaries, while the ground in the middle was filled with bones from the city's mass graves when their sites were needed for other purposes.

The oldest tree in Paris

The oldest tree in Paris can be found opposite Notre-Dame, on the Left Bank of the Seine, in square René-Viviani (25, quai de Montebello). This *robinia* (false acacia) tree was planted in 1636 and survives in part thanks to a "crutch" made from concrete that no doubt prevents it from collapsing completely. Its name is derived from Jean Robin, who was the first to introduce this American tree to France, in 1602.

NEARBY

Musée de l'Assistance Publique – Hôpitaux de Paris ⑨
Hôtel de Miramion, 47, quai de la Tournelle
Tel.: 01 40 27 50 05 • www.aphp.fr/histoire/musee.htm
Open Tuesday to Sunday 10am–6pm (closed on public holidays and during August) • Admission: €4, free first Sunday of every month

Installed since 1934 in the handsome Hôtel de Miramion, the townhouse where François Mansart once resided, the Musée de l'Assistance Publique – Hôpitaux de Paris is the oldest hospital museum in France. Mothers will be particularly interested in the collection of feeding bottles and dummies dating from antiquity to present times, a touching testimony – and sometimes a frightening one (certain bottles, veritable nests of bacteria, are characterised as lethal) – of timeless everyday preoccupations. From inside the museum, it is possible to see the small garden attached to the townhouse. This is a beautiful example of a hospital garden from the Middle Ages, a period when four was the perfect number, representing water, earth, air and fire, the four elements composing the universe. In relation to this figure, the garden, like abbey cloisters, was composed of four alleys, symbolising the four rivers of paradise and the four cardinal virtues (justice, prudence, fortitude and temperance).

The flag over la Tour d'Argent

Some Parisians will have noticed that a flag sometimes flies above *La Tour d'Argent* restaurant. This indicates that the owner is on the premises.

The oldest sign in Paris

The oldest sign in Paris (1380) is to be found at No. 42, rue Galande. It shows a man and a woman rowing a boat, with another man between them. The sign evokes the superb legend of Saint Julien l'Hospitalier: after accidentally killing his parents, he decided to leave everything and become a river ferryman. A leper presented himself one day and was accepted aboard by the saint, despite his illness. This leper was none other than Christ himself who gave eternal life to the man who would become Saint Julien l'Hospitalier.

NEARBY

The inner courtyard of the former Séminaire des 33 ⑩
34, rue de la Montagne-Sainte-Geneviève

This charming little paved courtyard is located on the site of a former seminary founded by Claude Bernard. After the death of a friend in a duel, he took holy orders and became the follower of Saint Vincent de Paul. He prophesised the birth of Louis XIV and in gratitude Queen Anne of Austria made a donation that allowed the creation of the Collège des Trente-trois (in reference to the age when Christ died), a seminary reserved for prisoners. It was not until the beginning of the 19th century that this college was finally transformed into private dwellings. In theory, the door is locked, but a martial arts club now occupies the premises and nothing prevents you from entering the building to ask for information.

A vestige of the crossing-point of the Bièvre in Philippe Auguste's wall ⑪
30 bis, rue du Cardinal-Lemoine • Visits first Wednesday of every month at 2.30pm

Once a month, the post office at the corner of rue du Cardinal-Lemoine and boulevard Saint-Germain organises a visit to its basement: there you can see an interesting remnant of Philippe Auguste's wall. At this very spot, a branch of the Bièvre river (supplying the gardens of the Saint-Victor abbey with water) crossed the wall, through the so-called "Bièvre arch".

The former horse market at 5, rue Geoffroy-Saint-Hilaire ⑫

Dating from 1760, this ravishing pavilion possesses a façade where you can still see a handsome horse's head as well as the inscription, *Marchand de chevaux, poneys, double poneys et chevaux de trait* (Trader of horses, ponies, double ponies, and draught horses). The building was constructed at the request of the *lieutenant de police* Sartine to house the agents charged with watching over the horse market located here. The market remained in business until 1907.

MUSÉE DE MINÉRALOGIE

A treasure trove

4, place Jussieu
Métro: Jussieu
Tel.: 01 44 27 52 88 • Open daily except Tuesday 1pm–6pm
Admission: €5, concessions €3

Located since 1970 in a basement of the Jussieu university science faculty, the Musée de Minéralogie has 24 panoramic display cases containing a selection of 2,000 minerals from its holdings of 24,000 specimens, with special lighting and a constant temperature to preserve them from deterioration. This choice allows the public to view the most beautiful pieces in a relatively small space. Based on rarity, quality and beauty, the selection presents the surprising riches offered by the mineral world with the aim of awakening the interest of a public often ignorant of the subject, but able here to discover what lies behind mysterious names such as "cummengéite", "cuprosklodowskite", or "phantom quartz". Those who are passionate about minerals can pursue matters further by visiting the Musée de Minéralogie des Mines, in the 6th *arrondissement* (see page 113), which has over 80,000 samples! Affected by the plan to remove dangerous asbestos from the Jussieu science faculty, the museum moved to new premises in June 2006, and now has disabled access.

© Collection de Minéraux de Jussieu/ J.-P. Boisseau

NEARBY

Façade at No. 1, place Jussieu

34, rue de la Montagne-Sainte-Geneviève

A very handsome neo-Renaissance building constructed in 1842 by the architects Totain and Vigreux, together with the sculptor Giraud.

THE DODO RIDE

A prehistoric ride

The Jardin des Plantes
Sunday from 11.30am to the garden's closing time
Wednesday - Saturday: from 1pm to the garden's closing time

Set up in 1992 in the middle of the Jardin des Plantes, this 1930s-style carousel was specially conceived for this location on the theme of animals that have now vanished or are threatened by extinction. It thus gathers together members of rare or extinct species, such as the famous dodo from Mauritius, the Tasmanian wolf, the sivatherium (an elk-like precursor of the giraffe), and the triceratops (one of the last dinosaurs).

Although children are not always aware of the history of the animals they've climbed upon, they seem to be delighted to ride in a gondola carried by a panda, in the shell of a horned tortoise, or on the back of a Madagascan aepyornis (the biggest bird ever recorded).

NEARBY

Microclimate in the alpine garden at the jardin des plantes ⑯

The Alpine garden at the Jardin des Plantes is an amazing place first conceived in the 1930s. Constructed 3 m below the level of the rest of the botanical gardens, and thus protected from both heat and cold, by means of the interplay of rocks and irrigation it mimics the microclimates of several mountainous regions. Within a confined space, there are temperature differences of up to 20°C. The garden can thus take pride in over 2,000 different plant species, including the famous but rare edelweiss, all cohabiting in an area measuring less than 4,000 m^2.

Buffon's "*gloriette*" (gazebo), at the summit of the maze in the Jardin des Plantes, is the oldest metallic construction in France. Born in the town of Montbard, Buffon directed the famous foundry there, which produced the steel used to build these metal structures.

A lion devouring a human foot - la Fontaine aux lions

The lion fountain located in the Jardin des Plantes near the gate in rue Geoffroy-Saint-Hilaire, was built by Henri Jacquemont in 1863. Astonishingly, a lion is seen here devouring what appears to be a human foot... The sculptor, particularly keen on naturalism, also conceived the sphinxes for the fountain in place du Châtelet, the lions in place Félix-Éboué (12th *arrondissement*), and the dragons in place Saint-Michel.

NEARBY

Bonnier de la Mosson's "Cabinet de Curiosités"

Bibliothèque Centrale du Muséum d'Histoire Naturelle
38, rue Geoffroy-Saint-Hilaire – Métro: Place-Monge or Jussieu
Tel.: 01 40 79 36 33 • Open Monday to Saturday 9.30am–7pm (Tuesday 1pm–
7pm) • Admission free • bcm@mnhn.fr • http://mussi.mnhn.fr/

Hidden behind the white wall of the media library in the Muséum d'Histoire Naturelle, this *"cabinet de curiosités"* (chamber of curiosities) is a little-known gem that is the work of a wealthy art lover, Joseph Bonnier de la Mosson (1702–1744). A knowledgeable collector, Bonnier ruined himself gathering together its contents, to the point that his creditors recovered part of the amounts he owed by auctioning off the collections after his death in 1745.

Bonnier nevertheless managed to acquire one collection, the so-called *"Cabinet des insects et autres animaux desséchés des plus remarquables"* (The most remarkable set of insects and other dried animals), which he had installed in the king's garden. Dismantled in 1935, the display cases were restored and moved to their present location in 1979. They were listed as a historic monument in 1980. Today, the cabinet is composed of five magnificent display cases carved in Dutch wood, decorated with entwined serpents and surmounted by animal heads bearing real horns. They present a collection of multicoloured insects and butterflies, gaudy birds, dried animals, horns of narwhales (once believed to be those of the legendary unicorn) and rhinoceroses, tarantulas, giant millipedes, etc. It is strongly recommended that you consult the detailed list of these curiosities. This can be found in catalogue 069.95 BON, available at the reception desk.

The "Cabinet de Curiosités", precursor of the museum

In the 16ᵗʰ century, with the development of exploration and the discovery of unknown lands, many scientists, art lovers and persons of wealth began to collect curiosities originating in these new places. This led to the emergence of *"cabinets de curiosités"* as a sort of mirror of the world, gathering together a multitude of rare and strange objects that not only reflected human endeavours, but also the three natural kingdoms: animal, vegetable and mineral. By the mid-17ᵗʰ century, the fad for these collections of curiosities began to wane, in favour of what would be called in the following century *"cabinets d'histoire naturelle"*, and then, the first museums.

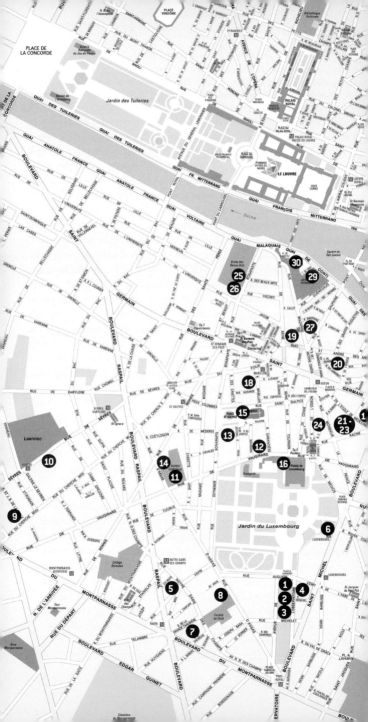

6th *Arrondissement*

Constructed in 1894–1896 to a design by the architect Maurice Yvon, this building at the corner of avenue de l'Observatoire and rue Auguste-Comte is one of the finest examples of Islamic architecture in Paris. Possessing a superb Moorish-style entrance on avenue de l'Observatoire, it has an attractive interior patio and a magnificent library that have maintained their original appearance. Strange that this gem is not better known. Originally built to house the École Coloniale, which trained those who would administer France's overseas colonies, it now houses the ENA, which trains those who administer France itself.

Islamic architecture in Paris

The first official contacts between France and the Orient came in 1669–1670, when ambassadors were exchanged between the courts of Louis XIV and the Ottoman emperor. Subsequently, the publication of Antoine Gaillard's translation of *The Arabian Nights* at the beginning of the 18th century made the Orient all the rage in the capital. Around the middle of that century French travellers rediscovered the beauties of Greece and then moved on to Egypt (see page 47), with the result that travel throughout the whole of the Muslim world became more common. The Spanish Alhambra and the mosques of Cairo would have an equal influence on the architects of the famous Marseilles church of Notre-Dame-de-la-Garde and even on the design of the crematorium at Père-Lachaise cemetery. Other than the beautiful **Great Mosque** in the *5th arrondissement*, the most striking example of the influence of Islamic architecture in Paris is probably the former École Coloniale at **2, avenue de l'Observatoire** (see above). Other fine examples are to be seen at **4bis, avenue Hoche** (a large Moorish-style salon built in 1892); **68, rue Ampère** (a Moorish-style salon, 1895); **44, rue Servan** (in the 11th *arrondissement*, this dates from 1870–1890 and has a façade adorned with material probably recycled from the pavilions for the Universal Exposition); **9, rue Fénelon** (a private house with an Arab-style vestibule and ceramic decoration produced by the Gillet ceramic works); and **16, rue Bardinet** (in the 14th *arrondissement*, dating from 1908). At **18, rue des Mathurins** you can also see the typical Arab-style windows of what used to be a hammam, while the **Maison du Maroc in the Cité Universitaire** has a magnificent carved wood ceiling from Morocco itself. Finally, two buildings in which the influence is less marked can be seen at **35, rue de Charenton** (in Moorish-Gothic style and dating from 1840) and **4, rue de la Cossonerie** (an elephant head that reveals a Muslim-Indian influence).

MUSÉE DE LA MATIÈRE MÉDICALE ②

A rare experience

Collections from the analysis laboratories of the Faculty of Pharmacology
4, avenue de l'Observatoire
RER: Luxembourg
By appointment for specialist professional groups (Tel.: 01 53 73 98 04). Open to
the general public during the Journées du Patrimoine (September) and the Fête
de la Science (October)

A visit to the Museum of Medical Specimens is a rare experience. This fine hall – complete with carved wooden decoration, old-style display cabinets and historical flasks and carboys – even incorporates materials recycled from a pavilion constructed for the Universal Exposition of 1889. Within this timeless ambiance, the museum has more than 25,000 different compounds and "simples" (natural substances that were dried and then used in the preparation of medicines). Professor Tillequin, who is usually the guide for those visiting the museum, is a veritable mine of information, supplying endless anecdotes regarding the substances present. For example, you learn that theine is the same as caffeine. Similarly, the subtle differences between various sorts of coffee (Arabica, Robusta, etc.) are explained, as is the truth about Brazilian guarana and Amazonian curare. The cabinet dedicated to Vin Mariani is particularly interesting. One day, Mariani, a Corsican, created a drink based on coca leaves (the source of cocaine) and wine. The beverage was a great success, in part due to Mariani's undeniable talent for marketing; he used to send bottles of the drink to the great and powerful, publishing in his advertisements letters of thanks from the more famous of them. In the United States, a local chemist took his inspiration from this concoction to produce one of his own, in which coca leaves were replaced by an extract of coca beans and wine by a fizzy drink. In 1892, the rights to this recipe were bought by Asa Chandler, and Coca Cola was born. Just behind this display is another with quinine bark, a substance which is still used to treat malaria. It was first brought back to Europe by the Jesuits, and an illustrious early user was Louis XIV, who had contracted malaria in the marshy areas around Versailles.

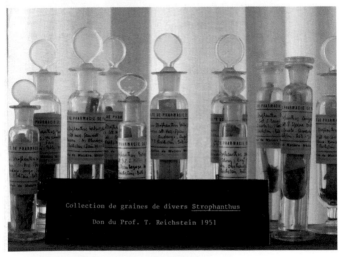

Collection de graines de divers Strophanthus
Don du Prof. T. Reichstein 1951

JARDIN BOTANIQUE OF
THE FACULTÉ DE PHARMACOLOGIE

Garden of Simples

4–6, avenue de l'Observatoire
RER: Luxembourg or Port-Royal
Open Monday to Friday, 9am–7pm

O riginally intended for students of pharmacology (the study of medicinal plants is part of their first-year course), this stunning and slightly neglected botanical garden is now open to the public. It has a rather nostalgic and romantic atmosphere, which makes it the perfect place for a first date (or perhaps to ask for a first date).

The garden is reached by the entrance at 4, avenue de l'Observatoire, from where you follow the pathway and then turn left. Formerly, the Paris École de Pharmacie was located in rue de l'Arbalète, which was also the site of the city's first "Garden of Simples", created by Nicolas Houel, a 16th-century apothecary.

When the Faculty of Pharmacology was transferred to avenue de l'Observatoire, the garden too was replanted (in 1880). Originally its surface area was almost 8,000 m^2, but now it occupies about half that. Nevertheless, it is still delightful to wander around the plant beds and old-style greenhouses, which contain about 500 different species of medicinal plants, toxic plants and plants that are used in the production of perfumes and cosmetics.

Each one is identified with a little label fixed into the ground; however, the abundance of weeds sometimes makes these difficult to read.

NEARBY

The elephants ④
at 1, avenue de
l'Observatoire

Directly opposite the former École Coloniale (see page 107) stands a very attractive building which, in spite of its exuberant façade, is easily missed by passers-by. Note, in particular, the carved elephant decoration on the first floor.

War-wounded Palm trees

The palm trees which during the summer months are placed near the large pond in the Jardin du Luxembourg are war veterans. The holes in the trunks of some of the trees were caused by shell shrapnel during the First World War.

BUILDING AT 26, RUE VAVIN

Building in tiers

Métro: Vavin

T his is one of the first houses in which the architect Henri Sauvage experimented with a tiered design. Built in 1912, it applies the principles that would find full expression in the more ambitious building in rue des Amiraux in the 18th *arrondissement* (see page 339). As the façade "retreats" gradually, each level has a terrace and even the lower floors are open to the light; the effect is enhanced by the use of white tiling, similar to that used in the métro.

NEARBY

Musée de minéralogie at the École des mines

60, boulevard Saint-Michel
RER: Luxembourg
Tel.: 01 40 51 91 39 • musee@mines-paristech.fr • Open from Monday to
Friday, 1.30pm–6pm - On Saturday, 10am–12.30pm and 2pm–5pm
Founded in 1794, this rather old-fashioned museum occupies a fine panelled gallery that stretches 100 m along the Hôtel de Vendôme. Aligned along the walls, the 19th-century display cabinets contain a dazzling collection that is one of the most important in the world and unique in France. You could spend many happy hours here inspecting the 80,000 exhibits, including some spectacular rarities. There is, for example, a large boleite specimen, a cube of radioactive thorianite and even the world's most wonderful specimen of haureite crystals (under cover in a wood-sided display case because continuous exposure to light would destroy them),

Reid Hall ⑦

4, rue de Chevreuse
A polite request to the porter may gain you admission to the Paris premises of Columbia University. These have a beautiful garden and a quite amazing lecture hall; built in the English style, Reid Hall can seat up to 200 people and is also used for evening lectures. The programme of events can be found on the website www.textes-et-voix.asso.fr or at the Tschann bookshop on boulevard Montparnasse.

Musée Zadkine ⑧

100 bis, rue d'Assas
Open daily from 10am–5.40pm. Closed Mondays and holidays
Tel.: 01 55 42 77 20 • musee.zadkine@paris.fr
Tucked out of sight of the street, this charming museum covers the work of the Russian-born sculptor Ossip Zadkine. Having emigrated to Paris in 1908, he lived and worked in this house-studio from 1928 until his death in 1967. The small entrance garden is particularly pleasant and contains a number of works specially adapted for the blind.

CHAPEL OF THE SOEURS AUXILIATRICES DU PURGATOIRE

A neo-Byzantine cupola

Accueil Barouillère
14, rue Saint-Jean-Baptiste-de-La-Salle
Métro: Duroc, Vaneau or Falguière
Tel.: 01 53 69 61 00
Telephone for appointment

In 1856 Eugénie Smet, Sister Marie de la Providence, founded the Congregation of the Auxiliary Sisters in Paris, adopting a Rule based on the spiritual exercises of St Ignatius Loyola. The Barouillère house is the mother house of this order.

You can meditate and pray here in a 19th-century chapel surmounted by a neo-Byzantine cupola; the edifice has recently been restored, inspired by the theme of hope. Contemporary in style, the altar combines wood and perspex and is particularly interesting. You can also visit the rooms where the founder of the order lived and worked until her death on 7 February 1871. These have been left just as they were and are imbued with a pleasant sense of calm and quiet.

NEARBY
Relics of Saint Vincent de Paul

⑩

Lazarist Church of Saint-Vincent-de-Paul
95, rue de Sèvres
Tel.: 01 45 49 84 84
Open 7am–12.30pm and 1.30pm–6pm
Weekday mass at 7.15am. Sunday mass at 10.30am

The chapel of the Lazarist Fathers in rue de Sèvres has, since 1830, housed the relics of Saint Vincent de Paul. These are contained in a dazzling silver shrine – made by the silversmith Odiot and paid for by the people of Paris – which dominates the chapel choir. Steps adorned with bas-reliefs lead to a scene that will powerfully affect the more sensitive visitor: the skeleton of the saint, with the face and hands modelled in wax. The body is clothed in priestly vestments and the hands hold the cross said to be the actual one with which St Vincent attended Louis XIII on his deathbed.

Statues of Liberty in France

Apart from the two Statues of Liberty in Paris (in the Jardin du Luxembourg and on the Île des Cygnes), there are another five versions of the famous New York statue in France: one at Roybon (Isère), one at Barentin near Rouen (it appears in Gérard Oury's film *Le Cerveau*, with Bourvil and Jean-Paul Belmondo), one in place de la Liberté in Poitiers, one in Colmar and one at Saint-Cyr-sur-Mer (see our guide *Secret Provence*).

The original statue in New York was presented to the USA by France (or rather, a collection of individual subscribers) in 1886. The statue itself is by Frédéric-Auguste Bartholdi, although it was Gustave Eiffel who designed the internal metal structure to which the copper plates are riveted. The figure symbolises "Liberty enlightening the world".

CRYPT OF SAINT-JOSEPH-DES-CARMES CHURCH

Blood-stained flagstones

70, rue de Vaugirard
Métro: Rennes
www.sjdc.fr • Visits to the crypt: Saturday at 3pm

AYANT PRÉFÉRÉ LA MORT A LA VIOLATION
DE LA SAINTE LOI DE DIEU ILS ONT ÉTÉ MASSACRÉS

Every Saturday at 3pm, groups of five or six people can visit the macabre and little-known crypt of Saint-Joseph-des-Carmes. Before the Revolution, the Carmelite monastery was a peaceful place nestling in a garden where the monks produced the distillation of lemon balm that became well known as *Eau des Carmes*. This is still on sale today under the name *Eau des Carmes Boyer*. The monastery church was also famous for its cupola, which had been the first in Paris.

After a law of 17 August 1792 ordered the closure of all monasteries and convents, the building was converted into a prison, whose inmates included some 160 clerics (three of them bishops). Having refused to take the oath of allegiance to the republican Constitution, which the Assembly had introduced for the clergy in 1790, these clerics would ultimately be massacred in prison. You can still see the steps to the garden where, summoned on Sunday 2 September 1792, these so-called *réfractaires* were killed by the pikestaffs and bayonets of a mob led by *Commissaire* Maillard. The accounts of that event subsequently written by the few survivors can be read on the website www.bxmartyrsde1792.com.

When rue de Rennes was laid out in 1867, it sliced through the monastery garden and resulted in the destruction of the Martyrs Chapel and of the well where the bodies had been thrown. Subsequent excavation recovered their remains, and these are now preserved in the church crypt. Aligned in rows, a number of the skulls bear clear traces of the murderers' blades.

The model of the demolished garden chapel also brings to mind the horrible scene (some of the blood-stained flagstones have survived).

The visit ends with a message that Josephine de Beauharnais, herself imprisoned here during the Revolution, wrote on the wall of her cell: "Liberty, when will you cease to be an empty word? It's seventeen days now since we were locked up. They tell us that we'll get out tomorrow. But isn't that just a vain hope?"

After the guided tour, you can wander around the garden and church, which is open to the public all day and contains a very fine *Virgin and Child* by Bernini.

THE LAST "STANDARD METRE"

An absolute standard

36, rue de Vaugirard
Métro: Saint-Sulpice or Mabillon

Achild of the Enlightenment and the French Revolution, the 'metre' was defined for the first time by the French Académie des Sciences in 1791 and was intended to replace all those units of measurement that made reference to the human body (*pouce*/inch; *pied*/foot, etc.). Given that individual bodies tend to vary, it had been frequent practice to take the body of the sovereign as the standard of reference, something that was clearly unacceptable to those opposed to the very idea of monarchy. The metre was finally adopted as the official unit of measurement in France in 1795. Subsequently, in 1796–1797, the Convention had sixteen standard metres engraved in marble and installed in various parts of the city, so that the population should become familiar with the new system. The plaque that can still be seen under the arcade of rue de Vaugirard (to the right of the porch to No. 36) is the only one still in its original position. The one other surviving standard metre in Paris was relocated in 1848 to 13, place Vendôme, to the left of the entrance to the Ministry of Justice; it had previously been fixed into the wall of the building that housed the Agence des Poids et Mesures (Bureau of Weights and Measures).

How is a metre defined?

It is all too often forgotten that the metre is a French invention, being defined by the Paris Académie des Sciences in 1791 as one ten millionth of a quarter of a meridian of the earth. By this definition, the circumference (that is, meridian) of the Earth was 40,000km. After the establishment of the first standard metre (see above), it was 1875 before seventeen other nations signed the "Convention du Mètre". In 1899, the Bureau of Weights and Measures had a standard metre cast in platinum-iridium alloy, which was held to be subject to only infinitesimal variations; that original bar can still be seen at the Pavillon de Breteuil in Sèvres (Hauts-de-Seine). With the advent of laser technology, the Conférence Générale des Poids et Mesures (CGPM) in 1960 gave a definition of the metre that is rather less comprehensible to the layman: 1,650,763.73 wavelengths of orange-coloured radiation emitted by the krypton 86 atom. In 1983 came an even more esoteric definition: the metre is the length of the path travelled by light in vacuum during a time interval of 1/299,792,458 of a second. According to the theory of relativity, the speed of light in vacuum is the same at all points, so this definition is considered to be more accurate.

NEARBY

Cloister of the former Séminaire de Saint-Sulpice ⑬

9, place Saint-Sulpice
Métro: Saint-Sulpice

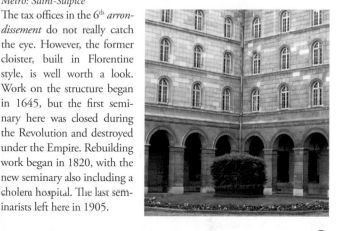

The tax offices in the 6th *arrondissement* do not really catch the eye. However, the former cloister, built in Florentine style, is well worth a look. Work on the structure began in 1645, but the first seminary here was closed during the Revolution and destroyed under the Empire. Rebuilding work began in 1820, with the new seminary also including a cholera hospital. The last seminarists left here in 1905.

Musée Édouard-Branly ⑭

Institut Catholique de Paris (ground floor)
21, rue d'Assas
http://museebranly.isep.fr/index.php • Contact: France Charles at 0149545 40

The three rooms occupied by the laboratory of Édouard Branly, inventor of radio conductors and former professor of physics at the Catholic University, have been converted into a museum. The exhibits include some of his inventions: the first remote control device and his magnificent "Nautilus Chamber", a Faraday cage coated with copper to block external electrical fields. You can also see the professor's study overlooking the Carmelite monastery, unchanged since Branly's day.

Remains of two brothels in Saint-Sulpice

The number plate at 36, rue Saint-Sulpice is deliberately larger than normal; this is a detail which serves to identify the location of most of the publicly-registered brothels in Paris. Note also the narrowness of the building, with just one window per floor. The madame here – a certain Miss Betty – will undoubtedly have had various clerics among her clients, given the large number in this area; the same was probably true at 15, rue Saint-Sulpice, where the tiled entrance still bears the name of the madame, Alys. The kitchen of the private apartment on the second floor occupies what was the brothel's hammam and is adorned with fine ceramic decorations, including a particularly shapely blonde ... (see page 49).

GNOMON IN THE CHURCH OF SAINT-SULPICE

An astronomical instrument "used" by The Da Vinci Code

Place Saint-Sulpice
www.paroisse-saint-sulpice-paris.org
Open daily 7.30am –7.30pm

Now attracting numerous pilgrims eager to verify what is said in T*he Da Vinci Code*, Saint-Sulpice church contains a real 18th-century gnomon. Standing in the north transept, this astronomical instrument consists of a vertical upright that, in sunlight or moonlight, casts a shadow on a horizontal surface which makes it possible to determine how high the sun or moon are above the horizon. The gnomon consists of a white obelisk about 12 m high. This is surmounted by a sphere from which a copper line runs down to floor level and then continues some 40 m across the choir and north transept.

Commissioned in 1727 by the parish priest, who wanted a more accurate means of determining the March equinox and thus the date of Easter Sunday, this instrument was designed by the clockmaker Henri de Sully, who had wanted to create a way of marking twelve noon within the city of Paris. However, he died before he could complete the task, and his work was subsequently modified, in 1743, by the astronomer Charles Le Monnier, assisted by the engineer Claude Langlois; these changes led to the creation of the famous pink copper line fitted into the floor between bands of white marble. Today, the sundial is only partially functional, as one of the "lenses" set in the window for the passage of sunlight was badly placed; however, the way it works is explained in detail in a text on a lectern not far from the gnomon.

Given the various claims made about this famous meridian in Dan Brown's book, another text has been added alongside this explanation for the benefit of the curious. It begins:"Contrary to the far-fetched allegations made in a recent novel of some success, the meridian line of Saint-Sulpice is not the extant trace of a pagan temple which, it is claimed, once stood here ..."

Corbelling: a real fire hazard

The medieval habit of constructing buildings with overhanging storeys was prohibited in Paris in the 1550s. Corbelled structures reach towards each other from either side of a street, so this building technique was a major factor in the spread of fires between wooden houses.

Why does rue de Rennes start only at Nos. 41 and 44?

Nos. 1 to 40, rue de Rennes simply do not exist. When originally planned, the street was to run up from the Seine itself. However, when work finally began the street started where it does now. By the time it was clear that it would not extend to the river, it was too late to renumber the existing houses.

VISITING THE FRENCH SENATE

The treasures of the Senate building

Palais du Luxembourg
15, rue de Vaugirard
Métro: Saint-Sulpice or Mabillon
Bookings: 01 42 34 20 01
Admission free

To designs by the architect Salomon de Brosse, work on the palace began in 1615 at the behest of Queen Marie de Médicis, who wanted a building in a style that reminded her of the Pitti Palace in Florence. Now housing the French Senate, this is one of the finest – even if least known – of the public buildings of the Republic. Too often people forget that it is very easy to visit the palace, without having to wait for the *Journeés du Patrimoine* when it attracts huge crowds. Article 33 of the French Constitution lays down that parliamentary sessions must be open to the public; in fact, any citizen can attend the sessions of either the Senate or the National Assembly. However, while places are expensive and very hard to come by at the Assembly, the Senate is much more readily available (at no charge whatsoever) for anyone who wants to fulfil their conscientious duties as a citizen (see box for conditions of admission). Before housing the Senate in 1799, the Palais du Luxembourg had been used as a museum (1750–1780) and even as a prison during the Revolution. A visit to the modern-day building will give you the chance not only to see senators in full rhetorical flight or fast asleep

(both educational experiences), but also to admire the artistic wealth of the place: the 57 m long conference chamber, formerly the Throne Room, which was built in 1852 by Alphonse de Gisors; the famous Library, decorated in 1845 by Delacroix; and the 18ᵗʰ-century salons by Germain Boffrand.

© Photo Sénat/E. Poget

How to visit the Senate

• With valid identification, go to 15 rue de Vaugirard on a day when the Senate is sitting (generally Tuesday, Wednesday or Thursday, plus other days – even at night during the annual budget debate). For days and times of sittings, Tel.: 01 42 34 20 01. Tickets to the public gallery (*tribune*) are available on a "first come, first served" basis.

• Other days when the doors are open to the public (generally Saturdays): the *Journée du Livre d'Economie* (January), the *Journée du Livre d'Histoire* (June), etc. These are announced on the Senate website: www.senat.fr.

• Individual visits organised one Saturday a month, 10.30am–2.30pm, by the Centre des Monuments Nationaux (+33 (0) 1 44 54 19 49).

• Group visits: more information at www.senat.fr

• *Journées du Patrimoine* (generally the third weekend in September).

MUSÉE D'HISTOIRE DE LA MÉDECINE

Don't forget the flayed man

Université de Paris-V – René-Descartes
12, rue de l'École-de-Médecine
Métro: Odéon
Tel.: 01 40 46 16 93
www.bium.univ-paris5.fr/musee/
Summer opening hours: 2pm–5.30pm, except Saturday, Sunday and public
holidays • Winter opening hours: 2pm–5.30pm, except Thursday, Sunday and
public holidays • Guided tours every Tuesday at 2.30pm, except during school
holidays • Admission: €3.5 (concessions €2.5). Guided tours: €8

This very attractive hall of cast iron and glass on the second floor of the medical school houses the unusual History of Medicine Museum. At the entrance you are greeted by a life-size anatomical model of the human body – minus its skin; from there you pass through one of the oldest such collections in Europe, which traces the astonishing history of medicine and surgery from the days of classical antiquity to the 19th century. Scalpels, trepans and surgical saws can be seen alongside objects that are veritable works of art – for example, a 17th-century circumcision kit in silver and agate. Other items of interest include the scalpel that belonged to Louis XIV's personal surgeon, Félix, and the medical bag belonging to Doctor Antommarchi, who carried out Napoleon's autopsy.

NEARBY

Musée des compagnons du Tour de France

10, rue Mabillon
Open Monday to Friday 2pm–6pm
Admission free

Despite its name, the Museum of Apprenticeship has nothing to do with the cycle race: like another three apprenticeship museums in Paris, it documents the training that youths once had to go through to become journeymen (see page 348). The reception staff will be pleased to answer any questions you may have.

Star on the building at 12, rue de Buci ⑲

Here the stroller in quest of local interest will find a curious star carved into the façade of the building. In fact, this is a Masonic symbol, the "Flaming Star" indicating the second level in the hierarchy of Freemasonry. In 1732 the building housed the first Masonic lodge in Paris

Cour de Rohan ⑳

Access via cour du Commerce-Saint-André or rue du Jardinet (before 8pm)

Made up of three small communicating courtyards, the charming cour de Rohan owes its name to the Hôtel des Évêques de Rouen (Bishops of Rouen), with the name of the city being corrupted into "Rohan". It has been linked with cour du Commerce-Saint-André since 1791, and traces of the city walls dating from the time of Philippe Auguste (at Nos. 3 and 7) can still be seen. A tower from those walls – now a private residence – stands within the Maison de la Catalogne in Cour du Commerce-Saint-André. The second courtyard has an old "shoe step" in wrought iron, which served to help women and old people to mount their horses. The third courtyard, which gives onto rue du Jardinet, has an old well complete with pulley and waterspout.

MUSÉE DUPUYTREN

A little museum of horrors

15, rue de l'École-de-Médecine
Métro: Odéon
Tel.: 01 42 34 68 60
www.umpc.fr
patrice.josset@upmc.fr
Open from Monday to Friday 2pm–5pm
Admission: €5 (concessions €3)

The Dupuytren Museum of Anatomical Pathology is certainly not suitable for everyone; it could give nightmares to children or to those of a sensitive disposition. When it was first set up, in fact, only men were admitted ...

The museum opened in 1835 and was financed by a legacy left by Guillaume Dupuytren, a professor of surgical medicine. Initially it occupied the refectory of the monastery of the Franciscan Observatines (the Cordeliers), where it remained until 1935. At that date it was considered to have become obsolete, and the material was stored away in the basements of the Faculty of Medicine. The museum was then laid out again in its present location in 1967. One old-fashioned room contains more than 6,000 exhibits illustrating the diseases and malformations of the human body. The oldest pieces in the collection date back to the 18th century, while the most recent were added in the 1930s. Most of the exhibits are human organs, some actually conserved in glass bottles, some reproduced in casts. Some of the items are of real historical value for example, the brain from one of Paul Broca's patients, which helped

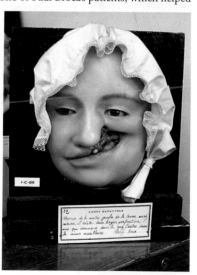

the physician to develop his theory regarding the cerebral location of specific functions.

The most disturbing exhibits are undoubtedly those of genital malformations: some, such as the cast of a penis covered with a fungal infection, or the genitalia of a hermaphrodite – are rather hard to take. There is also a startling collection of malformed foetuses preserved in jars, ranging from Siamese twins (two heads on one body) to an actual "cyclops"... We'll leave the descriptions at that.

STATUE OF DEATH

A striking portrayal of Death

15, rue de l'École-de-Médecine
Métro: Odéon

Already shaken by the contents of the fearsome Musée Dupuytren, you emerge into the open air and, just a few steps later, come across the discreetly placed Statue of Death. It is enough to make you wonder about the mental stability of the students and professors at "Réne Descartes" Faculty of Medicine.

Having crossed the cloister after leaving the museum, turn left and there, in a corner, is this strikingly realistic piece of sculpture. The work of Allouard (1910), the figure has all the classic attributes of Death – including the scythe – and treads upon all the symbols of human pride and vanity: a crown, a coffer of treasure, a sword, jewels and gems, a sceptre … As with the museum alongside: not for children.

NEARBY

Refectory of the Monastery of Les Cordeliers ㉓

15, rue de l'École-de-Médecine
Information on the temporary exhibitions held here at: www.mam.paris.fr
www.refectoire-cordeliers.paris-sorbonne.fr • Tel. 01 44 27 81 60

All that remains today of the famous Monastery of Les Cordeliers* is this refectory, a fine example of Flamboyant Gothic built at the end of the 15th century. A place of religious devotion, the monastery is best known for the fact that, from 1790 to 1794, it was home to the (in)famous Club des Cordeliers, whose members included Danton and Marat; after his assassination by Charlotte Corday, the latter was buried in the monastery gardens. Covering an area of more than 900 m², the fine refectory is lit by vast Gothic windows and has an impressive timber-work roof. Now the property of the City of Paris, it is a listed historic monument and is used for temporary exhibitions and other events.

House of Auguste Comte ㉔

10, rue Monsieur-Le-Prince. Tel. : 01 43 26 08 56
Open every Wednesday 2pm–5pm • www.augustecomte.org

Restored in the 1960s thanks to Paulo Carniero, Brazilian ambassador to UNESCO, Auguste Comte's apartment now looks at it did at the time of the death of this philosopher, the founder of Positivism (see page 63). Lasting some 5 to 10 minutes, the visit is a perfect opportunity to learn something about Positivism, and perhaps put a few questions to the staff on duty that day. There is nothing strange about the fact that the apartment was restored by a Brazilian: most adherents of Positivism today are to be found in Brazil, a country in which there is great interest in the spiritual and the esoteric.

---

* The official title of the order was the Franciscan Observatines; "Les Cordeliers" refers to the cord belt they wore with their robes.

SECRETS OF THE ÉCOLE DES BEAUX-ARTS

All the magic of Paris

14, rue Bonaparte
Métro: Saint-Germain-des-Prés
Tel.: 01 47 03 50 74 • www.monuments-nationaux.fr
visites-conferences@monuments-nationaux.fr
Possible visiting times: during the June "open days"; for groups with lecturer,
by appointment on Monday afternoons (except during school holidays):
01 47 03 50 00; for individuals, guided tours are organised by the Centres des
Monuments Nationaux (MONUM); for information on the schedule
(the guided tours are held about every three months),
Tel.: 01 44 54 19 30 or 01 44 54 19 35
Admission: €8 (concessions €6)

Occupying 2 hectares of land in the [...]main-des-Prés area, the École des Bea[...] es that are an essential part of the magic of [...] date back to the 17th century, and all aroun[...] dents themselves, giving the place a uniquely [...] oldest part of the art school is the chapel and [...] were built at the beginning of the 17th century [...] Petits Augustins friars and paid for by Queen [...] said to have been acquired dishonestly (*mal acquis*), nence the name of the nearby quai Malaquais.

When the chapel was deconsecrated in 1795, Alexandre Lenoir (1761-1839) used it to house a Musée des Monuments Français; when that closed in 1816, the building became part of the École des Beaux-Arts. Today, it houses various copies of works from the French and Italian Renaissance, including the *Gates of Paradise*, the original of which were produced by Ghiberti for the Baptistery of Florence Cathedral, and Xavier Sigalon's copy of Michelangelo's *Last Judgment*.

The glazed courtyard (1832) was the inspiration for Labrouste's design for the Reading Room at the Bibliothèque Imperiale (now the Bibliothèque Richlieu, see page 37). The so-called Amphithéâtre d'Honneur – also known as the Award Amphitheatre – is famous for the Paul Delaroche painting *La Renommée distribuant des couronnes* ("Fame Distributing Crowns").

The study hall, the exhibition space and the examination building are by the architect François Debret, whose work here was continued by his pupil and brother-in-law, Félix Duban; they were also respon-

sible for the restoration of the entrance courtyard, the chapel courtyard and the magnificent cour des Mûriers (Mulberry Courtyard), an authentic Florentine-style cloister. The final extension to the École des Beaux-Arts came in 1883, with the purchase of the Hôtel de Chimary and its annexes at 15 and 17, quai Malaquais. Conveniently, the porter at the rue Bonaparte entrance often mistakes visitors for students, so you can inspect the magnificent cloister – just to the right of the entrance – without being disturbed.

NEARBY
Lecture hall
16, rue Bona[...]
Tel.: 01 4[...]
subjec[...]
E[...]

of the Académie de Médecine

...arte

*...34 57 73 • Public lectures held on Tuesday afternoons; for times and
...s of lectures, see www.academie-medecine.fr*

...en if they are designed for a specialist audience, the public lectures given
on Tuesday afternoons are a perfect opportunity to discover a place which
is unknown to most Parisians, even though it is located just alongside the
École des Beaux-Arts. Note the magnificence of the lecture hall, which is
overseen by a large (2.7 m) statue of Hippocrates by Dimitriadis; there is
also a gallery of busts by such figures as Houdon and David d'Angers, as
well as a charming little library. The official function of the academy, set up
in 1820 at the behest of Louis XVIII, is to provide the government with any
information it requires on public health issues and to publish the results of
medical research in various fields.

NEARBY

Vestige of Philippe Auguste's city walls in an underground car park

27, rue Mazarine

The first level of this underground car park contains an important vestige of the Philippe Auguste city walls (see page 81). There is pedestrian access, and a plaque marks the location of the wall fragment.

A surprising concrete building: 1, rue Danton

15, rue de l'École-de-Médecine

Built by François Hennebique for himself, the structure at 1 rue Danton is surprising because it is entirely made from concrete even if looks as if it were in stone. Reinforced concrete was, in fact, invented by Hennebique's company, which took out a patent in 1892; the company moved into these premises in 1898.

Quebec in Saint-Germain des-Près

Standing at the junction of boulevard Saint-Germain, rue de Rennes and rue Bonaparte, place du Québec owes its name to the fact that Quebec's first bishop, Monseigneur François de Montmorency-Laval, was ordained just opposite, at the church of Saint-Germain-des-Près, in 1674. The strange fountain in the square is probably misinterpreted by most of the local residents: in fact, the upthrust rupturing the overlapping flagstones is intended to represent the rupturing of the ice on Canada's rivers. The nearby Café Le Québec adds to the area's references to this particular province of Canada.

HÔTEL DES MONNAIES PYRAMID ㉙

The one The Da Vinci Code forgot

11, quai de Conti
Métro: Pont-Neuf, Louvre-Rivoli or Odéon

More an obelisk than a pyramid, this is one of Paris's three indicators of noon set up on the meridian; the other two being the obelisk-gnomon at Saint-Sulpice and the Palais-Royal cannon-chronometer (when it was working). It stands in a corner of one of the courtyards of the Hôtel des Monnaies and probably dates back to 1768.

NEARBY

Bibliothèque Mazarine

23, quai de Conti
Tel.: 01 44 41 44 06 • www.bibliotheque-mazarine.fr
Opening hours: Monday to Friday 10am–6pm • Annual closing: 1–15 August
Open to the public, who can register on the spot; valid identification and two
passport photographs required • The temporary pass is free, the provisional card
costs €7.50 and an annual pass €15

This marvellous place is inextricably linked with the name of its founder, Cardinal Mazarin, whose coat-of-arms appears on the pediment of the façade, on the wood carvings of the Reading Room and on the morocco leather of the book bindings. All the public needs to gain access is valid identification and two passport-size photographs.

The core collection here was put together by the cardinal himself in his private mansion. In 1643, this library was then opened to scholars and men of letters, and is thus the oldest public library in France. To avoid his collection being split up after his death, Mazarin bequeathed it to the Collège des Quatre-Nations, whose entire left wing was given over to his library (not only the books but also the bookshelves and furnishings). Attached since 1945 to the Institut de France, which now occupies the buildings of the former Collège des Quatres-Nations, the Bibliothèque Mazarine is impressive not only for its collections of antique books but also for the splendid neoclassical staircase that leads up to a stunning Reading Room, 65 m long and 8 m high. Lit by eighteen windows, between which the bookshelves form thirty-two bays, the room is decorated with various *objets d'art* (most of them seized from private and royal collections during the Revolution).

Why the Académie Française had line 4 of the métro rerouted

The "hook" in Line 4 of the Paris métro, which makes a surprising detour eastwards to Île de la Cité as it runs from Saint-Germain-des-Prés to Les Halles, is due to the fact that the underground trains cause vibrations. If the route had run in a straight line, it would have passed beneath the meeting rooms of the Académie Française (Institut de France) and the vibrations would have disturbed the work of the *académiciens*.

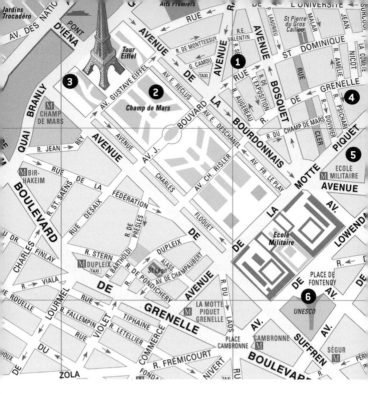

7ᵗʰ Arrondissement

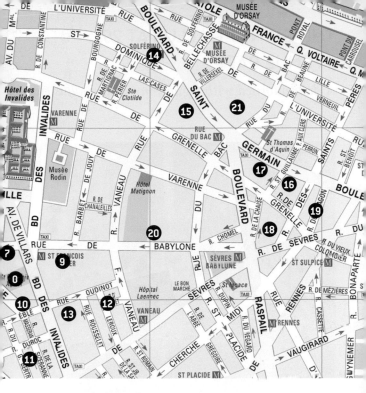

THE GIANT PHALLUS AT 29, AVENUE RAPP

A door adorned with a giant inverted phallus cloister

RER: Pont-de-l'Alma

A prize-winner in a 1901 competition for façade design, the building at 29, avenue Rapp is considered to be Lavirotte's masterpiece. Surmounted by a female head (perhaps a portrait of the architect's wife) and flanked by Adam and Eve driven out of Paradise, the main doorway is relatively well known to Parisians; however, there are few who have noticed that the door itself takes the form of an inverted phallus. To see this, just focus on the central part of the wooden door (the carving itself is significant), with the central glass panel and the two oval-shaped glass panels at the top. A fervent champion of sexual symbolism, Lavirotte also used the motif of a penis inside a vulva in the ironwork of the ground-floor window balconies.

Contrary to what is widely believed, the owners of the building were Lavirotte himself and a certain Charles Combes. It was never the home of the ceramicist Alexandre Bigot, whom many think used the façade to advertise his skills; however, there is no doubt that he did adorn the building with his famous stoneware ceramics, specially adapting them for use in architecture. Lavirotte himself lived on the fifth floor of the nearby building at 3, square Rapp.

Jules Lavirotte

One of the most famous architects of Parisian Art Nouveau, Jules Lavirotte (1864–1929) was undoubtedly the most flamboyant. He not only banished straight lines and right angles from designs in which curves predominate, but he also made free use of sexual symbolism – something which did not prevent him from becoming the only architect to win the "City of Paris" façade design award three times. However in 1907 he abandoned Art Nouveau, claiming that the imitations of his work were mere pastiches which betrayed the essence of the original movement.

His most famous buildings are to be found at 29, ave Rapp, 3, square Rapp, 12, ave Sédillot and 34, ave de Wagram (Hotel Céramic, see page 163). Other, less spectacular, buildings by him can be seen at 134 and 151, rue de Grenelle, 23, ave de Messine, 169, boulevard Lefebvre and 2, rue Balza at Franconville (95) (Villa Dupont).

Other ceramic phalluses

The building at 12, avenue Sédillot was the first fully designed by Lavirotte. That at 3, square Rapp contains quite clear sexual symbols (most notably, the ceramic phalluses in the window balconies of the fourth floor).

THE "RIGHTS OF MAN" MONUMENT ②

A Masonic celebration of the bicentenary of the Revolution

Champ-de-Mars
Métro: École-Militaire

The children who play football at its base may never have noticed that this is one of the most intriguing monuments in the capital. Commissioned in 1989 by the City of Paris to celebrate the bicentenary of the French Revolution, this "Rights of Man" monument in the Champ-de-Mars owes its dense esoteric symbolism to Michel Baroni, the former Great Master of the Grand Orient Masonic Lodge, who was responsible for organising the anniversary.

Designed by the sculptor Ivan Theimer, the structure itself is a small stone temple with decorative features inspired largely by Egyptian and Masonic motifs: a sundial, triangular obelisks, pyramids, solar images and other astrological and esoteric symbols. All this is heaped together with The Declaration of the Rights of Man and various scientific drawings. The side of the monument that looks out towards the Champ-de-Mars is lined by four statues of figures in togas. The most surprising figure of all is that of a little boy in a cylindrical cap, who is probably intended to symbolise apprenticeship in knowledge.

NEARBY

Chimney of the Eiffel Tower ③

RER: Champ-de-Mars

Tucked behind the western pier of the Eiffel Tower, few may have noticed a brick-built pillar surrounded by bushes. This dates from the work on the tower's foundations (1887) and was a chimney linked by a duct to the old machine room under the south pier.

Garden of the Lutheran Church ④

147, rue de Grenelle

A small and little-known garden laid out around the Lutheran Evangelical Church.

The porcupine at 82, boulevard De La Tour-Maubourg ⑤

The amazing crowned porcupine which stands above the entrance doorway was the emblem of Louis XII. The same motif is to be found on the exterior portal of the Louis XII wing of Blois Chateau.

Vertical gardens

Created by the botanist Patrick Blanc, these vertical gardens have become a cult in Paris. The various examples of Blanc's work can now be seen at: Musée du Quai Branly, 7ᵗʰ *arrondissement*; the Marithé et François Girbaud boutique, 6ᵗʰ *arrondissement* (see our guide: *Unusual Shopping in Paris*); the interior courtyard of the Hôtel Pershing-Hall, 8ᵗʰ *arrondissement*; the Fondation Cartier, 14ᵗʰ *arrondissement*.

Curiously, house numbers on quai d'Orsay begin with No. 33. This is because, in 1947, part of the quai was renamed after Anatole France. However, changing the address of the Foreign Ministry was out of the question, given that "Quai d'Orsay" is as synonymous with French foreign affairs.

WORKS OF ART AT UNESCO ⑥

Picasso, Miró, Calder, Giacometti, Tadao Ando ...

United Nations Educational, Scientific and Cultural Organization
7, place de Fontenoy
Métro: La Motte-Piquet or Ségur
Access only by appointment • Guided tours every Tuesday at 3pm (in English)
and Wednesday at 3pm (in French)
Identification required. Reservations at: 01 45 68 03 59
unesco.org/visit/fr/v4/index.htm • visits@unesco.org

A hidden Zen garden, a panoramic terrace, works by the greatest of modern artists ... UNESCO is crammed with art; on the walls hang more than 500 different works. There is even a remarkable space designed by the Japanese architect Tadao Ando, who was to have built the Musée Pinault of the Île Seguin.

As soon as the building was completed in 1958, famous artists were invited to make a contribution to the interior décor. Pablo Picasso, Joan Miró, Henry Moore, Alexander Calder, Jean Arp and Isamu Noguchi all responded, creating works especially for the site. In the foyer to the Conference Halls stands the largest work Picasso ever painted; a tragic *Fall of Icarus*, this acrylic on wood panel measures 10 m by 9 m. Outside, the work by Noguchi is probably the most famous of the contributions. The Japanese artist started with a few sculptures for the terrace, but ultimately transformed the place into an authentic "Japanese garden", a marvel of quiet and greenery. Other names encountered here are Giacometti, Brassaï, Appel, Tapies, Chillida and Bazaine. But it was not only painters and sculptors who made a contribution: no less than twelve architects played a part in the design of this Y-shaped building, which rests on 72 trapezoidal pillars in reinforced concrete and has three curved glass façades whose lines echo the semicircle of place de Fontenoy. The three main architects were Marcel Breuer, Pier Luigi Nervi and Bernard Zehrfuss, with input from Walter Gropius (the father of Bauhaus) as well as from Le Corbusier, Lucio Costa, Sven Markelius, Ernesto Rogers and Eero Saarine. One room was designed by the American Philip Johnson, one of the first exponents of the "International Style" of which the UNESCO building is an example.

More recently, in 1995, the Japanese architect Tadao Ando worked here on what is his sole completed project in France. This is a "meditation space" in the form of an inclined concrete cylinder, where thoughts, like the flowing water, can run on forever.

TINTORETTO'S *LAST SUPPER*

A little-known masterpiece by Tintoretto

Church of Saint-François-Xavier
Marriage Sacristy
Métro: Saint-François-Xavier
Open Sunday morning 9am–12pm, or by appointment
http://www.sfx-paris.fr/

The Marriage Sacristy in the church of Saint-François-Xavier unexpectedly contains a masterpiece by Tintoretto (1518–1594), one of the great masters of the Venetian Renaissance.

This *Last Supper* was painted in 1559 for the chapel of the Scuola del Santissimo Sacramento (Confraternity of the Holy Sacrament) in the Venetian church of San Felice. The inscription in the lower left names those who, at the time of the commission, were at the head of the confraternity, which was dedicated to the protection and veneration of the consecrated host. Thus we learn that the *gastaldo* (chamberlain) was Girolamo Diletti, the *vicario* (vicar) Salvador di Orsini and the *scrivano* (secretary) Marco de Marco. The painter also included their portraits in the picture. However, only those of the vicar and secretary (at the far right and left of the scene) survive; that of the chamberlain was removed by order of his successor after Diletti was accused of ill management of the confraternity's funds.

Though Tintoretto painted *The Last Supper* a number of times, this was not – as some say – because it was his favourite subject, but because it was much in demand among his clients. Anxious that his patrons should never feel they were getting "mass-produced" works, the artist did however tend to focus on a different moment in the gospel narrative each time he painted the scene. The San Felice work, for example, hinges on the identification of the apostle who will betray Christ. Jesus has just caused great agitation by announcing that there is a traitor amongst them; the apostles are looking at each other, trying to identify who the wretch might be. The painter also involves the spectator in the scene, by revealing something hidden from those within the picture: Judas faces away from us, but we see that behind his back he is clutching the purse with his thirty pieces of silver.

NEARBY

Religious plants in the garden of Saint-François-Xavier Presbytery ⑧

39, boulevard des Invalides

Open during the Parisian *Fête des Jardins* and every Thursday evening in summer (for fathers left alone in the city while their families are on holiday), this is a charming priest's garden which focuses on plants that have some sort of relation with the Church. These include: honesty (*monnaie-du-pape*), curate pears (*poirier du curé*), "red cascade" spindle trees (*fusain bonnet de prêtre*) and of course daisies (called *pâquerettes* in French because they flower around Easter, *Pâques*).

LA PAGODE CINEMA

A cinema in a Japanese pagoda

57, rue de Babylone
Métro: Saint-Francois-Xavier
Tél. : 01 45 55 48 48

The Far East was all the rage in late 19th-century Paris, and the owner of the Bon Marché department store, François-Émile Morin, had the brilliant idea of giving his wife an actual Japanese pagoda as a present. The architect Alexandre Marcel took his inspiration from the Toshogu sanctuary in Nikko (north Japan). However, shortly after receiving the gift, Madame Morin left her husband, who put the pagoda up for sale. The Chinese embassy was soon interested in the purchase as

it was looking for premises within the capital. It was only by a hair's breath that a possible diplomatic incident was avoided: not until the last minute did the Chinese emissaries realise that the frescoes inside the building actually depict Chinese defeats at the hands of the Japanese... Converted into a cinema in 1931, the pagoda was where Cocteau held the premiere of *Testament d'Orphée*. It has been a listed building since 1986. A charming little tea-room opens out onto a garden which is a particularly pleasant in the fine weather.

NEARBY

The indulgences plaque in the church of Saint-François-Xavier

In this church is a record of a religious practice that nowadays seems particularly anachronistic. Just to the right as you enter the room which houses Tintoretto's painting, there is a plaque with the following inscription: "By rescript of XXIII December MDCCCXCVII (1897), His Holiness Leo XIII has granted an indulgence ... for attendance at five services of the novena of grace celebrated from IV to XII March in the church of Saint-François-Xavier, and an indulgence of one hundred days for each service."

NEARBY
Musée Valentin-Haüy ⑪

5, rue Duroc
Métro: Duroc
Tel. : 01 44 49 27 27 • Open Tuesday and Wednesday 2.30pm to 5pm. Closed during school holidays • Admission free • museevalentinhauy@avh.asso.fr

Set up in 1886, the Musée Valentin Haüy is named after a man who founded a school for the blind in 1785; it charts the history of the blind and of the various methods developed to enable them to read and write – from the invention of raised cursive script to the introduction of Braille. This fascinating museum collection also includes a number of objects, machines and works of art created either for or by the blind or partially sighted.

A small area dedicated to the blind

The Musée Valentin-Haüy is conveniently located just next to the National Institute for Young Blind People, in boulevard des Invalides. A couple of steps away lies rue Valentin Haüy itself, which is officially part of the 15ᵗʰ *arrondissement*, and rue Maurice de la Suzeranne, which cuts across rue Duroc; the street is named after the founder of the Association Valentin Haüy, who as the result of an accident lost his sight at the age of nine.

NEARBY
23, rue Oudinot and 50, rue Vaneau ⑫

If one of the residents happens to be opening the door, take the chance to glimpse this little corner of paradise, with its low houses and cobbled streets.

Garden of the Saint Jean de Dieu Clinic ⑬

19, rue Oudinot

If you ask, you may be allowed through to see the magnificent garden of this private clinic which specialises in nosocomial treatment and surgery.

SHRAPNEL MARKS

Bulletholes in the ministry wall

At 231, boulevard Saint Germain
Métro: Solferino or Assemblée-Nationale

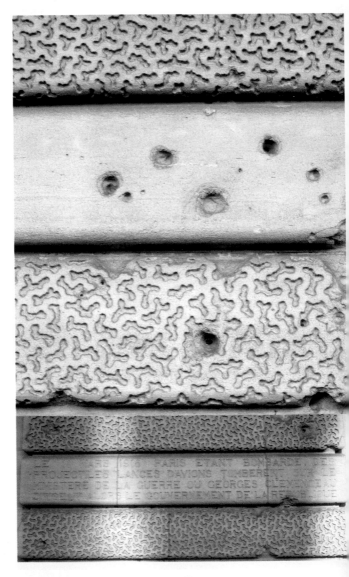

The former Ministry of War, which now houses the General Staff of the Armed Forces, bears disturbing witness to how close the First World War came to the centre of Paris. The damage to the walls was caused by shrapnel during the heavy bombardment of Paris on 11 March 1918. An inscription in the stone recounts details of the event.

If you are particularly interested in traces of past warfare, you will find numerous examples within the city. For example, shell damage can be seen on the Théâtre de l'Europe in the 6th *arrondissement* and on the façade of the Law Courts in the 4th. Even more astonishing is the small cannonball still embedded in the walls of the Hôtel de Sens (see page 85); this dates from the days of the 1830 revolution.

NEARBY

Garden of the Maison de l'Amérique Latine ⑮
217, boulevard Saint-Germain
Tel. : 01 49 54 75 10
Closed on weekends

This 18th-century town mansion has an exceptionally fine French-style garden. You can take advantage of the place either by visiting one of the numerous exhibitions held here, or by reserving a table on the terrace of the restaurant (menu at €37; see our guide *Secret Bars & Restaurants in Paris*).

© Maison de l'Amérique latine

PROTESTANT LIBRARY

A library of religion

54, rue des Saints-Pères
Métro: Saint-Germain-des-Prés • Open Monday to Wednesday 2pm–6pm,
Thursday 10am–6pm, Friday 1.30pm–5.30pm • Closed August
Tel: 01 45 48 62 07 • www.shpf.fr • shpf2@wanadoo.fr

ounded in 1885, the Protestant Library is a fine room open to the public. Though primarily a library, it also holds small exhibitions regarding Protestantism and its history.

The location is no accident, as the building stands some 50 m from the old embassy of the Netherlands, which in the days of religious persecution was where Parisian Protestants came to attend church services. The fine room is in a pre-Baltard style (Victor Baltard being the architect of the famous metal structures of Les Halles) and measures 21 m in length and 11 m in width. The library itself comprises more than 180,000 volumes, some of them extremely rare, together with various manuscripts, medallions, periodicals, etc.

NEARBY

House of Doctor Dalsace, ⑰
also know as the "House of glass"

31, rue Saint-Guillaume
Group visits possible upon application to the Association des Amis de Pierre Chareau
Tel: 01 45 44 91 21 • mdv.31@orange.fr

Hidden away at end of a courtyard, the house of Doctor Dalsace was a real novelty in its day. The work of the architects Pierre Chareau and Bernard Bijovet, it was built for the doctor in 1928–1931 and has been a listed historic monument since 1982.

The house occupies three floors but was actually conceived as a single space. The sophisticated design plays upon the transparency of the walls to create a fluid composition of space that was particularly avant-garde for the time. The façade giving onto the courtyard comprises glass panels held in a metal structure, whilst inside the private and public areas are divided by sliding or pivoting partitions. All the components of the structure, including pipes and conduits, are left visible so they also function as decorative motifs.

One curious detail: during building work, the aged occupier of the top floor refused to sell his apartment, so the "house of glass" had to be built within the old town mansion, with the result that the final ensemble is rather unusual.

Square Récamier ⑱

Even if the access road, rue Récamier, leads off the very busy rue de Sèvres, just a couple of steps away from the Bon Marché department store, the small Square Récamier is relatively unknown to Parisians, as it forms a cul-de-sac with access solely for pedestrians.

NEARBY

Garden of the École des Sciences Politiques

56, rue des Saints-Pères • Open during term

Known familiarly as *Sciences-Po*, the renowned Parisian School of Political Sciences has, as one of its premises, a 17th-century town mansion that was formerly the residence of Gabriel de Mortemart, father of the Marquise de Montespan. In theory, the magnificent garden is reserved for students and teachers, but sometimes a polite request can get you in to see it.

Garden of the Foreign Missions Institute

128, rue du Bac
Open to the public during the Journées du Patrimoine [Cultural Heritage Days]
and, by appointment, for group visits • Tel: 01 44 39 92 01
www.mepasie.org • 128ruedubac@gmail.com

This exceptional garden can be seen on those special days when parts of the city's cultural heritage that are usually private are thrown open to the public. It can also be visited by groups, by appointment. Mentioned frequently in Chateaubriand's writings, this enormous private garden - it occupies about one hectare of land – owes its existence to the founder of the Foreign Missions Institute, Bernard de Sainte-Thérèse, bishop of Babylon (whence the name of rue de Babylone just around the corner). Most of the numerous exotic plants here were brought back to France by missionaries returning from journeys to the far corners of the world; for example, the garden contains one of the two examples in France of the *Rosa soulieana*, this one having been brought back from Tibet in the 19th century.

A sphere of solid gold at the Palais Bourbon

Visible to the public from place de Palais Bourbon, the astonishing contemporary sculpture in the centre of the main courtyard of the National Assembly is by Walter de Maria. Standing on a base of white marble, the enigmatic sphere of black granite conceals within its core a second, invisible, sphere of solid gold.

A crooked bridge: Pont Alexandre III

Few notice that the axis of Pont Alexandre III is slightly skewed with respect to the river Seine flowing beneath it. Far from being a mistake by the architect, this was deliberate: it means that the bridge forms a perfectly straight line with esplanade des Invalides, thus becoming part of the "republican axis" which, during the Third Republic, was created for the Universal Exposition of 1900. The bridge is, however, named after Tsar Alexander III, whose son – Nicholas II, the last Tsar of Russia – laid the foundation stone during a 1896 visit to Paris. Not far away stands rue Franco-Russie, whose name commemorates the formal treaty between the two nations which was agreed during that same visit.

DEYROLLE

A veritable museum of the natural sciences

46, rue du Bac
Métro: Rue-du-Bac
Tel. : 01 42 22 30 07 • www.deyrolle.com • contact@deyrolle.fr
Open Monday 10am–1pm and 2pm–7pm, Tuesday to Saturday 10am–7pm

A veritable museum that is more a cabinet of curiosities than a shop, Deyrolle is extraordinary as the last surviving taxidermy* business in Paris, and one of the very few remaining in France as a whole (see our guide *Unusual Shopping in Paris*).

Housed in this fine town mansion of the 7th *arrondissement* since 1888, the Deyrolle business was actually founded in 1831 as a result of Jean-Baptiste Deyrolle's passion for natural history. His first and principal client was the State: the colour plates and stuffed animals that adorned the lecture halls of natural science faculties came from his studio. Nowadays, the premises are a treasure trove for collectors, decorators and set designers, with Deyrolle offering an amazing display of stuffed animals (lions, elephants, zebras …) and superb collections of insects, butterflies, fossils and minerals. Enthusiasts can also find originals or replicas of those famous teaching materials (plates, illustrations, etc). While the animals from all the continents of the world are available for purchase or hire, they do come at a price: a white rabbit costs €400, an immense Canadian elk €13,000, a magnificent golden pheasant or a coypu €480 … and the famous tiger €30,000. If your budget is more limited, you can always go for a butterfly – from €5 to €300, depending upon rarity – or an unusually shaped coleopteran. You can also have your favourite pet stuffed; however, this service is not available for protected species or those that require special hunting permits.

For any further information, see Yves, the charming salesperson who has been running the place since 1990.

The telescopic street on the Pont du Carrousel

Designed and created by the ironsmith/sculptor Raymond Subes in 1938, the Art Deco streetlamps of the Pont du Carrousel (itself built in 1935) were finally installed in 1946. So as not to obstruct the view of the Louvre, they were designed with a very special feature: their height varied from daytime to night-time. When darkness fell, the lamps extended to their full height, from 12 m to 22 m, so that they could efficiently illuminate the entire bridge. Unfortunately, the lamps have not been working for some years now and are awaiting restoration by the city's public works department.

---

* Taxidermy: the art of preserving (stuffing) animals so that they maintain a lifelike appearance. From the Greek taxis (order, arrangement) and derma (skin).

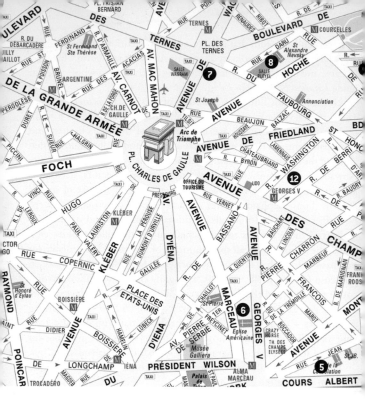

8th *Arrondissement*

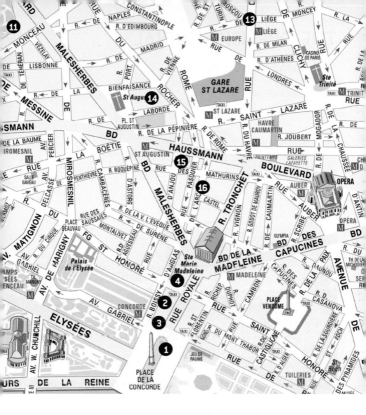

THE OBELISK-SUNDIAL

The world's largest sundial

Place de la Concorde
Métro: Concorde

Presented to France in 1831 by Mehmet Ali as a gift from Egypt, this obelisk was raised in place de la Concorde on 25 October 1836 in a ceremony attended by King Louis-Philippe. One of the two famous obelisks raised by Ramses II at the entrance to the Luxor temple, it has, since 1999, been part of the largest sundial in the world. In 1913, the astronomer Camille Flammarion, founder of the Société Astronomique de France, submitted to the Paris City Council a plan to lay out within place de la Concorde "the world's largest sundial", using the obelisk as the gnomon (see page 121) and carving the indications of the hours into the street paving itself. However, due to the 1914–1918 war the project was abandoned.

Twenty years later, in 1938, Daniel Roguet, the architect of the Juvisy Observatory, resurrected Flammarion's idea. Work began in spring 1939, but once again the project was interrupted by a war. Some traces of what was done are still visible: at the foot of the obelisk facing towards rue Royale are five radiating lines carved into the ground, one of them still with its original metal facing. The project was finally completed more than fifty years later, under Philippe de la Cotardière and Denis Savoie, with the sundial being officially opened on 21 June 1999.

Marked in bronze, the lines of the dial radiate from the foot of the obelisk and extend to the various divider strips in the square. At their end, Roman numerals from VII to XVII indicate the solar hour.

"Place Louis XVI" name plaque

Surprisingly, one of the original stone plaques identifying place Louis XVI still survives at the corner of place de la Concorde and rue Boissy-d'Anglas. This was the name given the square some time between 1826 and 1828, in commemoration of the fact that the king had been guillotined here on 21 January 1793.

Pont de la Concorde

The Pont de la Concorde was completed in 1792 using the stone from the Bastille prison, so that "the people would forever tramp the ancient fortress underfoot" every time they crossed the bridge.

MAXIM'S MUSEUM

Pierre Cardin's Art Nouveau collection

Entrance: 3, rue Royale, by the double door of the restaurant
Tel: 01 43 41 39 03
lacollection1900@maxims-de-paris.com
Guided tours by appointment, lasting approx. 1 hour
Admission: €15

Since 2004, the space above the famous restaurant *Maxim's* has housed the Art Nouveau objects and furnishings which Pierre Cardin began collecting some 65 years ago. Built in 1758, the city mansion at 3 rue Royale provides a perfect setting for the collection, given that *Maxim's* restaurant and reception rooms were refurbished in Art Nouveau style in 1899.

On the 3rd and 4th floors, Pierre Cardin has reconstructed the apartment of a high-class Parisian courtesan of the early 1900s, complete with salon, dining-room and bedrooms. The lighting is provided by fine lamps from Tiffany of New York; their shades, in polychrome glass paste, mute the rather stark light cast by the carbon filament bulbs used in that period.

In the main bedroom, the furniture of carved walnut is by Majorelle, whilst in the second bedroom the pieces are "Lyons School" marquetry in such precious materials as lemon, rose and amaranth wood. There is also period silverware, bronzework, linen and porcelain – a rich and fascinating record of the Belle Époque (see Art Nouveau feature, page 305).

NEARBY

The general mobilisation order, 2 august 1914 ③

1, rue Royale
Métro: Concorde

The walls of Paris bear various traces of war and episodes of bloodshed. Just to the left of the restaurant *Maxim's* you can still see a copy of the general mobilisation order dated 2 August 1914. Protected by a dusty glass panel, the poster reads: "The Mayor (Doctor Phillippe Maréchal) of the 8th arrondissement informs his constituents that a general mobilisation has been declared. The first day of the mobilisation has been set for Sunday 2 August (from midnight to midnight)." It seems, however, that the present poster is actually a photocopy dating from the 1970s.

The location of Alphonse Allais's home ④

Passage de la Madeleine - village Royal – 25, rue Royale

A wall plaque at the entrance to passage de la Madeleine reads "If in 1900 Alphonse Allais, by mistake, lived opposite here at 24 rue Royale, it is here that his spirit now resides" (Académie Alphonse-Allais). Raised by his admirers in 2004 to mark the 150th anniversary of his death, the inscription well reflects the spirit of the humourist … For more information, see the website www.boiteallais.com.

NEARBY

Façade of 40, cours Albert I ⑤

Given that cours Albert I is mainly used by motorists in a hurry, most Parisians have never noticed the building at number 40, built by the famous master glassmaker, Lalique. It was designed in 1911 to serve as his home, but then became a studio and showroom. The façade is a magnificent amalgam of plant motifs. Note the door made up of carved glass sections that form the branches of a tree.

Façade of 30, avenue Marceau ⑥

Built for himself by André Granet, Gustave Eiffel's son-in-law, the house dates from 1913 to 1914 and is a superb example of Art Nouveau architecture. Particularly striking is the upper part of the façade, which is entirely covered in sculpture of branches and pine cones.

Hôtel Céramic ⑦

34, avenue de Wagram

Designed by Lavirotte, this fine Art Nouveau hotel was built in 1904 and is entirely faced with ceramic stoneware. The interplay of volumes within the façade seems to herald modern architecture. Today, the building houses a comfortable three-star hotel, for which the façade serves as the best possible form of advertising.

ALEXANDER NEVSKY CATHEDRAL ⑧

The church where Picasso married the Russian ballerina Olga Koklova

12, rue Daru
Métro: Ternes
Liturgical services: Saturday at 6pm, Sunday at 10am

Listed as a historic monument in 1983, Alexander Nevsky Cathedral is undoubtedly the most famous of the numerous Orthodox churches in Paris. The initial scheme was promoted by Josef Vassiliev, chaplain at the Russian embassy, and paid for by funds collected not only in Russia (Tsar Alexander II gave the princely sum of 150,000 francs in gold) but also from among the Russian community spread throughout Europe. Designed by the architects Kouzmine and Strohm, the Cathedral was intended to provide Paris with an Orthodox church worthy of the name and was consecrated on 12 September 1861.

A great national hero, the Grand Prince Alexander Nevsky (1219–1263) was canonised for his humanity as a ruler, his military success against aggressors, his great wisdom and the fervour of his Christian faith. Placed under the jurisdiction of the Patriarchate of Constantinople (Istanbul) in 1931, this church is the archdiocesan seat of the Russian Orthodox Church in Western Europe.

In Byzantine-Russian style, it has a Greek-cross plan with a mosaic façade and five cupolas gilded "like the flames of candles" (the number symbolises Christ and the four Evangelists). The overall result is a building that stands out to striking effect within the urban landscape of Paris. Inside there are iconostases, icons and paintings with their traditional gold backgrounds. The services, maintaining a liturgy which has existed for some sixteen centuries, are celebrated to the chants of Orthodox priests amidst clouds of incense.

It is impossible to be present without sensing the fervour of the local Russian community who worship here.

The church, in fact, serves two parishes, so that each Sunday there are two Masses. One in French (in the lower church of the crypt) for the parish of Sainte Trinité, the other in Slav in the upper church for the parishioners of Saint-Alexandre-Nevski. One anecdotal curiosity regarding the church is that Picasso chose it for his wedding to the Russian ballerina Olga Koklova, where the guests included Jean Cocteau, Max Jacob and Guillaume Apollinaire. If, while respecting the silence of the place, you wish to attended a service, choose the great Easter Mass, which is certainly worthwhile, or the Mass held on 12 September to celebrate the feast day of the patron saint of the Russian community. That event is always followed by a pir, a magnificent Russian-style banquet.

An amazing gallery-museum housed in a pagoda

48, rue de Courcelles
Métro: Courcelles, Saint-Philippe-du-Roule or Monceau
Tel.: 01 45 62 53 15 • E-mail : ct.loo@hotmail.fr
Open without appointment on Thursday and Saturday, 2pm–6pm.
Other days by appointment

In the heart of the Monceau area an astonishing Chinese pagoda stands alongside the buildings typical of Baron Haussmann's urban redevelopment.

Occupying the site of a Louis-Philippe town mansion, it was built in 1926 by the French architect Fernand Bloch for the Chinese antique dealer Ching-Tsai Loo, whose company is still the oldest gallery of Asian art in Paris and the only truly Chinese antique dealer within the city. With 600 m² of space spread over six floors, the pagoda provides a unique architectural setting for the business. Details of the refined interiors include: Chinese lacquered woodwork dating from the 17ᵗʰ and 18ᵗʰ centuries; a ceiling in Art Deco glass tiles; a superb wooden gallery of Indian carving dating from the 18ᵗʰ and 19ᵗʰ centuries; and a lift entirely finished in woodwork and lacquer. The overall impression is of a Zen-like atmosphere, of a space where the passage of time has left its mark …

Within this unique gallery one encounters visitors from France and abroad (particularly from the United States). Customers include not only collectors and the curious, but also interior decorators interested in the contemporary lacquered furniture which the gallery produces. There is a vast range of goods on display: a 19ᵗʰ-century Chinese bench in elmwood (€1,500); a superb 18ᵗʰ-century painting on silk of ladies at court (€5,500); archaeological pieces in fired clay dating from the Han or Wei dynasties; a pair of 18ᵗʰ-century armchairs in hongmu, a sort of Chinese mahogany (€18,000). Those with a more limited budget will also find something to delight them, ranging from delicate Chinese prints of the 18ᵗʰ and 19ᵗʰ centuries (from €120 to €180) to such modern objects as a vase made from lacquered eggshells (€100).

© Galerie C.T. Loo & Cⁱᵉ

Note: some rooms in the gallery are hired out for cocktail parties, press conferences, fashion shows and receptions, etc.

THE PYRAMID OF PARC MONCEAU ⑩

A mysterious symbol

Parc Monceau
Métro: Monceau

Parc Monceau is crammed with curious follies: romantic ruins, truncated columns and – most curiously of all – a pyramid with a doorway flanked by two Egyptian heads. Probably a Masonic symbol of immortalty, the pyramid is the work of the architect and Freemason Bernard Poyet, who designed the various follies in the park.

Parc Monceau: "In a single garden, all ages and places"

In 1778 Carmontelle began designing this park for the future Philippe Égalité. It is the last remaining vestige of the various "Anglo-Chinese" gardens (known at the time as *fabriques*) which were laid out during this period; the parks of Bagatelle, Bastille and Clichy have long disappeared (though, outside the city, there is still the fine "Désert de Retz"). Laid out so that it formed a long journey of "initiation", Parc Monceau aimed to bring together all of knowledge, the most dazzling examples of human civilisation, in one place. Thus Venice was represented by a bridge (extant), Italy by a vineyard (at the time, the country had yet to be unified so Venice was an independent State), Egypt by a pyramid (see above), China by a stone lantern (extant) and Rome by a naumachia (this man-made basin for fake naval battles still stands to the north side of the park), Holland by a windmill (no longer extant), and so on.

NEARBY

Musée Nissim-de-camondo ⑪

63, rue de Monceau
Open Wednesday to Sunday, 10am–5.30pm. Closed Monday and Tuesday
Admission: €7 (concessions €5)

This superb museum attracts few visitors. Housed in a town mansion built in 1911–1913 by the architect René Sergent, it has a magnificent range of 18th-century furnishings and *objets d'art*.

Cité Odiot ⑫

26, rue de Washington

A haven of peace near the Champs-Élysées, the Cité Odiot stands on the site of the old city mansion of the goldsmith Jean-Baptiste Odiot, who made not only the shrine of St Vincent de Paul but also Napoleon I's imperial sword and sceptre. Far from the madding crowd, you can enjoy a space of wide lawns dotted with trees and lined by buildings dating from 1847.

LIÈGE MÉTRO STATION

One of the most beautiful stations of the Paris métro

Métro: Liège

Barrage de la Gileppe

Vallée de l'Amblève : Coo

Entirely faced with ceramic tiles, this – together with the Arts-et-Métiers station (see page 58) – is probably the most beautiful of the city's métro system. It used be the "Berlin" métro station, but the name was changed during the First World War. Closed for a long time, the station only reopened in 1968, with Welkenraedt ceramic decoration depicting the landscape and monuments of Liège in Belgium. Since December 4, 2006 completion of the modernisation work has meant that the station no longer closes at 8pm.

NEARBY

Boundary marker at 4, rue de Laborde ⑭
City limits in the 18ᵗʰ century

An unobtrusive plaque on the rear wall of the inner courtyard of 4, rue Laborde bears the following inscription: "1729, in the reign of Louis XV. By order of the king it is expressly forbidden to build in this road outside the present boundary and limit, upon pain of the sanctions contained in the edicts of His Majesty from 1724 to 1726."

Initially placed near rue de l'Arcade, this boundary marker set a limit to the area within which Parisians could build and was inspired by the need to maintain control over the population and guarantee supplies for the city. Clearly, people paid little heed to the ban, though its presence here is an interesting reminder of the limits of urban expansion at the time.

All in all, 294 boundary markers of this kind were fixed to the walls of 18ᵗʰ century Paris. Another surviving plaque can be seen at 304, rue de Charenton in the 12ᵗʰ *arrondissement*.

What happened to rue de Berlin and rue de Hambourg?

The area above Saint-Lazare is known as the "Quartier d'Europe" because all the streets are named after great European cities. However, the 1914–1918 war led to some changes in names here: rue de Berlin became rue de Liège and rue de Hambourg became rue de Bucarest. Similarly, after the Second World War, avenue de Tokyo in the 16ᵗʰ *arrondissement* became avenue de New York.

EXPIATORY CHAPEL

In memory of the king

Square Louis-XVI – Metro: Saint-Augustin
Open Thursday, Friday and Saturday, 1pm–5pm. Guided tours 1.30pm and
3.30pm, lasting approx. 30 min
Admission €5

Located in the charming square Louis-XVI, at the corner of boulevard Haussmann and rue d'Anjou, this expiatory chapel was built in 1816–1826 to commemorate Louis XVI. Remarkably quiet for somewhere right in the heart of Paris, it recalls a particularly dramatic period in French history.

After he had been guillotined in place de la Concorde, the king's body was brought here for burial in what was then the Cemetery of La Madeleine. Opened in 1721, that cemetery was at the time best known as the burial place of the 133 people who, in a sad presage of things to come, were crushed to death in rue Royale and place Royale (now place de la Concorde) during the firework display held on 30 April 1770 to mark the marriage of the future Louis XVI and Marie-Antoinette, Archduchess of Austria. The cemetery was also used to bury the 900 Swiss soldiers of the Royal Guard at the Tuileries who were massacred when the palace was attacked on 20 August 1792. Subsequently it was also the burial place of those guillotined between 26 August 1792 and 24 March 1794, on which date the cemetery was closed because of complaints regarding the pestilential odour.

Guillotined on 21 January 1793, Louis XVI was – like all those who had died a similar death – buried with his severed head between his legs, his body then being covered with quicklime. He was, however, accorded the right to an open coffin and buried in an individual grave (by the rue d'Anjou wall of the cemetery) rather than in a mass grave. The body of Marie-Antoinette was buried alongside him on 25 October 1793.

After the Restoration, King Louis XVIII had the bodies of his brother, Louis XVI, and his queen moved to the royal mausoleum of Saint-Denis on 21 January 1815. He himself then paid for the re-purchase of the areas of this cemetery that had been sold to private individuals so that the present commemorative chapel might be built there.

Modelled on a Graeco-Roman necropolis, the structure occupies the entire 900 m² of the old Madeleine cemetery. The courtyard leading up to the chapel proper is lined to north and south by a nine-arch arcade, each bay of which houses an empty tomb; the number commemorates the 900 Swiss soldiers of the Royal Guard. The altar in the crypt is in the form of a tomb and stands on the exact site of Louis XVI's grave. On January 21 each year a commemorative Mass is celebrated here.

NEARBY
Haut-Reliefs at 34, rue Pasquier

Note the haut-reliefs of sharks and camels adorning this 1930s-style building. The work of Alexander and Pierre Fournier, it was in fact built in the year 1927 for the *Société Financière Française et Coloniale*.

Traces of the monarchy in parisian place names

Although France is now a republic proud of its political achievements, its capital still preserves numerous traces of the country's past as a monarchy, most notably in the name of streets and boulevards and in the innumerable statues, busts and royal monograms adorning the facades of buildings.

Near the site where he chose to be buried, **Clovis** has a street named after him; **Charlemagne** has both a school and a narrow street, while **Henri IV** has a boulevard, a quai alongside the Seine, a footbridge, a bridge and a school, and **Louis-Philippe** has a bridge. The reference to **Louis XIII** is more indirect, given that rue Dauphine was named after him in 1607, when he was still heir to the throne. Similarly, the street and school named after **Louis XIV** are actually called Louis-le-Grand.

Rue François I is not actually named for the king, but for the reconstructed façade of a building in so-called "François premier" style. The female members of the royal family are not forgotten. Cours-la-reine owes its name to **Marie de Médicis**, who commissioned it, while rue Sainte-Anne is named after Anne of Austria and rue Thérèse after **Queen Maria-Teresa**.

Finally, rue de Berry, rue de Provence, rue Monsieur, rue Madame, rue Mademoiselle, rue d'Artois and rue Monsieur-le-Prince are all named after members of the royal family, just as rue Mazarin, rue Richelieu and rue Colbert are named after royal ministers.

Even **Louis XVI** receives due homage. Not only is there the expiatory chapel, but also the nearby rue Tronchet, rue de Sèze and boulevard Malesherbes, named after the three men who defended the king during his trial. Although it has since been renamed place de la Concorde, a stone plaque for "place Louis XVI" can still be seen at the corner of place de la Concorde and rue Boissy-d'Anglas.

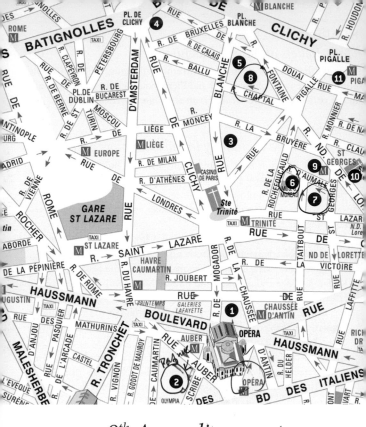

9ᵗʰ *Arrondissement*

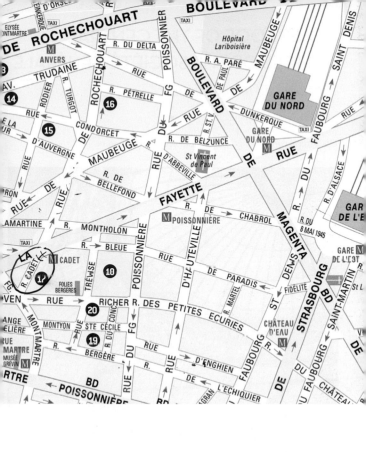

GLASS ROOF OF THE CENTRAL OFFICES OF THE SOCIÉTÉ GÉNÉRALE

①

A bank in all its splendour

29, boulevard Haussmann
Métro: Richelieu-Drouot
Open during office hours, and for Journées du Patrimoine

The Société Générale was founded in 1864, and its main branch occupies a magnificent ensemble of seven interconnected buildings dating from the Second Empire.

When the bank bought the premises in 1905, the architect Jacques Hermant demonstrated a clearly modern approach to structural conversion because he did everything possible to maintain the original façades, redesigning the interior space to create four underground levels for the vaults. The completed structure was opened in 1912.

In the centre of the bank is a large circular counter, known as le *fromage*; this stands under an immense cupola of iron and glass which measures 24 m in diameter and was designed by Jacques Galland. The mosaic floors were the work of the Gentil & Bourdet company of Boulogne-Billancourt.

Various parts of this bank (the exteriors; the glass and iron roof and hall; the main stairwell; the vault rooms) are all listed architectural features. Of particular note are the splendid strongbox rooms, the mosaics and the main door to the bank vault; weighing some 18 tons, this has 40 cm thick armour plating.

Visitors should be discreet as this is a place of work.

Glass and iron structures in the Opera District

Grand Hôtel, 2, rue Scribe
Galeries Lafayette, 40, boulevard Haussmann open Monday to Saturday
9.30am–7.30pm (Thursday until 9pm)
Printemps, 64, boulevard Haussmann open Monday to Saturday
9.35am–7pm (Thursday until 10pm)

There are three very fine glass and iron structures in this district which are much better known than the premises of the Société Générale. Each of them is an example of the luxurious Second Empire architecture associated with the massive urban-planning schemes undertaken by Baron Haussmann. Built in 1861, the Grand Hôtel has a vast hall that already hints at the use of colour in such structures. However, the real masterpiece here is the Reception Room, where a marvellous glass roof – a veritable blossom of gold and coloured glass – rests on double ranks of Corinthian columns. If it is not open, ask at the hotel's reception desk. Nearby, the two department stores of Le Printemps and Galeries Lafayette also have very fine glasswork. The roof at Galeries Lafayette rests on ten large metal pillars, while the glasswork on the sixth floor of Le Printemps is a fine example of Art Nouveau and was designed by Binet in 1911. The space now houses a tearoom and other areas used for receptions, etc. (see our guide *Secret Bars and Restaurants in Paris*).

NEARBY

Fragonard Perfume Museum

②

9, rue Scribe
Métro: Havre-Caumartin, Opéra or Chaussée-d'Antin
Tel.: 01 47 42 93 40
Open Monday to Saturday, 9am–5.30pm • Free guided tours only

Set up by the Fragonard Perfume Company in 1983, this museum traces the history of perfume-making from the ancient Egyptians until the 19th century. A miniature factory demonstrates the different processes used in extracting essences from raw materials. Unfortunately, the visit is very commercially oriented, and ends in the Fragonard shop, like all the worst tourist traps for groups of happy spenders.

Operatic Street Names

The names of the streets around the Garnier Opera House – Auber, Meyerbeer, Halévy and Gluck – are no accident; each one is named after a 19th-century opera composer. Scribe, a librettist, also has a street named after him. And Diaghilev, the Russian impresario who hired and fired choreographers and composers, has a city square that bears his name; it stands just behind the Opéra.

THE VINES OF RUE BLANCHE FIRE STATION

Wine-making firefighters

22-28, rue Blanche
Métro: Trinité
For the dates when the grapes will be picked, ask at the fire station from around the beginning of September

I f the firefighters of rue du Vieux-Colombier in the 6th *arrondissement* are well known for the ball they hold on July 14, those in rue Blanche also have their own very special public festivity: for a few days every year, their fire station is transformed into a vineyard.

The superb climbing vine on the façade of the building yields a generous harvest, from which is made a (non-alcoholic!) wine that is *mis en bouteille au château* and sold under the "Château Blanche" label. The quality of this *cru* might be debatable, but the tradition dates back to 1926; for the last thirty years in particular, the grape-picking has been a lively, colourful event involving firefighters, local residents, street urchins and even the girls from the Moulin Rouge.

More than 150 kg of grapes are harvested in just a few days, and these are used to make fifty or so full bottles of Château Blanche (each numbered) and 150 small bottles for the fire station itself.

Undoubtedly more authentic than the much more touristy event in Montmartre, the grape harvest in rue Blanche also has a small celebrity connection (Gérard Depardieu is the owner of bottle 24 of the 1997 *cuvée*). Still, the whole thing remains thoroughly convivial and the fire station chief is more than happy to talk to anyone about the curious traditions associated with the place. For example: to guarantee they will have children, the most recently married fireman and his wife must be the first to tread the grapes; the bottle labels depict the events of that particular year; and the name of the *cuvée* is that of the fireman who happens to be fire chief that year.

Origin of rue Blanche's name: plaster in Paris

It is the nearby quarries of Montmartre that resulted in rue Blanche getting its name: as the quarried plaster was being carted down to the barges on the Seine, it was not uncommon for small pieces to fall onto the road, which thus became covered in white dust.

It was due to the special heat-resistant qualities of this plaster that Paris avoided the catastrophic fires which so often ravaged cities like London: as early as the reign of King Philippe le Bel an edict was issued requiring every new house built in Paris to be faced with chalk. The abundance of the material has also meant that the city's buildings have that uniformity of colour so appreciated by visitors.

THE CLICHY-MONTMARTRE GAMING CLUB

A place to misspend your youth

84, rue de Clichy
Métro: Place-de-Clichy
Tel.: 01 48 78 32 85
Open all year • Billiard hall 11am–6am (cost per hour, from €4.80 to €11.70)
Gaming hall 4pm–6am (minors not allowed)

U ntil 1947 this building was a "Bouillon Duval", one of the city's first chain of restaurants to provide good-quality food at low prices; the nearby "Bouillon Chartier" still exists. Now it is home to the Clichy-Montmartre gaming club, whose billiard hall attracts professionals and amateurs of all ages; there are eight billiard tables, five French billiards tables, one snooker and two pool tables. Perhaps the customers do not fully appreciate the fine interior; this dates from the period between the two world wars and is lit by lamps and a large coloured-glass ceiling.

NEARBY
Hands at 82, rue Blanche   ⑤
The number of this building is indicated in a remarkable fashion, two hands on either side of the number seem to be stopping it from escaping.

Number 3: a simbol of the church of La Trinité
The architect Ballu played repeatedly upon the symbolic significance of the number three when designing the church of La Trinité. The central porch is divided into three arches; the large water basin has three separate fountains, each with three smaller basins. The central fount is surmounted by a statue of a woman, symbolising Hope, whose arms embrace three children, each of which has three bronze jars at its feet.

Impact of the advent of elevators
Before the introduction of elevators in Parisian buildings, in 1895, the most sought-after floor was the first above ground level. This explains why the height of the ceilings decreases as you move up the building, being highest in the most expensive floor and lowest in the cheapest.

That all changed after 1895, with the higher floors becoming much sought after: not only were they less noisy, but – being above the level of the trees – they also received more light.

STAIRWELL IN MUSÉE GUSTAVE-MOREAU

Paid for by the artist, and built in what had been his home

14, rue de La Rochefoucauld
Métro: Saint-Georges ou Trinité
Tel.: 01 48 74 38 50
Open daily from 10am–12.45pm and 2pm–5.15pm. Closed Tuesday
Admission: €4 (concessions €2.60). Admission free on the first Sunday of every month

Rather ignored by Parisians, the Musée Gustave Moreau is very special in that it was planned, designed and built by the artist himself in what had been his home. Three years before his death, Gustave Moreau, who had already asked himself the question of what would happen to his work, undertook to transform 14, rue de La Rochefoucauld with the aid of the architect Albert Lafon. Having decided to keep the first-floor apartment where he had lived with his parents as a sort of family museum of personal mementos and keepsakes, he had Lafon build the large studio one can see today. The magnificent spiral staircase gives access to a space which now houses his masterpieces along with all his preparatory sketches and thousands of drawings (these are conserved in cabinets with sliding panels). Intended as the masterwork of the artist, this museum gives an insight into his private genius, allowing each phase in the mysterious process of artistic creation to be followed. This unique museum still maintains the special enchantment that is a defining characteristic of Gustave Moreau's art.

> Born in 1826, Gustave Moreau went on to become an artist whose work was inspired by themes taken from mythology, literature and the Bible. The profusion of drawings he left makes it possible to chart the development of someone who was initially an academic artist but went on to become a symbolist and a modernist, producing towards the end of his life works that verge on the abstract.

NEARBY
Square d'Orléans   ⑦
Entrance at 80, rue Taitbout

Invisible from the street, this was the centre of a district of Romantic artists and writers which a contemporary newspaper christened *La Nouvelle Athènes*. One of the most unusual and peaceful parts of the district, the square d'Orléans was designed by the English architect Edward Cresy and took a whole twelve years to complete (from 1830 to 1842). The end result, based on the model of a London square, contained forty-six apartments and six artist's studios. The central garden, the fountain and the four square buildings around English-style courtyards were an immediate hit with artists and celebrities, who set up house – and salon - here, forming a sort of literary/artistic phalanstery. The best-known residents included the ballerina Marie Taglioni, the composer Marmontel and – most famously of all – George Sand (whose apartment was on the first floor of No. 5) and Frederick Chopin (at No. 9).

MUSEUM OF ROMANTICISM

Just what the name says

16, rue Chaptal
Métro: Blanche or Trinité
Tel.: 01 55 31 95 67 • Open daily 10am–6pm. Closed Mondays and public holidays
Free admission to permanent collection. Admission to special exhibitions:
full €5.50 (concessions €3.50). No charge for those under 14

An Italian-style roof (typical of the Restoration period), vines, wisteria, tree-lined paths, greenhouses, a fountain and a cobbled courtyard … everything here is redolent of Romanticism. Owned by the painter Ary Scheffer and his nephew – the writer Ernest Renan - the private house at 16, rue Chaptal at one time played host to a circle of Romantic artists and writers, attracting – and inspiring – such figures as Lamartine, Chopin, George Sand and Delacroix. These leading-lights of Parisian Romanticism would gather together in one of the two studios that Ary Scheffer had had built to either side of the courtyard.

Now owned by Paris City Council, the place – which is tucked away in a cul-de-sac – has been made into a Museum of Romanticism. The main body of the building houses mementoes of the daily life of the writer George Sand, together with paintings by Ary Scheffer and his contemporaries. On the other side of the courtyard, the painter's studio-salon has been restored to its appearance at the time these artists were alive. In good weather, from May to October, the tearoom occupying the conservatory and the terrace is an idyllic place (see our *Secret Bars and Restaurants in Paris*).

NEARBY

Hôtel Dosne-Thiers-Bibliothèque Thiers

27, place Saint-Georges
Tel.: 01 48 78 14 33
Group tours (10–15 people) by appointment
Library open on Thursday and Friday, 12pm–6pm (closed August). Access restricted to MA researchers and above. Manuscripts can be consulted only upon presentation of references from two members of the Institut

The Hôtel Dosne-Thiers houses a fine library of modern French history, run by the Institut de France. You can also see Adolphe Thiers's room and a suite of rooms on the ground floor, which are hired out for various kinds of events. Unfortunately, it is difficult to visit: apart from academic researchers, access is restricted to prebooked groups. There is a delightful and rather secluded garden behind the building.

Hôtel de la Païva ⑩

28, place Saint-Georges

One of the most picturesque buildings in this neighbourhood, this dates from 1840 but is named after the woman who lived here in 1850–1851: Thérèse Lachman, Marquise de la Païva, famed for her love of diamonds. In so-called *style troubadour*, the building is a mix of neo-Renaissance and neo-Gothic, with opulent external decoration intended to compensate for the narrowness of the façade.

AVENUE FROCHOT

A cursed villa

Private gateway; admission is a matter of luck
Métro: Pigalle

Though shut away behind a keypad-controlled gate, this little paradise can be admired through the wrought-iron railings. Laid out in 1830, the avenue is lined by opulent 19th-century residences surrounded by greenery. The mix of architectural styles here (neo-Gothic, Flemish, medieval, Palladian or neoclassical) has attracted the attention of artists of various periods: Victor Hugo, Alexandre Dumas senior, Toulouse-Lautrec and Victor Massé are some of those who succumbed to its charms. More recently, Django Reinhardt amused himself by burning some of his furniture in the fireplace of one of the houses, while François Truffaut used the avenue as the setting for a scene in his famous film *Les Quatre Cents Coups*.

A curious tale has been told of the house at No. 1 since the death of composer Victor Massé, who spent his last years here afflicted with multiple sclerosis. So it would seem that the house has brought nothing but ill luck to owners or occupiers. The director of the Folies-Bergères, who had bought it for himself, left it to his housekeeper, who was then savagely beaten to death with a poker. Having stood empty for thirty years, the house was bought by Sylvie Vartan, who lived here a very short time and then moved out abruptly. The next to buy the property was Mathieu Galev, and he too died – a victim of multiple sclerosis .. True story or urban legend?

To the left of the avenue, a pretty stained-glass window with Art Deco marine motifs, part of the former Théâtre en Rond, dates from 1837.

NEARBY
Cité Malesherbes
Private road, accessible via 59, rue des Martyrs
Laid out on the site of the former city mansion of the lawyer Lamoignon de Malesherbes, who was guillotined in 1794, the Cité Malesherbes contains some interesting buildings. Note the façade of No.11, covered with rich decoration in ceramic, enamelled earthenware and tufa. Commissioned by the painter Jollivet, this is the work of the architect Jal.
At No.17 is the fine rotunda of the private home of the architect Amoudru.Note also the cornice to the balcony, decorated with a female mask and two medallions with silhouettes.

Gardens at 41-47, rue des Martyrs ⑬
Partially hidden from the street, this carefully-tended lawn with rose bushes dotted here and there offers a pleasant breath of the countryside. Take advantage of it for a welcome pause.

THE PRIVATE COLLECTION AT THE "PHONOGALERIE" SHOP

A collection of talking machines

10, rue Lallier – Metro: Anvers
Tel./fax : 01 45 26 45 80 • Cell: 06 80 61 59 37
E-mail: aro@phonogalerie.com • www.phonogalerie.com
Open Monday to Saturday 10am–1pm and 2pm–7pm
Guided tours (without appointment) for groups of 3–4 people. More than
4 people, prior booking required

Jalal Aro is more than just a collector: he nurses back to life all sorts of instruments that have played a part in the history of sound recording. After a few years spent collecting the more amazing forms of "talking machines" produced since the invention of the technology in 1877 (cylinder recorders, horn gramophones, music boxes), he opened

a shop dedicated to all aspects of recorded sound. Here you can find advertising posters, musical postcards, old 78s and vinyl discs, and all sorts of rare and sophisticated apparatus for recording and playing sound. However, anything produced in the last thirty years is rigorously excluded. The proprietor will help you to choose the perfect gift (prices ranging from €5 to €15,000); he will also be happy to regale you with marvellously erudite anecdotes. Half-museum, half shop, "Phonogalerie" is ideally situated between the cabarets and nightclubs of Montmartre and the artist neighbourhood of *La Nouvelle Athènes*.

NEARBY
The owl at 68, rue Condorcet ⑮

68, rue Condorcet – Métro: Anvers
Under the balcony at 68, rue Condorcet, a sculpted owl perches atop a column. It is, in fact, a species known in French as *le grand duc*, and is a trademark identifying the building as the work of none other than the great Viollet-le-Duc. The architect designed this as his own home in 1862–1863, placing the owl under the windows to his studio.

NEARBY
Cité Napoléon
58, rue Rochechouart

Invisible from the street itself, the Cité Napoléon is a rare and fine example of a familistery, completed in 1853. Built to provide accommodation for 400 working families, its aim was to offer low-cost housing for those of modest means; not only was the rent affordable, but a doctor paid regular visits, free of charge. However, the families were expected to observe very strict discipline, and an inspector called frequently to verify the morality of their behaviour.

Familisteries and phalansteries

The familistery was a concrete expression of the utopian socialism Charles Fourier outlined in his theory of the phalanstery, a communal settlement in which accommodation was organised around a covered central courtyard. The name itself comes from the term "phalanx", which in classical antiquity referred to an elite corps of soldiers. As the very name "familistery" suggests, it provided accommodation for families alone.

NEARBY
Musée du Grand Orient de France
16, rue Cadet
Tel.: 01 45 23 20 92

Open Tuesday to Friday, 2pm–6pm and Saturday 1pm–5pm • Admission: €2

Built in 1889 on the site of the Hôtel Cadet, the Museum of the Grand Orient de France has a collection of more than 10,000 items (documents, Masonic symbols, badges of office, etc.) illustrating the history of the arrival and spread of the Order in France.

Cité de Trévise
Off rue Richer and rue Bleue

Characteristic of the various development schemes of the 1840s, the Cité de Trévise housing development still maintains a certain charm, in spite of the traffic. The neo-Renaissance buildings stand around a tree-dotted square, in the centre of which is a pretty drinking-fountain in the form of three caryatids holding hands.

Branch of Banque Nationale de Paris
14–20, rue Bergère

Built in 1881 by Corryer, this was long the home of the Paris Comptoir National d'Escompte, one of the four banks whose fusion gave raise to BNP Paribas. The stairwell and the trading hall with its magnificent glass ceiling are worth a visit. The three large façade sculptures are by Millet and depict Prudence, Commerce and Finance.

CHURCH OF SAINT-EUGÈNE-SAINTE-CÉCILE

Two patron saints, two liturgies,
two types of architecture ...

6, rue Sainte-Cécile
Church open Monday and Saturday 10am–8pm; Tuesday to Friday 7.30am–
8pm and Sunday 9am–8pm
Sunday Masses: Pauline liturgy at 9.30am and 7pm; Tridentine liturgy at 11am

This fine but little-known church is curiously dedicated to two saints: Saint Eugene (in honour of Napoleon III's wife, Eugénie, who was responsible for it being built in the first place) and Saint Cecilia (patron saint of music; the National Conservatoire is close by). Note that the church has no bell tower, so that the bells do not disturb the musicians.

Designed by Lussion and Boileau, who took their inspiration from 13th-century architecture, the church was built in 1854–1855 to meet the needs of the new suburbs being created as Paris expanded. Wherever you stand in the interior you get an overall view of the entire space, which is brightly painted and flooded with light; note also the Second Empire chandeliers.

The entire structure, including the columns, is in painted cast iron, creating a very original polychrome interior. The columns are steel blue and Florentine bronze, whilst the vaults are dotted with stars and the ribbing is painted a variety of colours.

Another peculiarity of the church is that since 1989 Masses here have been held according to two different liturgies – that introduced by Paul VI and that associated with Pope Pius V and celebrated in Latin. Up to 1998 the two liturgies were celebrated by two different priests, but now are the responsibility of a single priest. Thus it is not uncommon to find, in the same morning, a Mass in French (with the celebrant facing towards the congregation), then – a couple of hours later – the same priest, now in gold and purple vestments, celebrating a Latin Mass (complete with Gregorian chant) according to a rite that has him facing away from the congregation.

The Tridentine Mass. This is associated with Pope Pius V and was the liturgy which the Roman Catholic Church followed from the period of the Council of Trent (1563) – hence the name "Tridentine" – to the Second Vatican Council. Though opposed by some (most notably Monseigneur Lefèvre in France), the Pauline liturgy is considered as a step towards modernisation, a sign of the Church adapting to the 20th century.

The Pauline Mass. This is now the standard liturgy of the Roman Catholic Church and was introduced by Pope Paul VI following the Second Vatican Council (1962–1965).

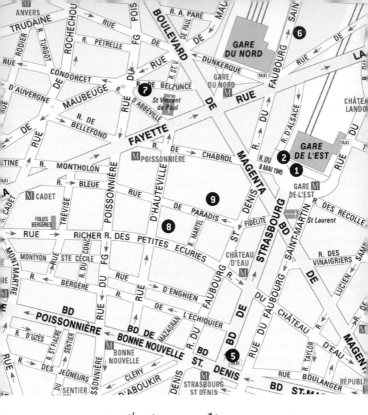

10th *Arrondissement*

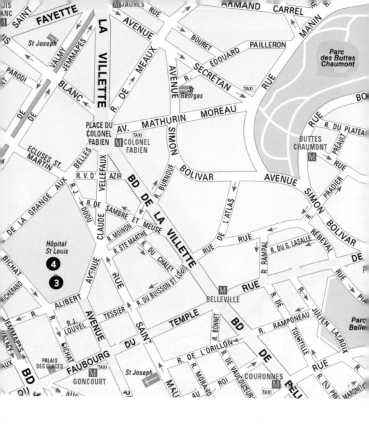

Phantom Stations of the Paris Métro

Although they no longer appear on the present-day map of the Paris transport system, a few stations still physically exist underground, some of them being put to uses very different from those for which they were built. The closure of most of these so-called "phantom" stations dates from the start of the Second World War in 1939, when – due to the call-up of some of the transport staff – the métro system was cut back. Later, when the war was over, it was decided not to reopen stations that had been little used or were too close to busier stations. As a result, the stations Arsenal, Croix-Rouge, Champs-de-Mars, Saint-Martin, Martin-Nadaud and Porte-des-Lilas disappeared from the Paris métro map; the first four, however, are on lines still in use, so if you keep your eyes peeled you may catch a glimpse of them from your train. Since being decommissioned, few of the stations have stood idle: Arsenal now houses facilities for the training of the network's electrical engineers and technicians; Saint-Martin – whose walls are still decorated with fine, period advertisements in ceramic tile – was used as a shelter for the homeless, then in 1999 became a social solidarity facility run by the Salvation Army. For its part, Croix-Rouge has had various roles: in the early 1980s, for example, an artist transformed it into a beach resort, complete with *chaises longues* and umbrellas; it has also been used for fashion shows. The situation at Porte-des-Lilas is rather different, as part of the station is still functional within the métro network. Behind the public platforms, however, facilities have been created for location filming. Depending upon the needs of the script, the station can become Pont-Neuf, Pigalle or whatever is required. Renamed Porte-des-Lilas-Cinéma, this part of the station used to serve the line which ran here from Pré-Saint-Gervais, a stretch of the métro which was opened in 1921 and closed in 1939; the shuttle along this line is still used for staff training and for the testing of new equipment. Two other stations – Haxo (between Porte-des-Lilas and Pré-Saint-Gervais) and Porte Molitor (located between lines 9 and 10) – suffered a different fate. No sooner were they built than they were abandoned, due to changes in the original plans for the transport system. The access stairways linking them with the street above were never even built.

Unknown aspects of parisian railway stations

There was a practical reason for the height and size of the glass roofs in most of Paris's railway stations : at the time they were built, trains were steam-powered and the high roofs were necessary to prevent passengers and staff being choked by noxious fumes.

The arrival of the railways in the city was not untroubled, and some engineers were very doubtful about the project. Arago, for example, predicted the most dire health risks for those who ventured into the Saint-Cloud tunnel. Furthermore, the railway companies were suspected of wanting to interfere in the city's business; as a result, it was decided to make métro tunnels too low to take railway trains, in order to prevent the two systems ever being interconnected. Similarly, as railways followed the English system of driving on the left, it was decided that métro trains were to drive on the right. It is no accident, therefore, that there is no direct métro line linking the various mainline stations. Indeed, the route one has to follow from one station to another is sometimes bizarre. For example, travellers arriving at Gare d'Austerlitz and wanting to continue their journey from Gare de Lyons (just over the Seine) have to carry bag and baggage there themselves. There is no métro link between the two stations. Perhaps now the time has come to remedy this situation.

The hollow columns of Gare du Nord

The metal columns bearing the structure of the Gare du Nord are hollow, allowing the rainwater that falls onto the roof to flow down directly into the drains below ground.

Apart from Paris, only four French cities have "line-head" stations, where the tracks come to an end rather than running through: Marseilles, Lyons, Tours and Orleans.

The influence of Napoleon III on parisian place names

The various military campaigns undertaken during the time of Napoleon III have left their mark on the toponymy of the city, with thirty-one roads and streets being named after cities or generals associated with the campaigns in the Crimea, Mexico or Italy – for example, Avenues Bugeaud, Malakoff, Magenta, Alma and Mac-Mahon. In the church of Notre-Dame-du-Travail in the 16th *arrondissement* (see page 263), there is even a bell from the Crimean War.

THE BUNKER AT GARE DE L'EST ①

A bunker under the railtracks

Gare de l'Est
Place du 11-Novembre-1918
Métro: Gare-de-l'Est
*Visits: publicised in the press (*Pariscope *and* Officiel des spectacles)
Otherwise, apply at the main information office at the station

Hidden under tracks 2 and 3 is an old bomb shelter which, strangely, is still intact. The place, from where the station was to be run in case of bombardment, is strikingly authentic: old train timetables lie on the floor as if they had just been dropped there, and the mechanical equipment appears to be in perfect working order (the Ministry of Defence still maintains the shelter). The signs reading *Notausgang* and other inscriptions on the walls reveal that the place was taken over by the Germans. However one question remains: was this command centre ever used?

We know that construction work began on July 20 1939, when the declaration of war was imminent, and that it was completed in 1941, during the Occupation. Hermetically sealed from the outside world, this concrete structure has a floor area of 120 m^2 and could accommodate up to 72 people. The three main rooms – telephone exchange, machine room and traffic-control room – are separated by three massive anti-blast doors. Bottled oxygen was also installed, for use in case of poison gas, and there were even pedal-operated generators to provide power should the electricity be cut off.

© Jean-Jacques Le-Roux

ASSOCIATION FRANÇAISE DES AMIS DES CHEMINS DE FER

For those mad about trains

(Association of French Railway Enthusiasts)
Gare de l'Est
Place du 11-Novembre-1918
Métro: Gare-de-l'Est
Access by the Alsace Car Park ramp, which runs alongside the station in rue
d'Alsace • http://www.railfaneurope.net/afac/indexfr.html
Open to members Saturday afternoon or by prior appointment
Tel.: 01 40 38 20 92

Founded in 1929, the AFAC is housed in the amazing underground space beneath Gare de l'Est. Upon entering, you are warmly welcomed by the club members operating the model train layouts. You will probably be invited to stand in the middle of one of these immense networks to understand the complex layout of rail signals, level crossings, marshalling yards, platforms, etc. – all reproduced to scale.

The association occupies two rooms. In one is a 1/87 scale model, while in the other are two layouts, one to a scale of 1/43.5 and the other 1/32. Lovingly created by AFAC members, these three rail networks can accommodate a number of trains, with traffic being handled with all the rigour of an actual rail system.

Louis Armand, a former chairman of the SNCF (French State Railways), was so impressed by the visit he paid here that he commented that the association was in some respects ahead of the SNCF itself!

Any member can run their own trains on these layouts, provided of course that they are compatible. This is one of the privileges you will enjoy if you join – and listening to the advice of your fellow members you may even learn how to build your own trains and carriages. A must for children!

MUSEUM OF DERMATOLOGICAL CASTS

Museum of Skin Diseases

1, avenue Claude-Vellefaux – Hôpital Saint-Louis
Métro: Goncourt
Open by appointment 9am–4.45pm weekdays
Tel.: 01 42 49 99 15
Admission: €3.50

Until recently reserved exclusively for doctors (due to a confidentiality clause that has now expired), this Museum of Dermatological Casts is extraordinary. Set up by Doctor Alphonse Devergies in 1865 as a "Museum of Skin Diseases", it received its first wax cast in 1867, the work of Jules Baretta.

The hospital also initiated the study of dermatology, so this collection was intended for teaching purposes, with almost 5,000 wax casts of heads or limbs showing the symptoms of skin diseases.

Produced over the period 1867–1958, these casts are exhibited in glass display cases against a black background and show the effects of such diseases as leprosy, gangrene, syphilis, naevus, scabies, dermatitis, eczema, shingles and pustules. Materials added since 1958 have been in the form of photographs.

THE SQUARE COURTYARD OF HÔPITAL SAINT-LOUIS

Place des Vosges – without the traffic

40, rue Bichat and 1, avenue Claude-Vellefaux
Métro: Goncourt
Open to the public 8am–6pm
Tel.: 01 42 49 49 49

This sublime interior courtyard is entirely on a par with place des Vosges – with the added bonus of having no traffic. Not to be missed for anything ...

Now a listed building, the hospital was set up in response to the great plague of 1562, which caused more than 68,000 deaths in the capital: given the overcrowding in the Hôtel-Dieu hospital and the fact that the disease was so highly contagious, it was essential that there be a a new *Maison de Santé* where patients could be isolated from the rest of the population.

The design that Henri IV chose for the building was by Claude Vallefaux, "master mason employed on the building projects of the king", and within a few years the Hôpital Saint-Louis was created. The central square measures 120 m by 120 m and is surrounded by a covered walkway, with each corner marked by large buildings in stone and bricks. There are also four other groups of free-standing buildings. The separation of each of the structures was intended to limit contagion and to prevent the patients from escaping.

The flowerbeds in the centre of the lawn are in the shape of a Maltese Cross. The Knights of Malta (now a hospitalier Order) occupy one of the buildings.

The numbering of Parisian streets

The number in a Parisian address can tell you if the house concerned is at the beginning or end of a street or on the left- or right-hand side of the road. The general principle is that the layout of the streets follows the course of the Seine: from right to left, that is from east to west (upstream to downstream). For the streets more or less parallel to the Seine, No.1 is therefore always to the east (to the right on a map of Paris), which is theoretically the beginning of the street. When you then stand looking down the street, the even numbers are on the right and the odd numbers are on the left.

For the streets that are more or less perpendicular to the Seine, the street "begins" at the river.

Adopted in 1805, this system was devised by the city prefect, Frochot, who gives his name to a very attractive private street (see page 193).

ATELIER HOGUET – FAN MUSEUM

Museum of an anachronism

2, boulevard de Strasbourg
Métro: Strasbourg-Saint-Denis
Tel.: 01 42 08 90 20
Open Monday, Tuesday and Wednesday 2pm–8pm, and during
school holidays also on Friday at the same times • Closed August
Groups must book in advance • Admission: €7

Occupying a very fine apartment near Barbès-Rochechouart, this private Fan Museum is well worth a visit, even for the charm of the setting.

Joseph Hoguet Duroyaume set up his workshop to make frames for fans in 1872, and since then four generations of the family have specialised in this craft. Given that there was a considerable drop in demand over the years, one way to prevent the disappearance of the Atelier Hoguet was the creation of this museum, which opened in 1993.

The collection contains around one thousand choice exhibits dating from the 18th, 19th and 20th centuries. In an extremely refined ambience, the museum actually occupies the display room which was designed in 1893 by the fan-makers Lepault & Deberghe. Now listed as of historic interest, this has maintained all its original Henri III decor: walnut display cases, a coffered ceiling, three tiered chandeliers, monumental fireplace and walls hung in blue fabric embroidered with gold-thread fleurs de lys. This large room contains the finest pieces in the collection, whilst a second room has exhibits that explain the making of a fan frame.

The last remaining master of this craft in France, Anne Hoguet continues her family tradition, producing new work that meets the highest standards of craftsmanship.

NEARBY

Garden of Hôpital Fernand Widal (6)
200, rue du Faubourg-Saint-Denis
Intended for geriatric patients, this green area of 1,000 m² is a very welcome surprise within this bustling area of the city, offering the chance of a pleasant moment of relaxation.

Art Nouveau façades at 14 and 16, rue d'Abbeville (7)
Métro: Poissonnière
Two superb Art Nouveau façades. The building at No. 14 was designed in 1901 by the architects Alexandre and Édouard Autant, with the ceramic decoration by Alexandre Bigot. Note the extravagance of the plant motifs: the central bay of the building swarms with what look like real climbing vines, whilst the loggia on the fifth floor is decorated with leaves, chimeras and slim columns in green ceramic.

PETIT HÔTEL DE BOURRIENNE

The marvel of a merveilleuse

58, rue d'Hauteville
Métro: Bonne-Nouvelle, Poissonnière or Château-d'Eau
Visit by appointment
Tel.: 01 47 70 51 14

During the late 18th century, faubourg Poissonière saw the construction of numerous city mansions in the neoclassical style of the day. Often hidden behind massive *porte-cochères* or by rented properties, these have maintained a more intimate feel than the mansions of faubourg Saint-Germain and yet are largely unknown. A fine example is the superb Hôtel de Bourrienne, which was built in 1787 and nestles behind a rather rustic-looking garden. The interiors, designed by the same architect who worked on the Bagatelle, reflect the tastes of two successive owners: Madame Hameline, one of the most famous of the so-called *merveilleuses* (elegant ladies) of the Directoire and Consulate periods, and Louis Fauvelet de Bourrienne, private secretary to Bonaparte. Still intact, the apartments on the ground floor are a rare example of the Directoire and Consulate styles in Paris. Opening onto a garden which is reflected in the wall mirrors, these still have all their furnishings and painted wood panels; the delightful frescoes were inspired by the contemporary vogue for the art of ancient Egypt and classical antiquity. The salon, dining-room, dressing room, bedroom and winter gardens can be visited only by appointment and with the authorisation of the present owners, who are keen to maintain the private, intimate atmosphere.

This remarkable place can be hired for special receptions, etc.

NEARBY

An old faience shop: Hippolyte Boulanger de Choisy-Le-Roi ⑨

18, rue de Paradis

In the late 19th/early 20th centuries, rue de Paradis was considered the place in Paris to buy glassware, porcelain and ceramics. It was one of the last examples in the city of a street given over entirely to the interests of one particular economic activity. Built in 1889–1892 by the architects Georges Jacotin and Ernest Brunnarius, the building at No. 18 housed the offices and the shop of the faience manufacturers Boulanger de Choisy-le-Roi. The company's moment of glory came during the creation of the Paris métro, for which they provided about two-thirds of the wall tiles. Today, the interior and exterior of the building are still covered by immense ceramic tiles; since 1981 this has been a listed building. A polite request will get you a look inside, even if the building is not officially open to the public.

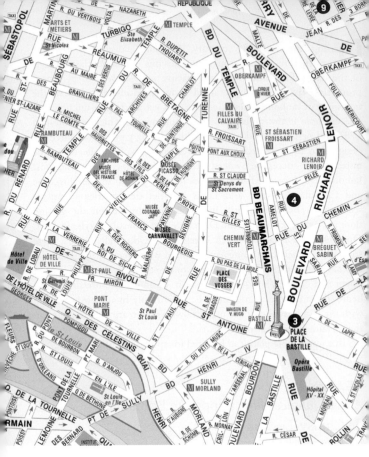

11th Arrondissement

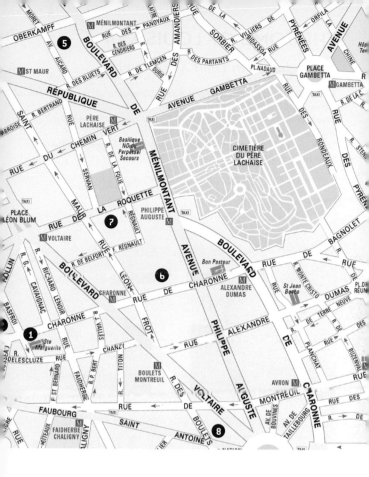

THE TOMB OF LOUIS XVII

Who is buried in Louis XVII's tomb?

Sainte-Marguerite Cemetery - Église Sainte-Marguerite, 36, rue Saint-Bernard
Métro: Ledru-Rollin • Tel.: 01 43 71 34 24
Church open from Monday to Saturday (except school holidays) 8am–12pm
and 2pm–7.30pm. Sunday 8.45am–12.45pm
To see Louis XVII's tomb, apply at the reception desk: Monday to Friday,
9am–12pm and 4pm–7pm

C losed in 1804, the cemetery attached to the church of Saint-Marguerite contains a small tomb with the inscription "L XVII – 1785-1795". There is a mysterious story associated with this, as for a long time it was taken to be the tomb of Louis XVII.

The son of Louis XVI and Marie-Antoinette, Louis-Charles was shut away in the prison of Le Temple on August 13, 1792, when he was just seven years old. After the execution of his father on January 21, 1793, he was entrusted to the keeping of the cobbler Simon until January 1794. Thereafter all trace of him is lost, and the official story runs that the Dauphin fell ill and died on June 8, 1795 and was buried in secret. The mystery surrounding this death led to no fewer than forty-three false "Dauphins" coming forward over the following years.

Research carried out at Sainte-Marguerite cemetery, traditionally used to bury those who had died in the prison of Le Temple, revealed that a child was buried there on June 10, 1795 – that is, two days after the supposed death of Louis XVII. A first exhumation was ordered in 1846, but the body discovered in the lead coffin was that of a youth aged 15–18. This gave rise to various rumours: some said that the prince had been saved from the prison by royalists, and that the body had been placed there to cover his escape; others argued that he had actually died in Le Temple but in 1794, and that no one was informed of the fact until a year later (in order to avoid a scandal, a burial was then held with another body).

The truth would seem to be that Louis XVII did actually die in the dungeons of Le Temple, and that his heart was removed and concealed during the autopsy. The prince's body was apparently then buried in Sainte-Marguerite cemetery, before being exhumed by order of the government of the day for reburial in the cemetery of Calmart. Over the coming years his heart would pass from owner to owner, until in 1975 it was laid to rest in the crypt of Saint-Denis, the burial place of many of France's kings. DNA analysis carried out in 2000 confirmed the authenticity of the attribution to Louis XVII, and a funeral urn containing the heart was placed in the Bourbon Chapel of the cathedral on June 8, 2004. However, one question still remains: who is buried in the tomb at Sainte-Marguerite?

NEARBY

Mosaics at 1, passage Rauch ②

Close to the cemetery, a rather nondescript building is enlivened with a number of ceramic decorations: a lion, a camel, a bear …

STROLLING AND EXPLORING THE ALLEYS AND COURTYARDS OF FAUBOURG-ST- ANTOINE

Starting point: the Bastille or Ledru-Rollin métro station (depending upon whether you want to stroll up or down rue du Faubourg-St-Antoine)

Note: Some of the courtyards are closed at the weekend and some are actually located within the 12th *arrondissement*, as they are on the even-number side of rue du Faubourg-Saint-Antoine.

The **passage du Cheval-Blanc at No. 2 rue de la Roquette** is a good place to start. Comprising a sequence of six fully-restored cobbled courtyards – named after the first six months of the year – this leads to the **cité Parchappe** area giving directly onto rue du Faubourg-St-Antoine. Take the opportunity to glance into the cobbled courtyard of **No. 33** in this street, the gate generally being open during the daytime; the Parisian radio station Radio Nova is located here. At **No. 50** on the other side of the street (and therefore in the 12th *arrondissement*; Baron Haussmann's redevelopment scheme divided the street between two arrondissements), **No. 9 passage de la Boule-Blanche** houses the premises of the *Cahiers du Cinéma* under a fine glass roof draped with greenery. From here you can, during the week, pass through to **rue de Charenton** (the passage is closed at weekends). A little further on, at **No. 56 rue du Faubourg-St-Antoine**, is the **cour de Bel-Air,** which is even prettier since its restoration; in autumn the façade vines here are full of grapes. This is home to the famous bookshop *L'Arbre à Lettres*, which is entered from No. 62, rue du Faubourg-St-Antoine. One of the houses in the courtyard also has a fine staircase in black wood which is known as "The Black Musketeers Staircase". At No. 66, take **passage du Chantier**, which still looks as it did in the 19th century, with large cobble-

stones, narrow pavements, and various workshops and shops; some of the premises still house woodworkers. At No. 71, on the 11th *arrondissement* side of the street, the cour des "Shadocks" (its unofficial name) is a fine example of what restoration can achieve, creating a place with its own, very special atmosphere. A little further, at No. 75, the **cour de l'Étoile-d'Or** takes its name from the *À l'Étoile d'Or* sign. Here you can still see a small 17th-century *pavillon de plaisance*; a sort of pleasure pavilion, which used to stand between the courtyard and the garden beyond (the latter was paved and made into a second courtyard in the 18th century). Reference is often made to the face of a sundial dated 1751 which is supposed to be engraved on the right side of the pavilion's façade, but nowadays it is completely invisible. If you have still managed to avoid getting run over as you cross back and forwards over rue du Faubourg-St-Antoine, try your luck once more to see **cour des Bourguignons** at No. 74. Here, the workshops bristle with large signs but still house a good number of artists and craftsmen. The courtyard has a fine porch decorated with sculpture and carved medallions; the fine brick chimney rising above a large glass roof is now a listed architectural feature. Crossing the road (yet again!), take the time to glance into **cour des Trois-Frères** at Nos. 81–83, it is a veritable hive of industry; **cour de la Maison-Brûlée** at No. 89 (the entrance has two fine mascarons); and finally **cour de l'Ours** at No. 95 (there is a relief of a bear carved on the façade). Moving away from the rue du Faubourg-St-Antoine, this stroll should also take in **passage Lhomme** in the nearby rue Ledru-Rollin (on the 11th *arrondissement* side). A verdant, cobbled street now occupied by art galleries and craft showrooms, this links rue Ledru-Rollin with rue de Charonne, where at No. 37 you can admire the last stop on our brief tour: **cour Delépine.**

NEARBY

Cour du Coq ④

60, rue Saint-Sabin, Métro: Chemin-Vert

Closed behind a wrought-iron gate decorated with a cockerel (just in case you had missed the name on the street sign), Cour du Coq owes its name to the strutting pride felt by a former owner at possessing a cobbled stretch of rural France right here in the centre of Paris. If the gate is closed, you can still gaze through the openwork railings to admire the quiet calm of the place.

Why are wood crafts located in Faubourg-St-Antoine?

The establishment of wood crafts in the Faubourg-St-Antoine district is due to the fact that the wood transported into Paris by river entered the city by the nearby fluvial port of La Rapée. Firewood and building timber were thus stored nearby, so it was only natural that people would soon have the idea of setting up wood-working crafts in the neighbourhood.

MUSÉE ÉDITH-PIAF

A hymn to the Little Sparrow

5, rue Crespin-du-Gast
Métro: Ménilmontant
Tel.: 01 43 55 52 72
Admission free; visits by appointment only

Including stuffed toys, Marcel Cerdan's boxing gloves, letters, pumps and the famous black dress that the singer wore on stage, these mementos of Édith Piaf were all donated by her friends and family. Visits must be prebooked by phone. This small, two-room museum is the life's work of a dedicated fan of the French chanteuse; retiring and discreet, he is also one of those who maintains the singer's tomb at Père-Lachaise cemetery. Visitors cannot help but be touched and moved by this collection of heterogeneous objects lovingly brought together in what was for some time the singer's own home. Even if this small apartment was not Edith Piaf's only home in Paris, you come away feeling that some of her spirit and generosity still pervade the place.

NEARBY

Garden of Doctor Belhomme ⑥
159, rue de Charonne

Hidden away behind some tall buildings, this pleasant area of greenery extends around three pretty little houses. These are all that is left of the Pension Belhomme, a clinic founded in 1769. Initially intended to house the mentally ill, the buildings would also provide refuge for the fortunate few during the period of the Terror.

Are there Egyptian mummies under the Bastille?

Along with the obelisk in the place de la Concorde and a giraffe called Zarafa, the vice-regent of Egypt presented Charles X (reign: 1824–1830) with a dozen carefully embalmed mummies. After a brief period of display in the Louvre, the mummies began to feel the effects of the Parisian weather, giving off a nauseating odour. So, in 1827, it was decided to bury them in the Louvre gardens. Three years later, the same spot was used to bury thirty-two victims of the July 1830 revolution who had died there. After that rebellion, King Louis-Philippe decided that the insurgents who had died bringing him to the throne should be given a more dignified burial, so the bodies were moved to the Bastille. At the time, no one seems to have been particularly concerned about the fact that some bodies were in a much better state of preservation than others. It was not until 1940, during the repairs to the vault, that the error came to light: the number of bodies present exceeded by two the number of insurgents officially buried there ... No one knows what happened to the other mummies.

The tomb vault in question is visible from the riverside promenade that passes over canal Saint-Martin beneath boulevard Richard-Lenoir.

SITE OF THE GUILLOTINE

Blood on the streets

Corner of rue de la Roquette and rue de la Croix-Faubin
Métro: Voltaire or Philippe-Auguste

Very discreetly set into the tarmac, four granite flagstones commemorate a very macabre time in the city's history: in 1832 the guillotine was transferred from place de Grève (Hôtel-de-Ville), where it had stood since 1792, to the barrière d'Arcueil (located above the present Saint-Jacques métro station), where it stood until 1851. This new location put the guillotine some 5 km from the prison of La Grande Roquette, where the condemned were held, which meant that their journey to their execution took some time. Finally aware that this added to the torture of those about to be beheaded, the government decreed (on 29 November 1851) that the executions should take place in the street at the entrance to the prison. To bear the weight of the guillotine, five large granite flagstones were set into the cobbles, forming a cross. The place would soon become known as the *"abbaye de cinq-pierres"* (playing upon the similar pronunciation of St Pierre [St Peter] and *cinq pierres* [five stones]). A total of sixty-nine people were executed on this spot. When the prison was decommissioned in 1900, the guillotine was moved to a position in front of – then inside – the prison of La Santé. The former governor of La Roquette prison had the five flagstones ripped up and tried to sell them to the Musée Carnavalet, which was not interested. However, when he then set them back in the road surface, he made a mistake: which is why pedestrians nowadays walk across not a traditional Latin cross in black granite but what is in fact St Andrew's cross.

Invention of the guillotine

In a certain sense, three people could claim the "credit" for having invented the guillotine. The godfather of the instrument was undoubtedly Doctor Guillotin, who was the first to propose decapitation using a machine of which he would say: "Gentlemen, with my machine you can cut off a head in the blink of an eye and without feeling the least pain." Finally approved in 1791, the project was then entrusted to the great surgeon Louis, Secretary to the Académie de Chirurgie, who was appointed to resolve the various technical problems posed by this type of execution. He worked out the basic principles of the guillotine and then called for "tenders" from those who were to build it. This is where the joiner Schmidt comes into the story. He, too, made various modifications to the machine, testing it in cour de Rohan using sheep and bales of hay. Schmidt even managed to fraudulently claim paternity of the guillotine and register a patent that would earn him a fortune, thanks to the orders that flooded in from all over France: at one point a total of eighty-three guillotines were at work. However Schmidt could not prevent this malevolent machine taking on the name of its real inventor.

NEARBY

Rue des Immeubles-Industriels ⑧

Métro: Nation

Inspired by Fourier's notion of phalansteries, the industrialist Jean-François Cail commissioned the architect Leménil to build the nineteen residential buildings that make up rue des Immeubles-Industriels. Constructed in 1872–1873, these offered a novel model of accommodation for working families. Within one and the same building were workshops (in the basement and lower levels) and family homes (on the upper floors), the whole thing being designed to be both modern and comfortable. A 200 horsepower steam engine provided the craftsmen (most of whom were woodworkers) with the energy necessary to drive their equipment. Unfortunately the only housing development of its kind in the capital, this experiment would be a great success; by the end of the 19th century there were almost 2,000 people living here. The nineteen buildings are admirably designed, with repetition making for elegance rather than monotony; the façades are adorned with painted and decorated cast-iron columns and the windows on the first floor have a fine arcade motif. The entire design won a Gold Medal at the 1878 Universal Exposition.

The streets named after Faubourgs …

Rues du Faubourg-Saint-Antoine, du Faubourg-Saint-Honoré, du Faubourg-du-Temple, du Faubourg Montmartre, du Faubourg-Poissonnière, du Faubourg-Saint-Denis, du Faubourg-Saint-Martin, all of these names have the same origin: they were given to streets that lay outside the Charles V city walls and the so-called *Mur des Fossés-Jaunes* [Yellow Ditches Wall] built as an extension to those defences (see page 42).

NEARBY

Ceramics at 4, rue Pierre-Levée ⑨

Built between 1880 and 1884, this formerly housed the Jules Loebnitz ceramics factory; it is still decorated by the fine ceramics for which the place became famous at the time.

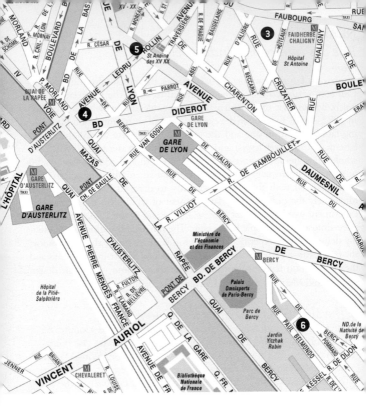

12th Arrondissement

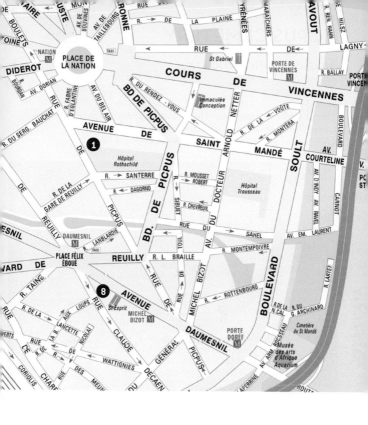

PICPUS CEMETERY

An aristocratic cemetery

35, rue de Picpus
Métro: Picpus
Open all week in summer 2pm–8pm (except Saturday and public holidays);
in winter 2pm–4pm (except Saturday and Sunday).
Admission fee, except during the Journées des Parcs et Jardins

Picpus cemetery is now cared for by the priests and nuns of the Sacred Heart who, committed by their vows to perpetual veneration of the Holy Sacrament, here watch over the repose of the earthly remains of some 1,306 victims of the Terror. A visit here is a very solemn and moving experience. Guillotined between 14 June and 27 July 1794 in what was at the time called place du Trône renversé (Overturned Throne) – now place de la Nation – these 1,306 victims were buried in two of the three mass graves dug in the gardens of the former Convent of the Augustinian nuns. In 1795 the cemetery was then closed and filled in – shortly after the fall of Robespierre – and two years later was secretly repurchased by Princesse Amélie de Salm de Hohenzollern-Sigmaringen, whose brother had been one of those guillotined. In 1803, it was thanks to the Marquise de Montagu (née de Noailles) that the entire grounds of the former convent were bought by an association of the families of the victims, with one area being set aside for the creation of a private cemetery reserved for relatives of those guillotined. The mass graves cannot be visited although they can be seen through the railings, whereas the rest of the cemetery is open to the public. The tombs here are adorned by the armorial bearings of all the great French aristocratic families. One of the most famous is that of the Marquis de La Fayette, husband of the Marquise de Noailles and hero of the American War of Independence. This latter fact explains the presence of the American flag in the cemetery; in fact, La Fayette was so attached to the country for whose independence he had fought that, at his request, the soil covering his tomb comes from America.

"Permission to die, Mother Superior?"

Amongst those buried in one of the mass graves of Picpus are sixteen Carmelite nuns from Compiègne, whose tragic story inspired Georges Bernanos play *Dialogue des Carmelites*, which in turn inspired Poulenc's opera of the same title. Sentenced to execution, their courage would earn them a place in history: along the entire route to the guillotine, they sang psalms and canticles, without anyone managing to silence them. Just as she was about to mount the scaffold, each of the nuns kneeled before the Mother Superior (who had been given the sad privilege of dying last) and asked "Permission to die, Mother Superior?", receiving the answer: "*Allez, ma fille.*" The Mother Superior, Mother Mary Lidoine, then mounted the scaffold in her turn, chanting the *Laudate Dominum*.

Caryatids at 199–201, rue de Charenton ②

The winner of a 1911 architectural award, this fine building was designed by the architects Brandon and Morlon. The unusual caryatids each represent a specific trade: a miner, a peasant, a craftsman and a sailor.

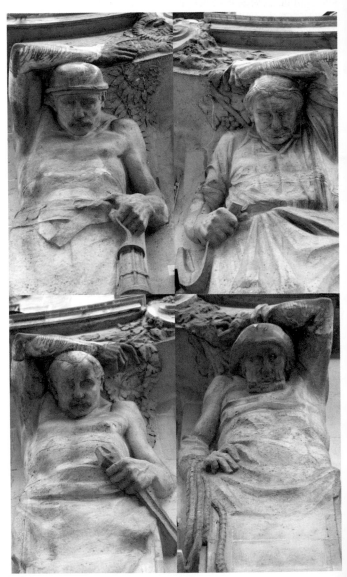

La Fayette

Born in Auvergne in 1757, La Fayette was still a very young man when he enlisted on the side of Washington and those fighting for American Independence. As part of the expeditionary force led by Rochambeau, he made a real contribution to the victory at Yorktown in 1781 and thus to the independence of the United States of America. It was La Fayette who, together with Condorcet and Sieyès, drew up the French Declaration of the Rights of Man, voted by the National Assembly on 26 August 1789.

The Tricolour Flag

The red and blue come from the coat-of-arms of the City of Paris; the white was the colour of royalty. The flag owes its existence to La Fayette, who had it adopted by his troops on 17 July 1789.

A Vegetative Building

While it may not be a great architectural triumph, the building that houses the headquarters of the National Forestry Office (2, avenue de Saint-Mandé) is said to have been inspired by the circular form of a tree trunk.

NEARBY

Aligresse Communal Garden ③

41, impasse Druinot

Created on a piece of wasteland, the Aligresse communal garden is a fine example of how a neighbourhood can come together in cultivating flower beds and vegetable plots. For the *jardin partagé* scheme, see p. 353.

The Giant Sliding Gate at 94–96, quai de la Rapée ④

Designed by Aymeric Zublena in 1992, the building at 94–96, quai de la Rapée has a very striking peculiarity: the entire façade is covered by an enormous sliding gate (weight: 84 tons; height: 25 m; width: 33 m). The spectacular opening and closing of the gate can be seen at around 7.00 and 19.00. For reasons of security, access to the building has, for some years now, been by the rather anonymous entrance on avenue Ledru-Rollin.

The Egyptian Columns of viaduc Daumesnil ⑤

Where it crosses avenue Ledru-Rollin, viaduc Daumesnil rests on curious columns with lotus flower capitals. These are a leftover from the 19ᵗʰ-century craze for Egyptian artefacts (see page 47). The viaduct was originally built to serve the old Vincennes railway, which opened in September 1859.

CINÉMATHÈQUE FRANÇAISE

"A dancer lifting her tutu"

(formerly The American Center)
51, rue de Bercy
Métro: Bercy
Exhibitions, Monday to Friday, 10am–7pm, and 10am–8pm at weekends.
Late night (until 10pm) on Thursday. Closed Tuesday
Film library: open Monday to Friday 10am–7pm
Prices and schedules for lectures and screenings at www.cinematheque.fr

The Cinémathèque Française, together with the National Film Library, moved into this building in 2005, after it had stood empty since 1996.

Designed by the American architect Frank O. Gehry, the structure had been built in 1994 to house the American Center, which the US president of the day had intended as a "cultural declaration" between the New and Old Worlds.

To meet this requirement, the Californian architect, renowned for designs that apparently tumble volumes together, suggested a building with two totally different façades: a rather sombre street façade in white stone, which fits in perfectly with its Parisian surroundings, and a Jardins de Bercy façade that is a deconstructed composition in which the architect fully demonstrates his virtuosity in playing with light and space.

Frank O. Gehry also designed two entrances, with that from the garden side offering a view of the whole interior and of the multiple floors and levels overlooking the atrium. At its opening, the *New York Times* hailed the building as "a love poem on the relation between liberty and tradition"; the architect himself coined the rather wittier comparison of "a dancer lifting the hem of her tutu".

Frank O. Gehry

Born in 1929 in Toronto, Frank O. Gehry was the son of a Polish-Jewish family (his real name was Owen Goldberg). His mother was a lover of music, his father a trader in building materials. After an adolescence spent in Ontario, the young man moved to California to study architecture and design, going on to work for various renowned studios, most notably in Paris. In 1962 Gehry set up his own studio in Los Angeles, subsequently being awarded the Pritzker Prize (a sort of Nobel for architecture).

The hallmarks of Gehry's iconoclastic work are deconstructed form and the use of richly contrasting materials. He has said: "I try to compose in a positive manner, using construction techniques and materials in the same way as an artist plays with his brushstrokes." Most famous amongst his remarkable designs are the two towers (Ginger and Fred) in the centre of Prague, and – above all – the Guggenheim Museum in Bilbao, which has received plaudits from around the world.

In 2012, another building designed by the architect should open in Paris: the Fondation Louis Vuitton in the Bois de Boulogne.

The Thiers City Walls

After the defeat of Napoleon, invasion by the "allied" forces of Austria, Russia and Prussia and then the occupation of Paris by foreign troops in 1814 and 1815, various French governments studied how the capital could be fortified. A compromise solution was ultimately found in 1840, when Adolphe Thiers decided on bastioned defences that would extend for 34 km and enclose a total area of 7,800 hectares with a population of 2.5 million. The average width of these earthworks was 140 m, including a paved roadway that would ultimately become the various "boulevards des Maréchaux". The ramparts proper consisted of an external ditch and raised earthworks, beyond which there was a 250 m wide zone in which all building work was forbidden. Placed between 1,500 m and 5,000 m in front of these defences were so-called "Vauban forts", in areas now occupied by the suburbs of Paris. In 1860 the city of Paris would incorporate the area between the walls set up by the Fermiers Généraux (tax collectors for the king) and these new Thiers defences, swallowing up all or part of a number of villages (Auteuil, Passy, Les Batignolles, La Villette, Belleville, Ménilmontant, Bercy). The customs and excise gates were at this time moved to the gateways in the later fortifications. These imposing and modern city defences withstood siege by the Prussians and, in spite of the defeat in 1870, saved the city from further depredations. Generally, however, the area beyond, where building work had been prohibited, was occupied by shacks of all kinds. After 1945, the defences were gradually demolished, the area being replaced by subsidised housing projects, sports stadiums, university campuses, gardens, etc.

Surviving remains of the Thiers defences are: Bastion No. 1 (see above) - A stretch of wall in the upper gardens of Malesherbes (bastion No. 44) (see page 325) - The layout of the Thiers defences is reflected in the course of the modern-day boulevards des Maréchaux.

Paris city walls

Throughout its history, Paris has been enclosed – for commercial and military reasons – within city walls. There were, in fact, seven different rings of walls; of some, physical ruins remain, while traces of others can only be seen in the city's street plan.

– Gallo-Roman walls (4th centery) (see page 71)
– 10th and 11th-century walls (see page 75)
– Philippe Auguste walls (1190–1215) (see pages 80–81)
– Charles V walls (1356–1420) (see pages 42–43)
– *Fossés Jaunes* walls (1543–1640) (see page 42)
– Fermiers Généraux walls (1785–1790) (see page 321)
– Thiers walls (1840) (see opposite)

BASTION NO. 1

A remnant of the Thiers City Walls (1840–1845)

Boulevard Poniatowski (Seine side), near rue Robert-Etlin
Métro: Cour Saint-Émilion or Porte-de-Charenton

A t the edge of the city ringroad stands what is left of bastion No.1 of the Thiers city walls.

A rather anonymous terre plein about 100 m high, this is one of the last traces of the city defences that were built from 1841 onwards (see opposite).

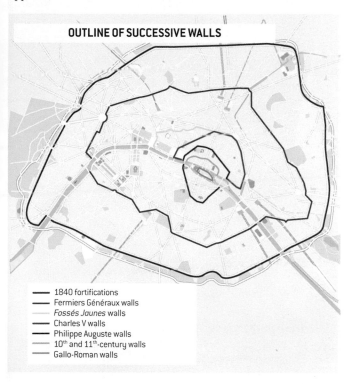

OUTLINE OF SUCCESSIVE WALLS

— 1840 fortifications
— Fermiers Généraux walls
— *Fossés Jaunes* walls
— Charles V walls
— Philippe Auguste walls
— 10ᵗʰ and 11ᵗʰ-century walls
— Gallo-Roman walls

CHURCH OF SAINT-ESPRIT

A replica of the famous Santa Sophia in Istanbul

186, avenue Daumesnil
Métro: Daumesnil
Tel.: 01 44 75 77 70
Open daily 9.30am–7pm

Built in 1928–1935 to designs by the architect Paul Tournon, this church has a spectacular interior that cannot fail to impress. It is, in fact, a small-scale replica of the famous basilica of Haghia Sophia in Istanbul, with burgundy-red bricks facing a reinforced concrete structure built by François Hennebique. At the time, the use of concrete was itself a demonstration of technical prowess – particularly in the creation of the cupola, whose height (33 m) is a reference to Christ's age at his death. The crypt of the church measures 33 m by 27 m.

Over seventy artists worked on the decoration of the church, making it one of the most important examples of Christian religious art in the period between the two world wars.

The church now figures in the supplementary register of listed buildings.

Other examples of Byzantine architecture in Paris

In the period between the two world wars, Cardinal Verdier launched a massive campaign to "reChristianise" the area of Paris. The dozen or so churches which he commissioned were often inspired by Byzantine architecture, which at the time was considered the "Christian" style *par excellence*. Thus, along with the church of Saint-Esprit, there is the church of Sainte-Odile (2, avenue Stéphane-Mallarmè, 17th arr.), the church of Sainte-Jeanne-de.Chantal (16th arr.) and the chapel of the Auxiliary Sisters (see page 115).

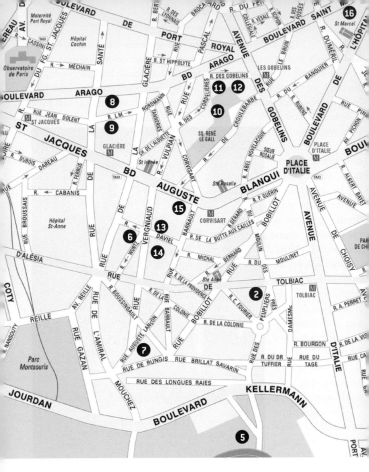

13th Arrondissement

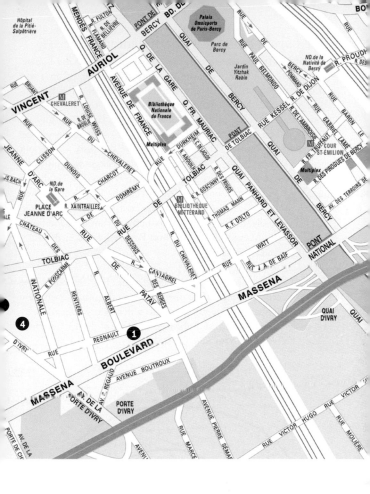

The Layout of Paris Arrondissements

The city's first *arrondissement* is the central area around the Louvre. From there, the twenty *arrondissements* of the city unfurl in a sort of clockwise spiral. This layout dates from the 1860s, when the faubourgs beyond the old Tax-Farmer city barriers were incorporated within the city. Some villages – such as Belleville, Grenelle, Vaugirard and La Villette – were absorbed entirely; some – such as Auteuil, Les Batignolles-Monceau, Charonne, Montmartre and Passy – were split between Paris and other outlying towns. Other villages were only partially annexed: Aubervilliers, Bagnolet, Gentilly (the Glacière district in the 14th and the Maison-Blanche district in the 13th), Issy (the Javel district in the 15th), Ivry, Montrouge (the Petit-Montrouge district in the 14th), Neuilly (the Ternes district in the 17th), Pantin, Le Pré-Saint-Gervais, Saint-Mandé (the Bel-Air and Picpus districts in the 12th), Saint-Ouen and Vanves.

Before 1860, Paris had twelve arrondissements. The 13th took a long time to accept its number: not only was there the usual superstition over the number 13, but there was also a derogatory contemporary expression – "to be married in the registry office of the 13th" – which meant "to be living in sin".

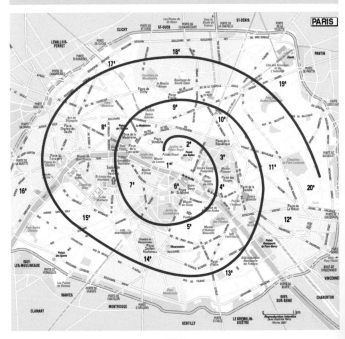

VILLA PLANEIX

①

An exercise in style

26, boulevard Masséna
Visits by appointment, at weekends only. Contact Hèlene Planeix
at 09 79 28 02 41

This is perhaps Le Corbusier's most complex composition of architectural volumes, with the architect meeting the challenge posed by creating a living space of a total area of 300 m² on a site measuring only 200 m². Commissioned by the self-taught artist Antonin Planeix, the villa was built in 1924–1928. At the time, this was an area of market gardening and "land was still cheap", says Antonin Planeix's granddaughter, Hèlene Planeix, who still lives here. Due to its slope, the site was a difficult one, with walls adjoining other houses. Initially, Le Corbusier designed the house to stand on pilotis 4.5 m high, intending to use the upper level for the apartment and the artist's light-filled studio. "However, my grandfather had already gone way beyond his budget, so asked the architect to stop at the ground floor and use the space for two studios that could then be rented out." Despite these changes, the main apartment has maintained all the characteristics of Le Corbusier's style, with 8 m of the living-room walls given over to windows, and non-weight-bearing partitions cleverly converted into storage units. The bathroom is tucked away in a specially designed curved wall.

Le Corbusier (1887–1965)

Widely considered one of the greatest architects of the 20ᵗʰ century, Le Corbusier was born Charles-Édouard Jeanneret-Gris in French-speaking Switzerland (later becoming a French citizen). He made his name with his theory regarding the "five points" of modern architecture, designing buildings that are characterised by the use of open-plan layouts, curtain walls, pilotis, window strips and roof terraces. Le Corbusier is equally famous for his *Modulor* system based on the proportions of the human body. His most famous works include: the city of Chandigar (India), the Cité Radieuse housing development in Marseilles, the chapel of Notre-Dame-du-Haut at Ronchamp (Franche-Comté) and the Villa Savoye in Poissy. Besides Villa Planeix, Le Corbusier's works in Paris are the Salvation Army Buildings at 12, rue Cantagrel and 29, rue des Cordelières in the 13ᵗʰ *arrondissement*; the Villa La Roche (see page 309) and Villa Jeanneret; his own apartment-studio at 24, rue Nungesser-et-Coli (on the borders of the 16ᵗʰ *arrondissement* and Bois de Boulogne; see our guide *Banlieue de Paris insolite et secrète*); and the Pavillon du Brésil and Maison de la Suisse in the Cité Internationale (14ᵗʰ *arrondissement*).

A Country Stroll around Porte d'Ivry
Métro: Porte-d'Ivry

Just like Tour Montparnasse or Tour Jussieu, the tower blocks of the Olympiades district do have one great advantage: when you are inside them, you do not see them. Still, even if you are not lucky enough (!) to live there, you can still find traces of the countryside within the city; not by spying down upon it, but by strolling around it. Leaving the Porte-d'Ivry métro station and walking back up rue Nationale towards rue de Tolbiac, you soon reach **passage Nationale**, a small unpretentious street which it is a pleasure to stroll along. A bit further on, you come to the charming **cul-de-sac Bougoin**, which is open to those who manage to be both curious and discreet. Still further on, at **36, rue Nationale**, is another little cul-de-sac, bedecked with flowers and plants. And at 56bis, avenue Nationale is the entrance to **impasse Nationale**. If you then

walk down the street on the even number side, you come to **passage Bourgoin**: lined with low houses, each complete with garden, this even has an small area for pétanque– right in the centre of Paris! Leaving passage Bourgoin by **rue du Château-des-Rentiers**, walk up to No. 70 in that street: if you are lucky, one of the residents will be entering and you can slip in to see the fine courtyard (you need the keypad code to open the gate).

NEARBY
Square des peupliers
②

74, rue du Moulin-des-Prés

Created in 1926, this small area of rich vegetation has a number of pretty houses and buildings organised around a maze of charming little streets. Not far away is place de l'Abbé-Hénocque, surrounded with quiet streets lined with pastel-coloured workers' cottages built at the beginning of the 20th century.

TEMPLE FOR RESIDENTS OF CANTONESE ORIGIN

Temple in an underground car park

37, rue du Disque
Métro: Porte-d'Ivry
Access is easiest from avenue d'Ivry, opposite No. 66
Open daily 9am–6pm
Admission free
Tel: 01 45 86 80 99

W hile the Buddhist temple of the Teochew Association is loc
the "Dalle des Olympiades" concourse (see below), this t
for residents of Cantonese origin is actually built below it: rue du Dis
is in fact more of an underground car park than a street proper, and
has the odour of trash cans to prove it. However, the interior of this, th
only other Buddhist temple in Paris, is in sharp contrast to its setting: the
visitor is warmly welcomed, and the atmosphere is just right for personal
reflection or for initiation into the world of Chinese Buddhism.

NEARBY
Temple of the Teochew Association ④
44, avenue d'Ivry
Open daily 9am–6pm
Admission free

Around 1975 hundreds of thousands of Chinese fled Vietnam to settle
in the four corners of the earth. About 80,000 of them were Teochew
(pronounced Ti-chew) from Guangdong Province who came to Paris,
where they settled and prospered in the 13ᵗʰ *arrondissement*. In 1985
the community founded the French Teochew Association's Centre for
Buddhist Meditation, with the aim of providing "mutual assistance to
further the social integration of its members and promote the cultural
identity of the Teochew". This place of worship for both Thai and
Chinese Buddhists is open to everyone, irrespective of their religious
beliefs. It is reached by passing along the market gallery (where the
merchandise on display already gives you a sense of another culture) and
then turning left onto the Olympiades concourse (known as the *Dalle
des Olympiades*) and finally turning right. Inside the temple there is an
altar dedicated to Buddha, where you can meditate or make offerings of
incense and fruit. However, some just come here for a cup of tea and to
leaf through the newspapers. If your Chinese is good enough, you can
also catch up on the local gossip.

...ing from beyond the grave

...ue de Sainte-Hélène
...ER B: station Cité-Universitaire
Tel.: 01 47 40 58 08 • www.ville-gentilly.fr
Cemetery open:
Summer: Monday - Sunday 8am–5.45pm
Winter: Monday - Sunday 8am–4.45pm

"To my esteemed healer" from "his grateful patients". This is undoubtedly the most adorned and bedecked tomb in the Gentilly cemetery. Even a century after his death, Jacob the Zouave (the Zouaves were a sort of light infantry) remains a very intriguing figure. As you can see from the votive plaques and bouquets of flowers, there are still those who believe in the healing powers of this Belle Époque warrior, who, it was said, cured people with an intangible fluid that emanated from his person. There were even those who came for his help after his death. Jacob the Zouave was just one of the numerous figures who reflect the 19th century's fascination with hypnotism, magnetism and other esoteric arts. His tomb is to be found in the allée du Sommet (near the top of the cemetery), between the allée Principale and the allée des Acacias. Lovers of oddities will not miss the chance to visit this cemetery, which despite the name is located in Paris not Gentilly. The sloping site is clearly visible from the ring-road, squashed between it and the fine Charléty Stadium.

Square René-Le Gall: an island in the middle of the Bièvre River

This square was built in 1930 on the southern part of the Île aux Singes, which itself lies between the two branches of the old *Bièvre river*: the *Bièvre* morte to the west and the *Bièvre* vive to the east. The route of the two is still visible between the boulevard Auguste-Blanqui and boulevard Arago, with the branches splitting apart around the area of the former boulevard.

– The *Bièvre morte* ran by the present-day rue Paul-Gervais, then into the square Renè-Le Gall and along the back walls of the Lycée Rodin, of the Salvation Army's Palais du Peuple and, further on, behind the Mobilier National.

– The *Bièvre vive* ran by the present-day rue Edmond-Gondine, rue de Croulebarbe and rue Barbier-de-Metz, forming the bend in the river. Even nowadays, it is easy to imagine the Bièvre running by the buildings to the east of square René-Le Gall, which included taweries and the famous Gobelins factory.

Le Cabaret de M. Grégoire. Now higher than it was, this restaurant can still be seen at 41, rue de Croulebarde. Inside is a 19th-century painting showing Victor Hugo, Chateaubriand and La Fayette dining on the banks of the Bièvre.

Arcimboldo in square René-Le Gall?

In the area near the Gobelins factory, the square is decorated with curious pebble compositions that are reminiscent of the Renaissance paintings of Arcimboldo.

The river Bièvre and its impact on the geography of contemporary Paris

The river has now been rerouted in its course within Paris and the old beds through which it once flowed are dry. However, numerous traces of the Bièvre are still to be found in Parisian topography and toponymy. The river itself flows from some thirty or so small springs located at Guyancourt, 5 km from Versailles and at an altitude of 135 m. In the past, it ran for a total of 32 km and entered Paris at Poterne des Peupliers, beneath the old 1840 fortifications and the site of the modern-day boulevard Kellerman (at an altitude of 38 m). It then formed a large "S" curve around Butte-aux-Cailles, with the dry branch following the route of **rue de la Fontaine-Mouchard, rue Brillat-Savarin and rue Wurtz.** (This stretch fed a number of small ponds that froze in the winter and supplied the ice that was kept in stone ice-houses (*glacières*) during the summer – hence the name of rue de la Glacière, immediately to the west of the Bièvre; such ice-houses fell out of use after 1890). Continuing on its course, the Bièvre then flowed beyond the Fermiers Généraux city walls; its exact location is indicated in boulevard Blanqui by the one pillar of the elevated railway that is higher than the others. At this point, its two branches split around the Ile aux Singes (see **square René-Le Gall** on the previous page). Beyond the faubourg Saint-Marcel, the Bièvre turned west to flow into the Seine near what is now the departures area of Gare d'Austerlitz. In prehistoric times, the Seine formed a large loop towards the north, between Bercy and l'Alma, passing by the foot of the hills of Belleville and Montmartre, while the Bièvre occupied what is the present-day route of the Seine from Gare d'Austerlitz onwards; the two rivers flowed into each other at l'Alma. In time of flood, the Seine occupied the bed of the Bièvre and abandoned its previous bed to the north; this became an area of marshes (*marais*), hence the name of the Marais district. The Bièvre was of great importance for the city's Left Bank. In the 12th century, channels were drawn off it to provide irrigation for gardens and waterpower for mills. The *Canal des Victorins*, for example, supplied water from the river to the Abbaye Saint-Victor; traces of this channel under the abbey walls can still be seen in the underground area of the post office at the corner of rue du Cardinal Lemoine and boulevard Saint-Germain (see page 98). In the 14th century, the purity of the river's water made it particularly appealing to dyers and brewers. In the 16th century, its banks were occupied by the tanneries and taweries which had been forcibly evicted from place de Grève. However, by the 19th century their growing presence had made the entire river both malodorous and unhealthy (a survey of 1860 numbered more than 100 industrial establishments present along its banks). After important rechannelling work carried out between 1824 and 1864, it became necessary to cover over the Bièvre, a project that was completed in 1910.

Contrary to expectations, the famous **rue de Bièvre** is not located along the old course of the river but on that of the channel drawn off it in the 12ᵗʰ century to serve the Abbaye Saint-Victor (see above).

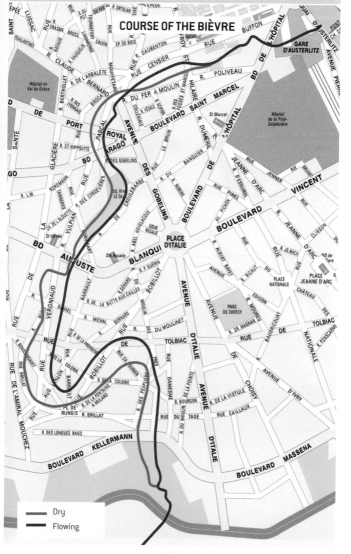

THE ANTOINIST TEMPLE

The Little House on the Prairie

34, rue Vergniaud
Métro: Corvisart
Readings of the Teachings of Father Antoine on Sunday at 10am; other days
(except Saturday) at 7pm
"Operation" (through prayer) in the name of The Father on Sundays and the first
four days of the week at 10am

This curious little yellow church belongs to the Antoinist movement, which believes in the fundamental healing power of prayer. A sense of great tranquility reigns in this small interior, worthy of something you might see in an episode of *Little House on the Prairie*: the men wear long black preachers' coats, while the women must wear not only a long black robe but also have their hair done in a style typical of the 19th century. Silence is de *rigueur* once you are inside; but if you want to, you may go into the *cabinet* with one of the "healers", who will pray with you for release from your mental or physical suffering. The struggle against pain is one of the main concerns of Antoinism, as one can see from the title of the principle work by "The Father" on sale here: *Deliver Us from Evil*.

The Antoinist Faith

Founded in Belgium in 1910, this takes its name from its founder, Antoine, known to the faithful simply as "The Father". In 1922 it was recognised as "A Foundation of Public Service" by the Belgian government. However, a parliamentary report into sects and cults in 1995 classified it as a 'healing movement', describing its beliefs in the following terms: "the very notion of sickness and disease is denied, as is that of death (belief in reincarnation). It is our intelligence which makes us suffer, and faith alone (not the intervention of doctors) which can suppress suffering." The Antoinists themselves deny any suggestion that theirs is a sect or cult: worship, they say "is a moral activity based on faith and self-sacrifice. It is public, and open freely to one and all". They also point out that "The Father" "received patients for over twenty-two years. When he started this activity, he had savings which enabled him to live without working; when he died, he no longer had any possessions". Today Antoinism has sixty-four temples and ninety reading-rooms worldwide, principally in France, Belgium, Australia and Luxemburg. There are around 2,500 believers in France and 200,000 worldwide.

NEARBY
Cité Florale ⑦
36, rue Brillat-Savarin

This development was built in 1928, on a former meadow that was often flooded by the Bièvre and therefore hardly suitable for large-scale constructions. The Cité Floral is, as a result, made up of small individual houses each with a garden of flowers. Access is by tree-lined, cobbled streets that bear the names of flowers: rue des Glycines, rue des Iris, square des Mimosas, etc.

CITÉ FLEURIE

A bouquet of artists

65, boulevard Arago
Métro: Glacière

Built in 1880 with materials "recycled" from the "Food Pavilion" at the 1878 Universal Exposition, the superb Cité Fleurie is the oldest artist community in Paris. Access is via a gateway, but you could wait until one of the tenants is leaving and then ask if you might have a look inside. In total there are twenty-nine studios, each with a white façade and all still occupied by artists. The famous names among past residents include Gauguin (who lived with Daniel de Montfreid), Modigliani (who lived with the Mexican painter, Zanaga) and Jean-Paul Laurens. Due to the personal intervention of the President of the French Republic, the cité Fleurie became a listed area in the 1970s.

NEARBY
Cité verte ⑨
147, rue Léon-Maurice-Nordmann
This houses artists in a total of twenty-four studio/homes aligned on either side of a tree-lined street. Built just after the Cité Fleurie, it has the same calm and rural atmosphere; however, it is more difficult to gain access to.

Château de la Reine Blanche ⑩
18 bis, rue Berbier-du-Mets
Entrance at 4, rue Gustave-Geoffroy • Free guided tours by the owners (April-September) each Wednesday and Sunday at 2pm, 3pm, 4pm and 5pm
Built in the 16th century for the Gobelins family, the château (a central block flanked by turrets) has recently been restored; based on information gleaned from contemporary documents, the work has preserved all the beauty of the buildings organised around the various paved courtyards. Trimmed with fine white masonry, the château has a number of admirable features: "pepper pot" towers with spiral staircases (one of these, dating from the 16th century, stands 17 m high and was carved in one piece out of the trunk of a single oak tree); arcaded galleries; and a superb wagon gateway with corbelled gables.

Hôtel de la Reine Blanche ⑪
17, rue des Gobelins
Not to be confused with the Château de la Reine Blanche, this city mansion is on the same block and has also maintained its charm and atmosphere; it has a fine spiral staircase.

3 bis, rue des Gobelins ⑫
Bought by the manufacturer Jean de Julienne, who was a great patron of Watteau, this former Hôtel Mascarini dates from the 17th century and occupies the back courtyard of the building; it still has its 18th-century garden and orangerie.

LITTLE ALSACE

The most attractive subsidised housing in Paris?

10, rue Daviel
Métro: Corvisart

Built from 1912 onwards by the architect Jean Walter, this is probably the most charming scheme of subsidised housing in Paris.

The forty houses, with pitched roofs in typical Alsatian style, are grouped around a flower-planted courtyard. The place is just as it was originally designed for the Habitation Familiale Association.

The Paris City Council Housing Department still runs the scheme, so – technically – you could even put yourself down on the waiting-list.

NEARBY
Villa Daviel ⑭
7, rue Daviel

As you leave Little Alsace do not miss Villa Daviel standing opposite, a pretty private street lined by houses adorned with plants and greenery.

Little Russia: homes for Russian taxi-drivers ⑮
22, rue Barrault

This is an amazing place, made up of two ranks of cottage-style homes designed from 1912 onwards to provide accommodation for Russian émigrés fleeing the Revolution. Mainly aristocrats, a large number of these newcomers would then take on work as taxi-drivers, using the garage below their homes to park their cars.

Unfortunately it is not easy to gain access here. If a resident does open the door for you, go up the staircase to the esplanade, lined by an amazing collection of cottages with raised ground floors. The view from the terrace is also worth the journey: to the south, it overlooks Little Alsace, to the left, the bed of the river Bièvre.

Remains of the old convent of Les Cordelières

Within the grounds of the Hôpital Broca stand these curious ruins surrounded by a garden. They are all that remain of the old convent of Les Cordelières, founded in 1289. The construction of new hospital buildings in 1974 further reduced the area around these ruins.

TEMPLE OF HUMAN RIGHTS

A mysterious Freemason temple

5, rue Jules-Breton
Métro: Saint-Marcel
Not open to the public
www.droithumain-france.org

Set in a discreet street of the 13th *arrondissement*, the facade of 5, rue Jules-Breton is truly astonishing: inspired by Egyptian architecture, it has lotus-flower columns and a balcony balustrade adorned with an ansate-cross motif. Above runs the inscription *Le Droit Humain* [Human Rights], which is the name of an Order of Freemasonry founded in 1893 by George Martin (1844–1916). The peculiarity of this Order is that it is a mixed one, and the inscription below the columns summarises the great principle which inspired its founder: "Within humanity, women have the same duties as men. They must have the same rights both within the family and within society." *Le Droit Humain* now has around 12,000 members. The temple is not open to the public.

The Ansate Cross

The ankh or ansate cross is the Egyptian hieroglyphic for "life". It probably originated as a stylised rendition of the vertebra of an ox, the animal that was a symbol of power and strength. The ankh appears frequently in Egyptian art, held in the hand of a god or goddess who is portrayed bestowing life upon the mummified body of the deceased. Mirrors, too, often had the form of an ankh. Nowadays, the ansate cross is used by the Coptic Church, mainly in Egypt and Ethiopia.

Joan of Arc in Paris and in the 13th arrondissement

There are five statues of the Maid of Orleans in Paris. Apart from the famous gilded statue by Frémiet in rue des Pyramides, these are to be found in: rue Jeanne-d'Arc (13th *arrondisssement*), on the esplanade of Sacré-Coeur (18th), outside the church of Saint-Augustin (the 8th) and on the façade of Saint-Denis-de-la-Chapelle (18th). There is also a bust of Joan of Arc in rue Saint-Honoré, by the plaque marking the place where she was wounded by an English arrow. The 13th *arrondissement* honours the saint not only with a statue and with a square and street named after her, but also in various other ways: rue de Patay is named after one of her important victories, rue Domrémy after the village where she was born, and rue La Hire and rue Xaintrailles after knights who fought alongside her.

14th *Arrondissement*

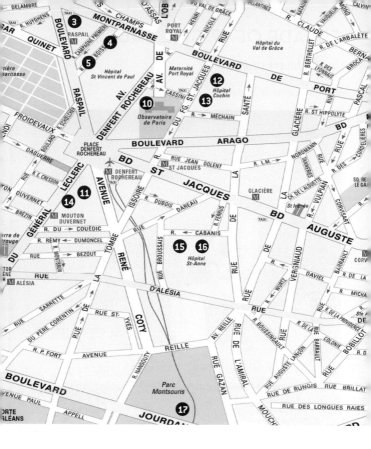

In the heart of Paris

Métro: Plaisance ou Pernéty

This magnificent door in the form of a double heart was designed in 1959 by the Hungarian-born artist Alexandre Mezei, who lived here. Clearly inspired by Art Nouveau, it shows a shepherd in the upper right panel playing a flute to an audience of sheep and sheepdog. This is a fine example of the charming little architectural details that are such a part of the magic of the city.

NEARBY

The menhir at 133, rue Vercingétorix ②

Between a basketball court and a children's playground, the small square opposite No.133 rue Vercingétorix contains – of all things! – a menhir. The plaque on the ground in front is almost illegible, but you can make out that "this menhir was presented to the City of Paris by the Chamber of Commerce and Industry of Morbihan. The work of seven Breton granite workers, it was unveiled by Monsieur Alain Poher, President of the Senate, on 13 (18?) December 1983 (1988?)". Lovers of Brittany can find another trace of the region on the other side of the railway tracks: an actual Breton lighthouse (see p. 279).

Unusual tombs in Montparnasse Cemetery

Less romantic than Père-Lachaise, the Montparnasse cemetery does contain some unusual tombs – for example, that of Tania Rasevskaya (allée Émile-Richard), home to Brancusi's sculpture The Kiss, produced by the Romanian artist in 1910, which depicts a lovingly embraced couple. There are also the remains of a windmill.Less impressive, perhaps, than the two windmills in Montmartre, that in Montparnasse is what is left of the Moulin de la Charité, which stood here before the creation of the cemetery. The windmill is in an area that was at one time used by the priests of Saint-Jean-de-Dieu to bury those who had died at their Hôpital de la Charité (in rue des Saints-Pères), hence its current name.

A Travelling Hotel

Initially occupying the site at the corner of the Champs-Élysées and rue de la Boétie, the Hôtel de la Massa was built in 1784 by Jean-Baptiste Le boursier. At the beginning of the 20th century it found itself in the middle of a property development scheme; however, rather than being demolished, it was simply dismantled, stone by stone, and moved to its present location – 38, rue du Faubourg-Saint-Jacques – in 1929. Nowadays it houses the Société des Gens des Lettres, founded in 1838 by Isidore Taylor, the man who was also responsible for the purchase of the Luxor obelisk and its shipment to Paris.

NEARBY

126, boulevard du Montparnasse ③

This fine complex of light-filled studios and apartments was the work of the architect and designer Louis Süe (1875–1968), who also designed various attractive studios in the nearby rue Cassini: at No. 3bis for the painter Lucian Simon, at No. 5 for the painter Jean-Paul Laurens and at No. 7 for the painter Czernikowski.

9, rue Campagne-Première ④

The gateway is operated by keypad, but it is worth waiting around to see if one of the residents leaves and is willing to let you have a look inside. All of the hundred or so artist's studios in this development were built using materials salvaged from the 1889 Universal Exhibition.

31, rue Campagne-Première ⑤

Designed by the architect André Arfvidson, this superb building dates from 1911 and was awarded a prize in the City of Paris Façade Design competition. It is a perfect example of the transition from Art Nouveau (the ochre and beige Bigot stoneware used in the façade) to the Modern movement.

NEARBY
Façade of 7, rue Lebouis

Built by the architect Molinié in 1913, the building at No. 7, rue Lebouis has a superb façade decorated with sgraffiti. This technique for the application of frescoes to the exterior of buildings is particularly common in Brussels (see our *Secret Brussels*). The building won an award in the 1913 Façade Design competition.

NEARBY
The Atlantique Hanging Gardens ⑦
Rue des Cinq-Martyrs-du-Lycée-Buffon
Métro: Montparnasse-Bienvenüe or Gaîté
Open daily; closed at night

The work of the landscape designers François Brun and Michel Pena, these Atlantique hanging gardens are invisible from the street, but offer a rewarding atmosphere of calm to those who search them out. The surest way of finding them is to make for the Memorial to the Liberation which still stands at the back of the gardens. This very contemporary melange of greenery, steel and wood (in the form of elevated walkways) is both unusual and effective. There are not only lawns and trees and shrubs of various kinds, but also a pond, ping-pong tables and any number of students basking in the sun. The charm of the whole place is made all the more striking by the fact that these gardens "hang" over the tracks into Montparnasse railway station; the sound of the trains seems to enhance rather than diminish the calm of the place. Even the towering masses of the buildings around the gardens play their part in adding to the tranquility, by cutting out the noise of the nearby traffic. At times, indeed, the curtain-wall façades of the buildings seem to give the whole place a rather surrealist air – like something you might see in *Blade Runner*. In fact, they do figure in numerous films by French "Nouvelle Vague" directors – for example in *Deux ou trois choses que je sais d'elle* by Jean-Luc Godard.

CHURCH OF NOTRE-DAME-DU-TRAVAIL

The first example of an ecclesiastical use of industrial architecture

59, rue Vercingétorix
Métro: Gaîté
www.notredamedutravail.net • Tel: 01 44 10 72 92
Open Monday to Friday from 7.30am–7.45pm; on Saturday 9am–7.30pm; on Sunday 8.30am–7.30pm • Masses on Saturday at 6.30pm and on Sunday at 10.45am • Mass in Portuguese on Sunday at 9am

From the outside this looks like many other churches, but the interior – the work of the architect Jules Astuc – is a remarkable example of the use of industrial architecture. Clearly influenced by the designs of Eiffel and Baltard, the metal structure of the nave is made from 135 tons of iron and steel.

Very atypical for a church, this interior was the brainchild of Abbé Soulange-Bodin, who was appointed to the parish of Plaisance in 1896. His ambition was to build a church that would "unite workers of all classes within the realm of religion". Designed to make the workers feel at home by reminding them of their factories, the new church was – perhaps inevitably – dedicated to Notre-Dame-du-Travail; however, the statue predates the church.

> The church is also home to a trophy of war. Weighing 552 kg, the bell was presented to the church in 1865 by Napoleon III; it comes from the city of Sebastopol and was seized during the Crimean War.

NEARBY

Place de l'amphithéâtre and place de Séoul ⑨
Entrance in rue Vercingétorix

Rebuilt in the 1980s, the place de Catalogne district is the work of the Catalonian architect Ricardo Boffil. While not everyone appreciates place de l'amphithéâtre and place de Séoul, there is no denying that they are a striking example of a contemporary reading of classical architecture. The point of access is not obvious, so many Parisians are not even aware of these two city squares, which have pleasantly quiet and peaceful gardens.

HEADQUARTERS OF THE KING'S HYDRAULIC ENGINEER

⑩

Royal water supplies

42, avenue de l'Observatoire
Métro: Denfert-Rochereau
www.paris-historique.org/maison.php • contact@paris-historique.org
Programme of events available at 01 48 87 74 31; also open during the Journées du Patrimoine *(Association Paris Historique)*

By telephoning beforehand for the lecture schedule, it is possible to arrange to visit this very curious HQ of the King's hydraulic engineer, built in 1619–1623 by the Gobelin brothers to a design by Salomon de Brosse. There is also a *regard* (peephole – see p. 366) through which it was possible to inspect the waters flowing from the Arcueil aqueduct.

Today, however, these waters no longer flow underneath the house but go directly to the Montsouris reservoir. The visit gives you some idea of the different methods used over the centuries to supply Paris with water. There are three ancient *bassins* [water tanks]: Bassin du Roi, de la Ville and Des Carmelites.

As their names suggest, these served different areas of the city: the Palais du Luxembourg, the Val-de-Grâce and the Carmelite monastery plus a total of thirteen different drinking fountains.

NEARBY

The peephole in avenue René-Coty   ⑪

Behind the fine building of the La Rochefoucauld geriatric hospital is a rather remarkable little structure (entrance by avenue du Général-Leclerc). It houses an inspection peephole that gave access to the water flowing from Arcueil (see above).

Arcueil Aqueduct

Contrary to what you might expect, aqueducts still supply Paris with water (see page 369), and the Arcueil aqueduct is one of them: every day, 145,000 m³ of water flow along it, across the Bièvre valley. The modern-day Arcueil aqueduct actually combines two structures dating from very different periods: the Marie aqueduct and the La Vanne aqueduct. The former was inspired by a project devised by Sully for using an ancient Gallo-Roman conduit that drew water from the Rungis and Wissous springs. It was built in 1613–1623 at the behest of Marie de Médicis, hence the name. When in operation, the Marie aqueduct filled a reservoir near Montagne Sainte-Geneviève and supplied the Fontaine Médicis at the Palais du Luxembourg. Nowadays, it still carries 2,000 m³ of water per day, from the Rungis springs to the water tanks of Parc Montsouris. The La Vanne aqueduct constitutes the upper level of the Arcueil aqueduct. Standing 14 m above the Marie aqueduct, it was built by the engineer Belgrand as part of Baron Haussmann's urban development scheme.

A hidden paradise

123, boulevard de Port-Royal
RER: Port-Royal
Officially closed to the public. Access possible by request to the hospital's
administrative staff

A little corner of paradise unknown to most Parisians, the cloister of Hôpital Cochin is a marvel that should not be missed.

Entering from boulevard du Port-Royal, follow the arrows to the chapel. The cloister was once part of the convent of the nuns of Port-Royal-des-Champs, a Cistercian order founded at the beginning of the 13th century in the Chevreuse valley.

This Parisian convent opened in 1625 under the abbess Angélique Arnauld and would, from 1635 onwards, become famous as a centre of Jansenism; Blaise Pascal, for example, was a regular visitor to this community of the Daughters of the Holy Sacrament.

Suppressed during the Revolution, the convent was converted into a prison, ironically known as "Port-Libre". The place was first used as a hospital in 1795.

The last vespasienne in Paris

In boulevard Arago, just in front of the prison of La Santé, is the last *vespasienne* in Paris. Dating from the beginning of the 19th century, these distinctive features of Paris owed their existence to the Prefect of the Seine region, Comte Rambuteau, who for obvious public-health reasons ordered the creation of urinals to replace the *barils d'aisance* (barrels filled with sawdust in which gentlemen had previously relieved themselves at street corners).

The *vespasiennes* were not only more sanitary, they offered more privacy, as the clients were shielded from public view by metal sheeting. Progress has led to the introduction of coin-operated public toilets that are self-cleaning and, more importantly, can also be used by women. However, though the city council voted for the removal of *vespasiennes* on 21 December 1959, it was not until 1980 that the first four coin-operated cabins were installed; note that progress has also put an end to a public service that had been free of charge. No one knows why this particular 19th-century *vespasienne* survived, but now there is talk of having it "listed".

The word "*vespasienne*" comes from the name Vespasian, emperor of Rome in AD 69. Renowned for his greed, he introduced a tax on urine and had urinals erected that the Romans had to pay to use. Unsurprisingly, he is also credited with the expression: "money has no odour".

THE CAPUCHIN QUARRIES

20 m underground: one source of the city's building materials

Hôpital Cochin
27, rue du Faubourg-Saint-Jacques
RER: Port-Royal
www.seadacc.com • association@seadacc.com
Well worth a visit. E-mail: jlhr-faure@wanadoo.fr (don't hesitate to write two to three times) or by letter to the Association SEADACC at the Hôpital Cochin (see address above). Applications by letter are often given priority over those by e-mail • Length of visit: 1–2 hours. Access impossible for persons of restricted mobility, and inadvisable for those suffering from claustrophobia

Perhaps a visit to the Denfert-Rochereau Catacombs is rather too conventional; but finding an illegal point of entry to undertake a do-it-yourself visit to Paris's underground passageways is definitely too risky …

The Capuchin Quarries provide the perfect happy medium. Located some 20 m underground, they still have an air of adventure about them, not having been too sanitised by the association of enthusiasts who, lamp and spade in hand, have spent years of passionate work restoring these ancient quarries. Now a listed site, this is a unique place, with no equivalent anywhere in the world.

It was here that in the 15ᵗʰ and 16ᵗʰ centuries workers quarried the stone that would be used to build the chapel of the Capuchin monastery. Injuries were frequent and, 20 m overhead, Jean-Baptiste Cochin had an infirmary built to treat the causalities, creating the institution that became the modern-day Hôpital Cochin.

The quarries also provided some 30% of the stone used in building Notre Dame, and were ultimately used to cultivate underground mushrooms: the manure from the horses drawing the city's carriages was often tipped down here, turning these humid tunnels into the perfect environment for growing tasty mushrooms.

Guided by one of the Association volunteers, the visit begins with the descent of a hundred or so steps, which brings you to tunnels "wide enough for a man pushing a wheelbarrow". The sodium lamps (designed to preserve the ecosystem) bathe everything in a strange light, in which the walls of the tunnels gleam with moisture (humidity levels here can be up to 90%). The climax of the visit is the extraordinary *Fontaine des Capucins*. Complete with steps that go down to the phreatic water level, this semi-cylindrical well was dug in 1810.

VILLA ADRIENNE

Artists in the countryside

Entrance in Avenue du Général-Leclerc
Métro: Mouton-Duvernet
At night the keypad gate is locked, but it is open during the day

Built from 1870 onwards to provide accommodation for clerics and soldiers, the Villa Adrienne housing development is a little paradise, offering its residents an oasis of calm just 2 m from the hectic place Denfert-Rochereau. It is laid out around a private garden that has all that one would expect of such a delightful park: well-tended lawns, fine trees, comfortable benches and imperturbable statues. Three sides of this green area are lined with fine buildings in brick and white stone; adorned with sculpted terracotta balconies, these are named after such illustrious figures as Racine and Corneille. The fourth side is lined by magnificent city mansions.

A stroll through the rural south of the 14th arrondissement

The southern part of the 14th *arrondissement* is full of tiny rural corners that are unknown to the public at large (some of them cannot be seen from the main streets); in certain cases there are even houses built by such leading figures of modern architecture as Auguste Perret and Le Corbusier.

29, rue Boulard. Private road. Ask one of the inhabitants if you can have a look around. A magnificent little street lined by houses, each with its own garden. Gauguin, at the time a mere bank employee, began his career as a painter here, in the studio of his friend, Émile Schuttneckar.

14 bis, rue Mouton-Duvernet. The entrance to the building jealously guards the secret of a pretty little winding path through greenery lined by houses, each with its own elegant glass porch.

Villa Hallé. 36, rue Hallé. A charming private street that served as a location during the filming of Catherine Deneuve's *Le bon plaisir*. A couple of metres away, at the junction of rue Hallé and rue d'Alembert, there is a pretty little area in the form of a half-moon.

Square Montsouris: the end house was built by Le Corbusier. The square is, in effect, a street – one of the most charming in all of Paris.

Rue Georges-Braque: No. 6 was built by Perret and was home to the painter Braque.

Rue du Parc Montsouris. Villa du Parc-Montsouris and Impasse Nansouty.

Villa Seurat: at 7bis is the house built by the famous architect Perret for the sculptor Chana Orloff. Soutine and Henry Miller also lived in this cul-de-sac.

Villa Alésia: 111, rue d'Alésia and 39bis, rue des Plantes.

Villa Jamot: 105 and 107, rue Didot. The gate is operated by keypad. Wait a few minutes to see if one of the residents is leaving, so that you can get a glimpse of this charming double alley with its cobbled street.

NEARBY

Musée Sainte-Anne

Centre Hospitalier Sainte-Anne. Building L, 2nd floor, 1, rue Cabanis
Open by appointment on Tuesday and Thursday 2pm–7pm
Tel.: 01 45 65 84 33 • Admission free
For the (free) guided tour, ask at the museum reception

Located in a former dormitory, this museum charts the life of the hospital since the admission of its first patient in May 1867. The collection of pictures, photographs and medical instruments cannot leave one unmoved. Look, for example, at the elegantly varnished and padded wooden case containing the blades which were used for sawing skulls. Unfortunately, it is no longer the famous Doctor Freddy who provides the guided tour. Still, the visit is recommended for those interested in the subject.

The Dibbets Medallions

In 1994, the City of Paris commissioned an original work from the artist Jan Dibbets: 135 bronze medallions (diameter: 11 cm) bearing the name "Arago" with the letters N (North) above and S (South) below. Laid out along the line of the Paris Meridian (which was the international meridian of reference before it was supplanted by Greenwich; see page 275), these medallions commemorate François Arago, who pursued his calculations of the meridian as far as the Balearic Islands. Set into the city's pavements, the medallions run for

a total of 17 km. Searching them out is a very good way of stimulating a child's interest in this scientific subject through the form of a game that can be played while walking around the city. Unfortunately, thirty of these medallions have already gone missing.

NEARBY

Musée Singer-Polignac

Centre Hospitalier Sainte-Anne, 1, rue Cabanis
Tel.: 01 45 65 85 41 or 01 45 89 21 51 • Open only during the Journées du
Patrimoine *or during temporary exhibitions (advertised in the press or on the
site www.centreetudeexpression.com) • http://centre-etude-expression.com*

During the regular temporary exhibitions held here, the Musée Singer-Polignac shows works produced by psychiatric patients, particularly those who over the last fifty years have attended art therapy
workshops.

The Medallions of the Green Meridian

This *Méridienne Verte* was a project devised by architect Paul
Chemetov (designer of the Ministry of Finance in Bercy) as part of
the celebrations for the new millennium.

The idea was to plant trees throughout France to mark out the
line of the Paris meridian (from Dunkirk in the north to Prats-de-

Mollo in the Eastern
Pyrenees).

Within Paris itself, the
line of the meridian
would be marked by
medallions: three to the
west of the large water
basin in the Jardin du
Luxembourg, one to
the south-east of Jardin
Marco-Polo (avenue
de l'Observatoire) and
the last at the corner
of avenue Denfert-
Rochereau and avenue
de l'Observatoire.

THE SOUTHERN MARKER

⑰

A surviving trace of the Paris meridian

Parc Montsouris (boulevard Jourdan side)

Known as the *mire du Sud*, this 4 m high stone bears a curious inscription: "In the reign of … [Napoleon's name has been erased], a marker stone for the observatory. MDCCCVI." Originally erected in the garden of the Paris Observatory, this served to align the instruments used in that institution. It was moved to its present site in 1806, though due to work in the park it is now slightly off-line with the Paris meridian.*

The Paris Meridian

Before being replaced by the Greenwich meridian in 1884, the Paris meridian was the meridian of reference for all the world's geographers. Work on plotting it began in 1669, just two years after the foundation of the Paris Observatory, through the centre of which it runs. That charting was completed in 1718 by the Cassinis (father and son) and by Phillippe de La Hire. Upon request from the Convention, the meridian was recalculated by Delambre and Méchain in 1792–1798 so that it might serve as the basis for determining the exact length of "one metre" (see page 118). All of these figures – Cassini, Delambre and Méchain – have streets near the Observatory named after them. Later, Arago and Biot would extrapolate Delambre and Méchain's measurements as far as the Balearic Islands. The meridian line is today charted on Parisian pavements by 135 medallions engraved with Arago's name (see page 273).

Within the capital itself, the northern limit of the meridian is marked by an obelisk (the *mire du Nord*) located at 1, avenue Junot in Montmartre; unfortunately, it is part of a private residence and so cannot be visited, even if listed as a historic monument. The original northern marker was a simple wooden pillar raised in 1675 by Abbé Jean Picard; the stone obelisk was raised in 1736 "by order of the king".

The *mire du Sud* is located in parc Montsouris in the 14th *arrondissement* (see above).

A further trace of the Paris meridian can be seen in the floor of the galeries du Carrousel at the Louvre, under the inverted pyramid.

Another alignment marker can be seen at Villejuif, on the outskirts of Paris (see our *Banlieue de Paris insolite et secrète*). It was raised in the 18th century by the topographer Jacque Cassini, son of Jean-Dominique Cassini who is credited with being the father of French astronomy.

---

* A meridian is an imaginary line running from the North to the South Pole which links all those points where at noon (solar time) the Sun is at its zenith.

15ᵗʰ Arrondissement

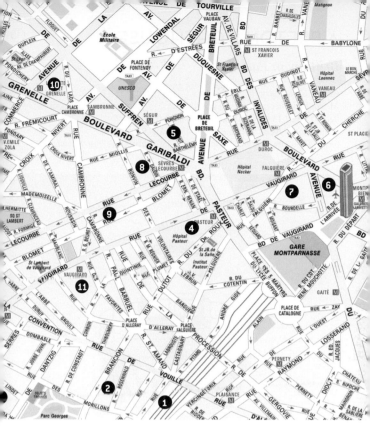

A BRETON LIGHTHOUSE

Brittany in Paris

69, rue Castagnary
Métro: Plaisance or Porte-de-Vanves
Tel.: 01 45 31 15 00 • www.lacrieeduphare.com
Fishmonger's open from Tuesday to Thursday, 9am–1pm
on Friday 9am–1pm and 3.30pm–7pm; Saturday 9am–7pm; Sunday
9am–1pm

The Eiffel Tower is not the only beacon within the city to guide aircraft and tourists who have lost their way. Since 1996 a genuine Breton lighthouse has stood guard over Parisians not far from the station of Montparnasse. Standing 10 m high, the structure was brought into the heart of the city direct from Brittany. At its summit fly the French and Breton flags, while on the back of the building – visible, therefore, only to those taking the train towards Brittany – is the slogan: "Glory to Fishermen and Sailors". The truth is that the lighthouse is an immense advertising sign for the fishmonger's 'La Criée du phare'; a veritable institution within the city, this covers some 1,000 m^2 and sells not only fresh fish, shellfish and crustaceans but also fruit, vegetables, flowers and wine at truly competitive prices. As well as being the largest fishmonger's in Paris, the place also has a very unusual interior. There used to be another lighthouse in Paris. Located on the avenue d'Iéna side of the Trocadero, it was part of the *Services des phares et balises* (Lighthouses and Beacon Services), whose building was destroyed one sad night in 1992.

NEARBY

Villa Santos-Dumont ②

Laid out in the 1920s on a plot that had previously been a vineyard, the beautiful villa Santo-Dumont development was the work of the architect Raphaël Paynot and quickly attracted various artists already resident in the Montparnasse district – for example, Zadkind, Léger and Brauner. Today, the residents are still mainly artists, who have worked to maintain the peace and quiet of this street.

Why are there so many crêperies in Montparnasse?

Most Parisians never think about it, but the high number of Breton crêperies around Montparnasse station is no accident: this is where the trains from Brittany arrive in the capital. The same transport link explains the number of restaurants around Gare de l'Est serving sauerkraut and beer: the trains from Alsace-Lorraine arrive there.

Brittany in Paris: a lighthouse, crêperies ... and even a menhir!

As well as a lighthouse and creperies (see above), Brittany has made its mark upon the capital in another way: on the opposite side of the tracks leading into the station there is an actual Breton menhir (see page 259).

LA RUCHE

A beehive of artists

2, passage Dantzig
Métro: Porte-de-Versailles or Porte-de-Vanves
Visits by appointment only
Contact Mr Herth at 01 48 28 16 38

Nestling discreetly in a magnificent garden of age-old trees at the opening of the cul-de-sac, **La Ruche** (literally, The Beehive) owes its existence to Alfred Boucher (1850–1904), a well-known sculptor and generous philanthropist, who in 1902 set up this phalanstery for struggling young artists. A *Prix de Rome* winner, Alfred Boucher stopped in Milan on his way home from Italy and sold several of his works. Returning to the capital, he immediately invested this small nest egg in a plot of land, where La Ruche would be created. The material for the main building was salvaged from the pavilions which had been erected for the 1900 Universal Exposition – most notably, the Kiosque des Vins du Médoc designed by Gustave Eiffel – and the structure owes its name of 'the beehive' to its polygonal form. At its centre is a wonderfully designed staircase that is flooded with light, with the three floors being occupied by small studios which, over the years, have been used by artists such as Léger, Zadkine, Soutine, Chagall and Modigliani. Nowadays, La Ruche consists of a total of four buildings, the second of which was also constructed using material salvaged from the Universal Exposition. At one point it was threatened with sale and demolition, but thanks a campaign of artists – headed by Chagall and Malraux – it survived. In 1971 the place was bought by René and Geneviève Seydoux, who set up a foundation that still manages the property as a community for artists. The buildings are now listed and provide accommodation for around 60 people (originally there were 140 residents). Alongside sculptors, painters and engravers, you will now find film-makers, set designers, cartoonists and graphic artists.

The beehives of Paris

Alongside the famous bees on the roof of the palais Garnier, there are a number of beehives in Paris. The temperature in the city is around three degrees warmer than in the surrounding area and bees flourish here, actually producing more honey than their country cousins on the Île-de-France.

The hives are to be found:

– on the roof of palais Garnier (not open to the public)

– in Luxembourg Gardens

– on the roof of Opéra-Bastille (not open to the public)

– in Parc Georges-Brassens (15th *arrondissement*)

– in Parc Kellermann (13th *arrondissement*)

– on the roof of the Eiffel Park Hotel (private)

– in La Villette (public gardens)

– at the statue of Casimir Périer in Père-Lachaise cemetery.

MUSÉE PASTEUR

Special presidential dispensation for the funeral chapel

25, rue du Docteur-Roux
Métro: Pasteur
Tel.: 01 45 68 82 83
www.pasteur.fr
Open weekdays 2.30pm–5.30pm. Closed at weekends
Admission: €3 (concessions €1.50)

Located within the premises of the Institut Pasteur, this fascinating museum was set up in 1936 and is dedicated to the famous scientist whose discoveries would revolutionise chemistry, agriculture, industry, medicine, surgical practice and notions of hygiene.

Famous for his work in crystallography and in the development of vaccines (particularly against rabies), Louis Pasteur is here commemorated by a room of scientific mementos and instruments that chart his work in various fields. This fascinating material is then followed by a reconstruction of the private apartments of the Pasteur family, where Louis spent the last seven years of his life.

All of this material came from the scientist's grandson, who donated furnishings and other objects that had belonged to his grandparents. Accurately recreated by the Institut in 1934–1936, these rooms provide a touching insight into the life and work of the great scientist, as well as offering a vivid picture of bourgeois life at the end of the 19ᵗʰ century.

Made up of a total of a ten rooms and two halls linked by a fine French-style staircase, the apartment is crammed with furniture and personal objects. There are also a number of more valuable pieces, which were either bought by the couple themselves or given by admirers – for example, the unique glass vase by Émile Gallé which was presented to the scientist on his fiftieth birthday by his students at the École Normale Supérieure. Just alongside this precious item lies some of Madame Pasteur's unfinished knitting….

This glimpse into Louis Pasteur's personal life ends with a visit to the private funeral chapel (made possible solely by a special presidential dispensation). The opulent neo-Byzantine decoration of the place is rich in symbolism, which the enthusiastic guide is happy to interpret for you.

NEARBY
The old Artesian well at Grenelle   ⑤
Place Georges-Mulot

This artesian well was sunk in the courtyard of an old abattoir. Its location is now marked by an elegant monumental drinking-fountain, complete with neo-gothic columns and medallions depicting various famous figures. Begun in December 1833 (see page 307), work on sinking the well was headed by the man who gives his name to the square.

MUSÉE DU MONTPARNASSE AND ESPACE KRAJCBERG

"I am talking of a time when those under 20 ..."

21, avenue du Maine
Métro: Montparnasse-Bienvenüe
Tel.: 01 42 22 91 96 • Open daily except Saturday, 12.30pm–7pm
Admission: €5 (concessions €4)
Espace Krajcberg: open daily except Monday, from 2pm-6pm
Free admission

Away from the noise and bustle of Montparnasse district, No. 21, avenue du Maine leads into a wonderful cobbled cul-de-sac lined with trees; originally this was the courtyard of an inn for the coaches serving the west of France.

At the beginning of the 20th century, the owner of this land had the brilliant idea of buying some of the buildings that were being dismantled after the 1900 Universal Exposition; these were then reassembled here, on either side of the street, to provide some thirty or so studios for penniless artists. From 1912 onwards Marie Vassilieff, who was the driving force behind the Académie du Montparnasse and the Académie Russe, offered accommodation here to the artists who were to form the École de Paris. She also set up a sort of canteen for the poorer among them; those who, in their times of direst need, profited from her hospitality included Picasso, Braque, Modigliani, Léger, Derain, Max Jacob and Fujita. Today, this place is still the haunt of artists (painters, actors, florists, set designers), who struggle valiantly to preserve the vitality of this oasis of greenery. Created in 1998, the Musée du Montparnasse centres around Marie Vassilieff's own studio; mounting temporary exhibitions dedicated to specific themes, it aims to make the illustrious past of this area better known.

Located at the end of the alleyway, the Espace Krajcberg opened its doors in 2003. It houses the works which the Brazilian sculptor donated to the city of Paris, together with a centre documenting his work. A place of encounter between French and Brazilian culture, this space aims, through art, to make visitors aware of environmental problems.

NEARBY
Musée Bourdelle   ⑦

16, rue Antoine-Bourdelle
Tel.: 01 40 26 77 94
Open daily 10am–6pm, except Saturdays and public holidays
Permanent collection: admission free. Admission to temporary exhibitions:
€4.50 (concessions €3) free

Built in 1961 on the site of the home of the sculptor Antoine Bourdelle (pupil of Rodin and teacher of Giacometti), this museum brings together numerous examples of the artist's works (bronzes, casts, large marble figures, monuments, bas-reliefs), some of which are truly monumental in scale. Some rooms house temporary exhibitions of work by other artists.

Saint Rita: Patron Saint of Desperate Causes

Born in Umbria (Italy) in 1381, Margerita (Rita) Mancini entered religious orders after the death of her husband and two children. One day whilst she was praying before an image of the crucified Christ, a thorn came away from his crown of thorns and stuck into her forehead. The wound started to give off a pestilential odour and Rita was isolated in her cell, where she later died. However, after death her face recovered its supernatural beauty and her body gave off a scent of roses that filled the entire convent. Perfectly preserved, her embalmed body is now in Cascia, near where she was born.

Saint Bonaventure: Patron Saint of Unmarried Women

If your unmarried state has not yet become desperate, then rather than turning to Saint Rita you should pray to Saint Bonaventure. At the foot of his statue are two cushions to which innumerable slips of paper have been pinned. These are the votive prayers of women looking for husbands ...

The Gallican Rite

The Gallican Rite is the Catholic liturgy that was practised in Gaul in the 8th and 9th centuries. Abolished by Charlemagne, the rite was reintroduced in the 20th century, with some additions from the Tridentine rite (see page 197). Its particular features are that it allows for the marriage of priests and bishops and for women deaconesses. With a present total of thirty or so priests, the Gallican Church is a member of the Ecumenical Council of Churches.

CHURCH OF SAINTE-RITA ⑧

A special Mass for animals

27, rue François-Bonvin
Métro: Sèvres-Lecourbe ou Volontaires
Tel.: 01 47 34 21 56 or 01 45 67 57 06 • Open daily (except Tuesday) 9am–
12.30pm and 3pm–7pm. Saturday 8.30am–1pm and 3.30pm–9pm

During celebrations dedicated to St Francis of Assisi, the saint who befriended animals, the church of Sainte-Rita holds a special Mass for them. On that occasion, it becomes a sort of Noah's Ark with dogs, cats, tortoises, hamsters, goldfish, and even such exotic animals as zebras, llamas and tigers. (Though it may spoil the image of the occasion, it should be pointed out that these latter generally come from circuses and zoos, they are not the pets of some eccentric Parisian.)

The almost mystical silence which the animals keep during the whole service always surprises newcomers to the event. Perhaps the animals themselves are surprised by the transformation that takes place within them: legend has it that that by the end of the Mass, the neurasthenic cat has regained its appetite and the manic-depressive dog soon regains a shiny, healthy coat.

Unless, of course, these near-miracles are due to the blessing which, at the end of a Mass celebrated according to the Gallican rite, the priest gives the congregation (animals included).

CHURCH OF SAINT-SÉRAPHIN-DE-SAROV

A tree within a church

91, rue Lecourbe
Métro: Volontaires
Visitors admitted on Saturdays, 2.30pm–5pm

Hidden away in the back courtyard of the building at 91, rue Lecourbe, the Orthodox church of Saint-Séraphin-de-Sarov is a little gem.

Totally invisible from the street outside (to reach it, go through the first courtyard into the second, then turn right), the church takes its name from a Russian hermit who had himself immured while still alive. The first parish church here, founded in 1933, was little more than a shack built around a tree; however, the present structure (built in 1974) has real charm. Standing amidst the weeds of this small garden, the church has wooden outer walls surmounted by a blue onion dome decorated with

the three-arm Orthodox cross. A place of touching simplicity, the interior is adorned with a multiplicity of icons; at the heart of the chapel you can also see the lower part of the tree around which the original structure was built. Serving the Russian community of the 15ᵗʰ *arrondissement*, the church of Saint-Séraphin-de-Sarov is well worth a visit for the warm atmosphere generated during religious services. Information is posted at the entrance; and if you are lucky, you might get to be present at one of the Russian banquets which take place during the course of the year.

Other Orthodox churches in the district

Fleeing the Russian Revolution, numerous White Russians, many of them aristocrats, came to France. A large number settled in the 15ᵗʰ and 16ᵗʰ *arrondissements* of the capital, where – desiring to maintain their culture and religion – they quickly founded the various Orthodox churches that today are dotted around the two districts. Also hidden away behind a block of buildings, the church of the Presentation of the Virgin (91, rue Olivier-de-Serres) is architecturally much less interesting (services on Saturday at 6pm and on Sunday at 10.30am). However, the spirit which informs Saint-Séraphin-de-Sarow can also be seen at the church of Trois-Saints-Docteurs-et-Saint-Tikhon (5, rue Petel), which again has a rather banal exterior but a richly ornamented interior. Three more Orthodox chapels are to be found in the 16ᵗʰ *arrondissement*: at 19, rue Claude-Lorain, 7, rue Georges-Bizet and 87, boulevard Exelmans.

NEARBY

The Cavalerie Pelota Courts

Club de Pelote Basque
8, rue de la Cavalerie – Métro: La Motte-Picquet-Grenelle
Tel.: 01 45 67 06 34 • http://peloteba.club.fr/index.html • Open daily. It is better
to go after 4pm. From 2pm to 4pm on Sundays the courts are given over to
children beginners (even those whose parents are not members)

Listed in the supplementary register of historic buildings in 1986, the superb pelota courts of La Cavalerie were set up in 1929 by a group of Argentineans; they occupy the seventh floor of the building. Though the sign says "Private Club" visitors are welcome and can watch from the gallery; only members are allowed to play (applicants require two existing members as sponsors). Membership also gives you access to a small bar and lounge worthy of an English gentlemen's club.

NEARBY

15, square de Vergennes   ⑪

Entrance by the porch of 279, rue de Vaugirard – Métro: Vaugirard
www.15squaredevergennes.com • Open Tuesday to Saturday 12pm–7pm
Closed August and public holidays • Guided tours by appointment:
01 56 23 00 22 • Admission: €5 (concessions €2.50)

Built in 1931–1932 by Robert Malle-Stevens for the master glassmaker Louis Barillet, this former workshop has recently been reconverted into a centre of contemporary art and design. The work done on the building by the previous owners totally failed to respect its character, but in 1993 the structure was included in the supplementary register of listed buildings and then purchased (in 2001) by an art lover who had it restored to its original condition. Now, the organisation of space within the interior is as it was intended to be, with massive windows extending over different levels and white Art Deco glasswork by Louis Barillet himself. The restoration is, in itself, a phenomenal achievement, given that there are only three extant photographs of that original interior.

Garden of clinique Blomet   ⑫

134–136, rue Blomet
Apply at reception or telephone the nursing sisters at 01 45 32 89 50
Mass on weekdays at 7.30am. No Mass on Sunday

Rather modern in appearance, the Blomet Clinic has a neo-Gothic chapel. The sisters of St Paul of Chartres who are in charge of it also tend the clinic's very pleasant garden, where a polite request will gain you the chance of a relaxing stroll.

Cité morieux   ⑬

56, rue de la Fédération
Pretty little cul-de-sac lined with country-style houses.

The Crow and the Fox   ⑭

A fine sculpture inspired by La Fontaine's fable of *The Crow and the Fox* adorns the façade of 40, avenue Félix-Faure.

FRESCOES IN THE CHURCH
OF SAINT-CHRISTOPHE DE JAVEL

St Christopher blessing pilots and racing drivers

28, rue de la Convention
RER: Javel
Tel.: 01 45 78 33 70 • www.scjavel.net

The façade of the entrance porch is adorned with extraordinary frescoes. Designed in the 1930s by Henri-Marcel Magne, they show St Christopher helping not just travellers but navigators, pilots, train drivers and motorists. This surrealist vision is an invitation to enter the church and admire the choir frescoes, the fine interior and the attractive modern stained glass (again by Magne). Javel is a district closely linked with the transport industries: not only were there the old Citroën works (on the site of the park of the same name), but also factories that produced locomotives, hot-air balloons and aerostats. Naturally enough, the new church was dedicated to St Christopher, the patron saint of travellers.

Built in 1926–1930, Saint-Christophe de Javel was the first church in the world designed to be constructed entirely in prefabricated reinforced concrete, which accounts for its low cost and the speed with which it was completed. The structure was financed by a subscription amongst motorists. Nowadays it seems quite incredible, but each subscriber to the project simply paid the equivalent of the cost of one can of petrol. The cardinal-archbishop of Paris used to come here to bless the cars of the owners who had gathered for a Mass in front of the church, attracted by the chance of protection this offered; more mundane forms of car insurance did not become obligatory in France until 1958.

Saint Christopher and the Golden Legend

Tradition has it that St Christopher bore Christ on his shoulders across a raging torrent. In fact, the Greek etymology of his name, *Christos phoros*, means: "he who carries Christ".

The history of the saint is told in *The Golden Legend* by Jacques de Voragine, a 14th-century Dominican from Genoa. One of the major works of Christian hagiography, this contains stories from the lives of 180 saints and martyrs, together with some episodes from the Life of Christ, all organised according to the Church's liturgical year.

Eau de Javel

At the end of the 18th century, industrialists were granted a licence to set up a plant near the Javelle mill (in the present-day district of Javel) to produce vitriol. It was here that scientists would first produce sodium hypochlorite, which would later become commonly known in France as *eau de Javel*.

16th *Arrondissement*

EIFFEL AERODYNAMICS LABORATORY

Eiffel's wind tunnel

67, rue Boileau
Métro: Exelmans
Tel.: 01 42 88 47 40
Group visits only (minimum 10; maximum 20), Saturday and Sunday by
appointment only • Contact: Mr Martin Peter (curator): 06 82 33 95 07
www.aerodynamiqueeiffel.fr

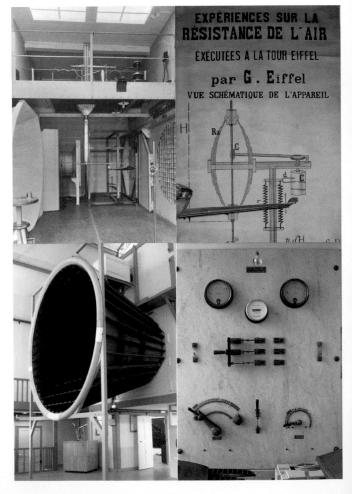

A listed historic monument, this laboratory is a remarkable piece of industrial archaeology that is now open to the public.

It remains intact thanks to the foresight of Gustave Eiffel, who in 1920 stipulated that the laboratory should not be closed down and demolished as long as the wind tunnel was operational; his wishes have been respected by the Société Aérodynamique Eiffel and, in particular, by the current curator, Mr Peter, who joined the company as an engineer in 1959. World-famous for the tower that bears his name, Gustave Eiffel was also a pioneer in the field of aerodynamic technology. Remarkably well preserved, this laboratory, which opened in 1912, is still operational. Eiffel himself ran it until 1920, using scale models of planes to compile the first scientific data on the nascent technology of aircraft and flight. As well as such aerodynamical experiments, the laboratory was to diversify and open its facilities to the automobile and construction industries. In fact, it was here that tests were carried out on the models of the Citröen ZX for the Paris-Dakar rally, the Amiens football stadium and the CNIT building at La Défense.

Comprising a vast hangar and various workshops, the laboratory constructs models and then measures their performance in various wind tunnel tests. Originally, the laboratory had two wind tunnels, but the smaller (diameter: 1 m) was dismantled in 1933. The larger (diameter: 2 m) has been operational for over ninety years and is still used to test the resistance of industrial models to winds of up to 100 km/h. If no model is undergoing tests the day you visit, take advantage of the opportunity to ask if you can feel the effects of the wind tunnel yourself; it is a phenomenal experience. Within the hangar there are also attractive displays of models of racing cars, aircraft and of the wind tunnels themselves. Note also the famous free-fall apparatus, which is used to measure the air resistance of objects by dropping them from the top of the tower.

VILLA MULHOUSE

Very special housing for workers

Villas Dietz-Monin, Émile-Meyer and Cheysson
Located between rue Parent-de-Rossan and rue Claude-Lorrain
Entrance at 84 and 86, rue Boileau
Métro: Exelmans

While the houses that make up this unusual group of rural-style streets are now far from cheap, this was not always the case. Émile Chasson (1836–1910) was, in fact, Inspector General with the state's Ponts et Chaussées (civil engineering) Department and published hundreds of articles and leaflets on the problems of social housing. At the beginning of the 20th century, this committed social reformer was the driving force behind the creation of what was originally an area of low-cost housing.

NEARBY

Hameau Boileau, Villa Molitor, ③
Villa de la Réunion

38, rue Boileau – 7, rue Molitor – 29, rue Chardon-Lagache
Métro: Chardon-Lagache or Michel-Ange-Molitor

This tiny area in the south of the 16th *arrondissement* contains a number of private roads, culs-de-sac and housing developments which are the stuff of daydreams for idle strollers or eager property investors in search of a haven of peace. The houses and city mansions of the Hameau Boileau, Villa Molitor and Villa de la Réunion nestle within their own private gardens and can only be glimpsed through the railings of gates which close off the approach roads. At each gate are ardent watchmen, keen to preserve the peace and quiet enjoyed by the residents (perhaps a famous singer or an optician who has made a fortune).

Church of Tous-Les-Saints-de-la-Terre-Russe ④

19, rue Claude-Lorrain
Métro: Exelmans • Tel.: 01 45 27 24 82 • Services daily at 6pm

The only external evidence of the presence of a church tucked away on the ground floor of this brick building is the wooden doorway; it is surmounted by a blind arcade in the form of the *kokoshnik* head-dress once traditional among Russian peasant women. The church itself does not come under the authority of the patriarchs of either Moscow or Constantinople, but is part of the patriarchate known as "The Russian Church beyond the Frontiers". Just a few hundred metres away stands another Russian Orthodox church, the Church of the Apparition of the Virgin (87, bd Exelmans). Equally close by, at 39, rue François-Gérard, there is a Russian Catholic church that observes the Byzantine rite. Many White Russians were fairly well off and liked this district.

The marquise: *one way to shelter from the rain*

A number of fine Parisian buildings, particularly in the 16th *arrondissement*, have these distinctive glass canopies fanning out over the main doorway. Such *marquises*, in fact, were designed to make it possible for those getting out of carriages and cars to reach the building without getting wet.

CASTEL BÉRANGER

a.k.a. Castel Dérangé

14, rue La Fontaine
Métro: Ranelagh or Jasmin

The full scope of Hector Guimard's talent was not widely known when he was commissioned to design this building in the heart of the then village of Auteuil. The owner of the site, however, showed great foresight in her decision, because the building (1897–1898) won the City of Paris Façade Competition in 1899 and immediately established the fame of its architect. Containing a total of thirty-six apartments, the structure makes use of stone, pale-pink brick, wood, cast iron, steel, glazed stoneware and ceramics – and is undoubtedly Guimard's masterpiece. The project embodies all the fundamental principles of Art Nouveau, with the architect even designing such details of the interior as carpets, wallpapers and doorknobs. While the public at large failed to appreciate the building – quickly turning "Castel Béranger" into "Castel Dérangé" (deranged) – some important contemporary figures (such as the painter Paul Signac) had no doubts, proclaiming Guimard to be a genius and choosing this building as their home.

NEARBY
45, rue Ribera ⑥
A superb bas-relief by the architect Boussard, dating from the end of the 19th century. Not far away are some unusual seated caryatids, at 1, rue de l'Yvette.

Hector Guimard

Born in Lyon in 1867, Hector Guimard is the central figure in French Art Nouveau. His most important artistic legacy is perhaps the métro stations which he designed between the years 1899 and 1904. Today, some 66 of the 380 which once existed still survive, the most famous being the stations of Porte Dauphine and Des Abbesses (which have splendid glass roofs). The master architect also designed numerous houses and apartment buildings in Art Nouveau style. Most of these are to be found in the 16ᵗʰ *arrondissement*, where Guimard himself lived. His works include:

In the 16ᵗʰ arrondissement:

– Castel Béranger: 14, rue La Fontaine (1897–1898) (see previous page)

– Group of 17–19 and 21, rue La Fontaine, 8 and 10, rue Agar (1909–1911) and 43, rue Gros

– Hôtel Mezzara: 60, rue La Fontaine (1910)

– Hôtel Roszé: 34, rue Boileau (1891)

– Hôtel Jassedé: 41, rue Chardon-Lagache (1894)

– École du Sacré-Cœur: 1, avenue de la Frillière (1895)

– Immeuble Jassedé: 142, avenue de Versailles and 1, rue de Lancret (1903)

– Hôtel particulier: 3, square Jasmin (1921)

– 36–38, rue Greuze (1927–1928)

– Villa Flore: 120, avenue Mozart (1924–1926)

– Hôtel Guimard: 122, avenue Mozart (1909–1913)

– Hôtel Delfau: 1, rue Molitor (1894)

– 18, rue Henri-Heine (1930)

– 11, rue Francois-Millet (1909)

– Atelier de Carpeaux, 39, boulevard Exelmans (1894); this is an early work, unrelated to Art Nouveau

Elsewhere in Paris and in France:

– Synagogue: 10, rue Pavée, Paris, 4ᵗʰ *arrondissement*, 1913 (see page 87)

– Villa La Hublotière (1896): 72, route de Montesson, 78810 Le Vésinet (Yvelines)

– Maison Coilliot: 14, rue de Fleurus, Lille, 1898–1900

– Castel Val: 4, rue des Meulières, Auvers-sur-Oise, 1903

– Castel Orgeval: 2, avenue de la Mare-Tambour, Villemoisson-sur-Orge, 1904

– Chalet Blanc: 2, rue du Lycée, Sceaux, 1904

– Villa Hemsy: 3, rue de Crillon, Saint-Cloud, 1913

Art Nouveau

The term itself comes from the name of the art gallery which the Hamburg dealer Samuel Bing (1838–1905) opened in Paris in 1895; his "Art Nouveau" would subsequently show work by all the great figures of this artistic movement. The German/Austrian equivalent, *Jugendstil*, was taken from the title of the satirical magazine *Jugend* launched by the German publisher Georg Hirth in Munich in 1896. He published numerous designs that exemplified new artistic trends, even if the term *Jugendstil* is now predominately used to refer to a more geometric type of design.

Elsewhere in Europe, Art Nouveau went by different names. In Austria it was the *Sezessionstil*, associated with the Secessionist movement founded by G. Klimt in 1897; in England, it was known as "Liberty Style" after the department store famous for its modern-design textiles. Later came the "Modern Style", which combined the two major trends in European Art.

As for more popular terms, the flowing forms of Art nouveau were sometimes referred to in France as examples of the "nouille style" (noodle style) or even "spaghetti style".

More than a simple artistic movement, Art Nouveau embodied a new way of thought and life, breaking with the accepted norms of existing society. Striving for liberation from exploitation, Church domination and the repression of women, it emphasised a level of eroticism and sensuality that would previously have been unthinkable. Look, for example, at the numerous stylised and sensual depictions of women that adorn the façades of Art Nouveau buildings.

However, having flourished in the years up to 1914, Art Nouveau was severely affected by the First World War and its aftermath. Given that the buildings designed by Art Nouveau architects were neither cheap nor easy to produce on a large scale, the movement was unable to satisfy the need for mass rebuilding required at the time.

In Paris itself, the undisputed leader of Art Nouveau was Hector Guimard; however, other architects – such as Jules Lavirotte (see page 139) – also made their mark in the city.

The Principle behind Artesian wells

Unlike traditional wells, the water in Artesian wells does not need to be pumped, but rises freely to the surface. The term "artesian" originates from the fact that the first to note this phenomenon were the monks of Lillers Abbey in Artois. The principle at work is similar to that exemplified by liquids in communicating vessels. It occurs in particular geological circumstances, when the point of exit of a well is located below what is known technically as the piezometric level (this corresponds to the highest level of the water table that supplies the water in the well).

HOW AN ARTESIAN WELL WORKS

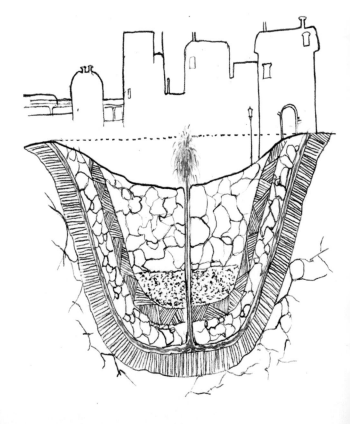

THE ARTESIAN WELL
IN SQUARE LAMARTINE

A survivor of the epic efforts to supply the
with water

Square Lamartine

Begun in 1855 and opened in 1866, the Passy well is the last fu
tioning artesian well in Paris. Sunk to a depth of 587 m, its aim wa
ambitious: to supply water not only for the local residents but also for
the complete irrigation of the Bois de Boulogne and for its two lakes.

Despite its current ferrous taste, due to the fact that iron pipes were
used in the well, the water is still perfectly safe to drink; it is tested regularly. The well's output has declined considerably since the 19th century,
however, falling from 25,000 m³ to 350 m³.

Artesian Wells in Paris

After the cholera epidemic of 1832, the city looked for unconta-
minated sources of water. One solution was the drilling of artesian
wells that would draw on water from a water table which was dee-
per (more than 500 m underground) and therefore less vulnerable
to bacterial infection. Five such wells were sunk. The first was the
Grenelle Well (see page 283), which emerged in place Georges-
Mulot (the square is named after the entrepreneur behind the scheme). Sunk to a depth of 587 m in 1866, the **Passy Well** stands
in what is now square Lamartine in the 16th *arrondissement*. The
Hébert Well (place Hébert, in the 18th) was sunk in 1863 then
redrilled in 1891, but it was covered over in 2004. The **Butte-aux-
Cailles Well** (rue Bobillot in the 13th) produced hot water and was
sunk to a depth of 678 m in 1863; redrilled in 1904, it was covered
over in 2002; contrary to popular belief, it is not the source of the
water for the Butte-aux-Cailles swimming pool. Finally, there is the
Blomet Well in the 15th *arrondissement*. This was completed – to a
depth of 587 m – in 1929.

Other private wells were also sunk within the city: that serving the
Say Refinery was sunk in 1869, whereas the **Maison de la Radio**
well dates from 1956.

Today only the Passy Well is operational; the phreatic level for all
the wells being the same, the drilling of any new wells would immediately lower the pressure in the others.

Built from 1926 onwards by Robert Mallet-Stevens, this housing development is a "manifesto" of modern architecture and comprises a total of five individual buildings. At No. 12 is the home and studio of the architect himself, while No. 10 was the home/studio of the sculptors Joël and Jean Martel, No. 8 was home to the pianist Mme Reifenberg, No. 7 was occupied by Daniel Dreyfus and Nos. 3/5 by Mme Allatini. At the end of the street, No. 1 is the caretaker's cottage. The design of each of these buildings plays upon the juxtaposition of smooth-sided white cubes in terraces, recesses, towers and jutting roofs; in Robert Mallet-Stevens' words, "the architect sculpts one single massive block: a house". Unfortunately, the listing of the buildings in 1975 came too late to save the furnishings and fittings which had been designed by the architect himself.

NEARBY

Villa La Roche

8 and 10, square du Docteur-Blanche
Tel.: 01 42 88 75 72
info@fondationlecorbusier.fr • reservation@fondationlecorbusier.fr
Open 10am–12.30pm and 1.30pm–6pm (closed Monday morning, open Friday until 5pm and Saturday 10am–5pm)

This is home to the Fondation Le Corbusier, and a visit here is a real aesthetic treat. With its interplay of volumes and partition walls, its raised platforms, walkways and sloping ramps, the space will give you some idea of the work of the architect, enabling you to appreciate the reputation he achieved in spite of the numerous, sometimes justified, criticisms levelled at his designs.

Modern Architecture in the 16ᵗʰ arrondissement

Along with the Art Nouveau buildings by Guimard, the 16ᵗʰ *arrondissement* – and particularly Auteuil district – was a place of experimentation for a number of early 20ᵗʰ-century architects. When the villages of Passy and Auteuil were incorporated within the city of Paris, the former was already substantially built-up, while the latter basically comprised just the three streets which linked it to Passy: the present-day rue d'Auteuil, rue Molière and rue La Fontaine. There was therefore space to build on and money to spend, and those who wanted to turn this into a little architectural paradise included not only Guimard, Le Corbusier and Mallet-Stevens, but also Henri Sauvage (the Studiobuilding at 65, rue La Fontaine), Ginsberg (42, avenue de Versailles) and the Perret brothers (25bis, rue Franklin and 51–55, rue Raynouard; the latter actually the brothers' home). Luckily for the curious stroller, most of these buildings are concentrated within a rather small area.

ENTRANCE TO PORTE-DAUPHINE ⑩
MÉTRO STATION

A dragonfly in Paris

Entrance opposite to 90, avenue Foch
Métro: Porte-Dauphine (!)

Created by the master of Art Nouveau, Hector Guimard (see page 303), this entrance to the Porte-Dauphine station on line 2 of the Paris métro is a real masterpiece. Opened on 13 December 1900, it has a glass roof ending in an upward fanning canopy, with curved borders resting on branching columns. The panels around the tunnel entrance are in orange-glazed ceramic. The particularly light and airy form of the structure has earned it the nickname "the dragonfly".

NEARBY

Square des Poètes

Avenue du Général-Sarrail
Métro: Porte-d'Auteuil

Squashed rather unhappily between the ring road and its approach slip roads, square des Poètes is home to forty-eight small steles in stone or bronze bearing lines of verse from the works of French poets. For the quirky melancholic, this place is on a par with the Auteuil glasshouses, where you can stroll peacefully in the warm and dry. Perfect for winter – and for children.

A blockhouse in the Bois de Boulogne ⑫

Just near the Porte Dauphine, at 45, avenue du Maréchal-Fayolle, is a blockhouse dating from the Second World War. It now accommodates the local scout troop

MAISON DE BALZAC

"I have some Belgian lace"

47, rue Raynouard
Tel.: 01 55 74 41 80
Métro: Passy
Open daily, except Mondays and public holidays, 10am–6pm
Admission free to permanent collections

Now converted into a museum, this is where Balzac lived from 1840 to 1847. The house was particularly suitable for the novelist as it served as a refuge from his creditors: there are two separate entrances, one on rue Raynouard and one, lower down, giving onto rue Berton. Visitors were not even admitted unless they knew the password, one of the most famous of which was "I have some Belgian lace". Nowadays, the charm of the place lies in this anecdote - and the delightful garden.

Inside, the museum has manuscripts, first editions and different depictions of the writer by artists who were his contemporaries; unfortunately, there are few personal objects, as most of these were sold off by Balzac's widow after his death. More than the collections themselves, it is the rather old-fashioned air of the place which makes it attractive. Note the large genealogical table that the novelist drew up to indicate all the family relationships between the various characters of his *Comédie humaine*.

NEARBY

A Wine Museum in ... rue des Eaux   ⑭

Musée du Vin
Rue des Eaux and 5, square Charles-Dickens
Tel.: 01 45 25 63 26
www.museeduvinparis.com • info@museeduvinparis.com
Open daily, except Monday, 10am–6pm
Admission: free for under 14s. Full price €11.90. Group visits possible for numbers over 15
Restaurant from Tuesday to Saturday 12pm–3pm

Opened in 1984 by the *Échansons de France* association of wine enthusiasts, this Wine Museum is ironically located in rue des Eaux. The place itself occupies a maze of tunnels which, in the 16th and 17th centuries, were used by the Minim friars of Passy, whose monastery produced a light white wine. Driven out during the Revolution, the monks abandoned the tunnels to the neglect they would suffer right up until the place was bought twenty years ago. Now the various niches house the equipment used in cultivating vineyards and in winemaking and tasting; there are even such comic objects as a left-handed carafe or wine glasses impossible to knock over. The visit ends with a glass of wine (included in the price). And if that leaves you feeling hungry, you can also stay for lunch (except on Mondays).

VILLA BEAUSÉJOUR

Russia in Paris

7, boulevard de Beauséjour
Métro: La Muette
Gate unlocked (just push) on Monday to Saturday 9am–8pm
Closed on Sunday, public holidays and in August

Despite its very French name, this is really a tiny Russian village of wooden *isbas* (including a typical coach inn). Originally created for the 1867 Universal Exposition, these characteristic wooden cottages were later reassembled here in the heart of the 16th *arrondissement*. Only one of the four came directly from Russia, the others were made in Paris to instructions and designs from the Russian Committee for the Exposition. Still inhabited, all four are now in the supplementary register of listed buildings.

NEARBY

Hameau de Passy ⑯
48, rue de Passy
A small rural-style passageway running from rue de Passy through to rue Vital.

Vegetable Gardens in rue la Manutention ⑰

Laid out by Robert Milin in 2002, this "residents' garden" is an attractive vegetable garden occupying what was once wasteland running alongside the Museé d'Art Moderne de la Ville de Paris. Created in response to a request from those responsible for the Palais de Tokyo, these gardens comprise sixteen plots that are rented out centrally by Paris City Council (see page 353). They end in a special "wild garden" laid out in the same year by the Dalto Studio (architects: M. Pouzol and L. Dugua). Closed behind a locked gate, this inaccessible garden runs below the road level of avenue du President-Wilson and along the side of the Palais de Tokyo. Note the quirky guardrail whose central band has been filled with grassy turf.

Remains of the old Hôtel de Ville and Tuileries Palace in Trocadéro Gardens

In the lower part of Trocadéro Gardens, on the Passy side, are some vestiges from the Hôtel de Ville (built by Domenico da Cortona for François I) and the Tuileries Palace (designed by Philibert Delorme for Catherine de Médicis). These were brought here after the two buildings had been destroyed by fires set at the end of the Commune in 1871.

NEARBY

The Benjamin Franklin Obelisk ⑱

66, rue Raynouard, at the corner of rue Singer

Imposing and yet little noticed locally, this bas-relief in the form of an obelisk is set into the wall of 66, rue Raynouard. It marks the spot where Franklin installed France's first lightning conductor. It was in the grounds of the (now destroyed) Hôtel de Valentinois, where he stayed during his time in Paris, that Franklin erected the instrument which he had first invented in 1756. The American Congress's ambassador to France, Benjamin Franklin was also one of the authors of the American Declaration of Independence. The neighbourhood pays tribute to him in various ways: nearby is rue Franklin; the Collège Saint-Louis-de-Gonzague is better known simply as "Collège Franklin"; and on the corner of avenue Paul-Doumer stands a statue of the American statesman.

The Chinese Salon of the Mona Bismarck Foundation ⑲

34, avenue de New-York
Métro: Iéna • www.monabismarck.org

Set up in 1986, the Fondation Mona Bismarck is housed in a fine city mansion that is open to the public during the frequent exhibitions that are held here. Don't miss the chance to enjoy the building's fine interiors, especially the wonderful Chinese Salon with its magnificent frescoes, a very beautiful red lacquer screen. In accordance with the wishes of its founder, who was American by birth, the Foundation aims to nurture Franco-American relations and, to this end, holds two or three exhibitions a year.

The Garden of the Buddhist Pantheon ⑳

Annex to Musée Guimet - 19, avenue d'Iéna
Open daily 9.45am–5.45pm, except Tuesday • Admission free • Tea ceremonies
per quarter (see www.guimet.fr) • Reservations must be made by e-mail at
resa@guimet.fr or by phone at 01 56 52 53 45 • www.guimet.fr

Since 1991 the area behind the Buddhist pantheon has been made over into a small Japanese garden. The small wooden tea pavilion regularly serves tea ceremonies carried out according to Japanese tradition – an exercise in social refinement that borders on the spiritual.

Paris's Statue of Liberty now faces towards the United States

Raised on the occasion of the 1889 Universal Exposition, the Statue of Liberty on the Île aux Cygnes was a gift from the United States of America to France. Nowadays it faces westwards, towards its more famous sister in New York harbour. Originally, it faced eastwards, so that its back was not turned towards the Élysée Palace. The change was made in 1937.

ICI
S'ELEVAIT UN
PAVILLON
DEPENDANT
DE
L'HOTEL DE

VALANTINOIS

DE
1777-1785

B. FRANKLIN

L'HABITA
ET Y FIT PLACER
LE PREMIER

PARATONNERRE

CONSTRUIT
EN FRANCE

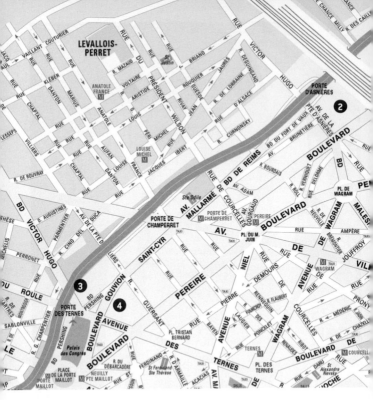

17ᵗʰ Arrondissement

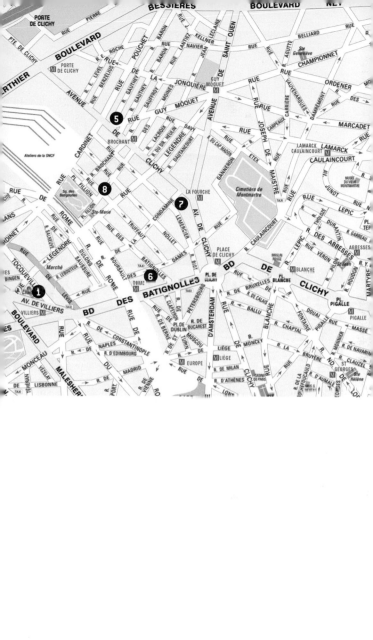

Rotonde de la Villette

The elevated railways: course of the fermiers généraux city walls

The course of the Fermiers Généraux city walls is now followed almost exactly by lines 2 and 6 of the Paris métro. This is particularly clear in the elevated railway sections of these lines: between Barbès and Belleville (line 2) and Pasteur and Passy (line 6).

The Ledoux Rotundas: la Villette, Monceau, Nation, Denfert-Rochereau

In the 18ᵗʰ century, the inhabitants of Paris paid an *octroi* [duty] on consumer products entering the city – everything from wine and meat to hay and wood – while in the countryside there was a *taille*, a tax on land itself. With the increased urban development of the city and its faubourgs, the fiscal limits between these two areas of taxation became more difficult to establish, and fraud was common. For this reason, the Fermiers Généraux, farmers who had either paid for or been granted the right to collect taxes, proposed that the city be enclosed within a new wall. In 1785 Louis XVI ordered the construction of this tax barrier and the redefinition of fiscal territories (faubourgs such as Chaillot, Villiers and Charonne were incorporated within the city proper). The architectural aspects of the new plan were entrusted to the royal architect, Nicholas Ledoux. Stretching more than 24 km, the new walls enclosed an area of 3,400 hectares with 600,000 inhabitants. The sixth ring of walls to be built in Parisian history (see page 232), the new structure was to be 3 m high and 1 m thick, with an interior ring road 12 m wide. The ban on construction outside the walls extended for 100 m, though there was a 30 m boulevard planted with trees. Taxes and duties were collected at fifty-five entrance "barriers", twenty-four of which were complete with accommodation for customs officers. For the scheme, Nicholas Ledoux drew his inspiration from classical architecture, producing structures of an opulence that bore little relation to their function. The magnificence of this scheme – plus the high cost of the land expropriated – meant that by 1787 the initial budget had been wildly exceeded. Still, despite the Revolution and the destruction it brought, the wall was completed and was fully operational by 1790. But there was widespread and violent opposition to what Victor Hugo would punningly call a "*mur murant Paris qui rend Paris murmurant*" [a wall enwalling Paris that makes Paris grumble]; it was even argued that the wall undermined the health of the city's inhabitants by blocking the free circulation of air. Furthermore, the structure proved incapable of ending the high levels of tax fraud (still around 20%), so on 1 May 1791 the National Assembly voted to abolish the octroi duties and the institution of the Fermiers Généraux. Due to the financial problems faced by the City of Paris, such duties were however reintroduced in 1798. In 1860, the collection points were moved to the entrances of the new fortifications that had been built in 1840. At that point, the classically-inspired barriers built by Ledoux were demolished, with the exception of the four that still survive: *the barrière de Chartres* (now in Parc Monceau), *de La Villette, du Trône* (at Nation) and *d'Enfer* (place Denfert-Rochereau). Duties on goods entering the city were not totally abolished until 1943.

POLONIA

A forgotten library

20, rue Legendre
Métro: Malesherbes, Villiers or Monceau
Open Tuesday to Saturday, midday and evening
Tel.: 01 43 80 10 06
restaurantpolonia@hotmail.com

The restaurant Polonia (see our guide *Secret Bars and Restaurants in Paris*) contains a small gem, which the current managers are happy to show to visitors: on the fourth floor of this old city mansion is a wonderful library which the Polish association "Concorde" (which now runs the place) had restored in 2003. The lift is broken and the stairs are steep, but you will not regret making the effort. Originally, the room must have housed an old chapel, which was then taken over by a Masonic lodge. Nowadays, the books have gone, but what remains is this superb neo-Gothic interior: carved wood, paintings, coffered ceiling and a remarkable fireplace. In a corner sits a piano, waiting to be played. For €500 the room can be hired for special events, and cold dishes can be brought up from the restaurant downstairs.

THE FLOWER TOWER IN HAUTS-DE-MALESHERBES GARDENS

Flower power

8, rue Stéphane-Grappelli and 23, rue Albert-Roussel
Métro: Wagram (then a 10-minute walk)

Occupying what was wasteland attached to the Gare Saint-Lazare, the Hauts-de-Malesherbes gardens were opened in March 2005. The project coordinator was the famous architect Christian de Portzamparc, and among the various astonishing features of this contemporary addition to Paris perhaps the most surprising is what looks like a building of plants, the Flower Tower. The work of architect Édouard François and botanist Patrick Blanc, each side of the structure is covered with large white plant holders overflowing with greenery and shrubs, creating the very real impression of the building being one huge flower.

Patrick Blanc also created the living walls at the Musée du Quai Branly and at Hôtel Pershing Hall (see page 143). Opposite the Flower Tower, the garden opens onto a stretch of the old Thiers city walls (see page 233).

Geography of Parisian Theatres

A number of Paris theatres – Théâtre des Bouffes-du-Nord, Théâtre de l'Atelier, Théâtre Hébertot, l'Européen, etc. – all lie to the north of the Grands Boulevards. This is due to the fact that this side of the boulevards lay outside the Fermiers Généraux city walls (the outline of which is, roughly, that of lines 2 and 6 of the Paris métro; see page 321). Beyond that barrier, theatres were classified as "provincial" and thus they had the right to put on the plays mounted by the "city" theatres just forty days after their *première*. Their location at the very gates of the city meant, however, that these theatres could attract larger audiences, and thus choose among the very best of the provincial actors, who saw such places as a springboard to work on the Paris stage. To the south of Paris, the same logic explains the location of the Théâtre du Ranelagh and the Gaîté-Montparnasse.

CHAPELLE ROYALE
SAINT-FERDINAND

A travelling chapel

2, boulevard Aurelle-de-Paladines
Métro or RER: Porte-Maillot
Tel.: 01 45 74 83 31 • paroisse.n.d.compassion@wanadoo.fr

S quashed between the ring road and the Concorde Lafayette Hotel, the Chapelle Royale Saint-Ferdinand is rather unusually located for a church. So it may come as no surprise to learn that this royal mausoleum, consecrated in 1843, no longer stands where it was first built (the original site now being occupied by the Palais des Congrès).

The chapel was built as a memorial to the duc d'Orlèans, Ferdinand-Philippe, the eldest son of Louis-Philippe, who died in 1842 at the age of 32 when the horses of his carriage bolted and he was thrown violently to the ground. It was moved here in 1968 when work began on the Palais du Congrès complex. The reassembly stone by stone took two years in all, and though the chapel is incongruous here, it has not lost everything in the move: it now has a parish crypt laid out in Greek Cross plan and designed in an attractively eclectic style.

The stained glass in the original chapel was the work of the architects Fontaine and Lefranc, to cartoons by Ingres. One intriguing detail is that the faces of all saints here were clearly inspired by members of the royal family – St Louis, for example, looks remarkably like Louis-Philippe.

NEARBY
Villa des Ternes   (4)
96, avenue des Ternes
39, rue de Guersant
Métro: Porte-Maillot

This magnificent housing development comprises a number of small avenues leading to wonderful private properties nestling in their own gardens: avenue de la Chapelle, des Arts, Yves-du-Manoir, des Pavillons and avenue de Verzy. No. 1bis, avenue de Verzy and No.13, avenue Yves-du-Manoir are, however, subsidised public housing, built in spite of the strenuous efforts of the other residents. Even these new additions have their own air of luxury, as the architects (B. Bourgade and M. Londinsky) have laid out the steps and pitched roofs in such a way that each apartment appears to be a small detached house.

The architect of 10, avenue Yves-du-Manoir strove to copy the Palace of Darius at Susa. A haut-relief is all that is left.

CITÉ DES FLEURS

Each of the original owners was required to plant three flowering trees

154, avenue de Clichy
59, rue de la Jonquières
Métro: Brochant or RER: Porte-de-Clichy

At though private, this road is accessible to the public; it is a wonderful oasis of greenery that has survived in the heart of Paris. When it was laid out in 1847, each property owner was required to plant three flowering trees or shrubs in their garden. Since then the plants have grown, and now it is very pleasant to enjoy the rural atmosphere of this little enclave of individual houses standing just a short distance from the bustling area of avenue de Clichy.

NEARBY

Museum of Freemasonry ⑥

8, rue de Puteaux
Métro: Rome
Tel.: 01 53 42 41 41 • www.gldf.org • Open daily 10am–1pm 2pm–5pm Guided tours by appointment • Admission free

For an introduction to Freemasonry: two temples and a library that houses some 100,000 works on the subject of Freemasonry, the esoteric and the paranormal.

Cour Saint-Pierre and Cité Lemercier ⑦

47, avenue de Clichy and 28, rue Lemercier
Metro: La Fourche

Two private streets, but open to the casual stroller. Both of them share a pleasantly provincial atmosphere that seems to date from another era. Cour Saint-Pierre is made up of two-storey buildings perfectly aligned on either side of the cobbled street, each one lovingly adorned with flowers and plants by the residents. Cité Lemercier is made up of detached houses, each standing in its own garden. Jacques Brel himself succumbed to the charm of the place, living for a time at Hôtel du Chalet.

Square Nicolay ⑧

77 bis, rue Legendre

A private square with a very attractive interior garden, visible through the railings. The other side of the square gives onto rue des Moines.

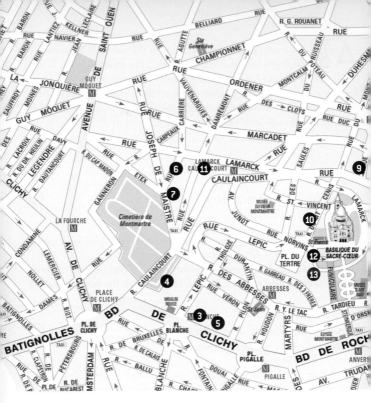

18ᵗʰ Arrondissement

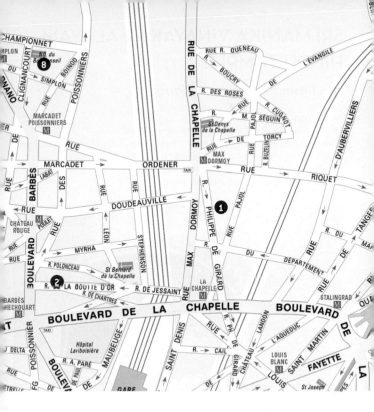

SRI MANIKA VINAYAKAR ALAYAM HINDU TEMPLE ①

Hinduism in the heart of Paris

17, rue Pajol
Métro: Marx-Dormoy, La Chapelle or Gare-du-Nord
Admission free, open 9.30am–8.30pm. Three poojas a day (10am, 12pm, 7pm)
Bathing ceremony (abhishekam) on Friday, Saturday and Sunday
Tel.: 01 40 34 21 89 and 01 42 09 50 45
www.templeganesh.fr • srimanicka@yahoo.fr

No need to take a plane to travel to exotic places: in Paris, a simple métro ticket gives the chance to experience the extraordinary and complex rituals of the Hindu religion. Dedicated to the god Ganesh, the elephant-headed son of Shiva, this is the only Hindu temple in the city. It was founded in 1985 thanks to the determination of one man, Mr Sanderasekaram, who on his arrival here noticed that within the uprooted and scattered Hindu community of France (which numbers more than 100,000) religious worship was limited to small domestic altars within individual households. Like other members of his family (see below) Mr Sanderasekaram founded a temple – Sri Manika Vinyyakar Alayam – which quickly became a central gathering point for the Sri Lankan Tamil community.

Though now too small to house the whole congregation, the temple still offers a remarkable welcome to outsiders. A vegetarian meal is generously served to all of those present at the ceremonies on Saturday and Sunday.

Temple-building seems to run in the Sanderasekaram family. The father had a temple and statue to Ganesh raised in Jaffna (northern Sri Lanka), while his brother did the same in London and his niece in Australia.

The *pooja* is a ritual that each Hindu performs in the morning after having washed and dressed but before eating. Though there are individual variations, the ritual basically involves the chanting of a special mantra and the offering of food and drink to specific deities. The rite of *abhishekam* is basically a bathing ceremony. The statue of the deity is undressed, sprinkled with water, then with milk, honey, rose water and curdled milk in order to purify it. Once its robes have been replaced, a garland of flowers is placed on the statue, while priests (*pujaris*) chant mantras.

NEARBY
Villa Poissonnière ②

41, rue Polonceau and 42, rue de la Goutte-d'Or
Métro: Château-Rouge or Barbès-Rochechouart

In the middle of the Goutte-d'Or district stands the Villa Poissonnière development. Built in 1840, this pretty cobbled street is lined by small houses standing in their own gardens. Entrance is by an almost hidden *porte cochère* that gives on to rue de la Goutte-d'Or; the rue Polonceau entrance is often closed.

VILLA DES PLATANES

In the shade of flowering plane trees

58, boulevard de Clichy
Métro: Blanche or Pigalle

Boulevard de Clichy is not only sex shops; there are also some pleasant surprises here. Unfortunately, Villa des Platanes (at No. 58) is shut away behind a wrought-iron gate. Still, if one of the residents is leaving, you might be lucky enough to see more than can be glimpsed through the railings. Built in 1896 by the architect Deloeuvre, the development is laid out around two courtyards, which are entered by passing through a passageway with a coffered roof. A fine spiral staircase in the first courtyard leads up to the second, where the buildings are distributed around a wonderfully quiet garden.

NEARBY
7, Impasse Marie-Blanche　④
Tucked between 19, rue Cauchois and 9, rue Constance, this charming cul-de-sac contains a very surprising house. Built in 1835, the house at 7, impasse Marie-Blanche has a pink, medieval-style façade, complete with a machiolated tower and half-timbering.

Cité du Midi　⑤
48, boulevard de Clichy
A few yards away from the villa des Platanes is another oasis of quiet that can make you forget all about the bustling boulevard and its shops. One can still see the white ceramic façade of the old Pigalle public baths.

Foundation of the Jesuits in Montmartre
On 15 August 1534, Ignatius of Loyola – together with Francis Xavier and five other companions – went to the Chapel of the Martyrium, located on what was supposed to have been the site of St Denis's martyrdom. During a Mass celebrated in the crypt, at the moment of Holy Communion they pronounced vows of poverty and chastity, dedicating themselves to the welfare of souls. This was the beginning of the Society of Jesus, which would become more famous under the name of the "Jesuits".
The chapel was destroyed during the Revolution, but then rebuilt on what was supposed to have been its original site at 11, rue Yvonne-le-Tac.

Cocteau Light Fittings
The Cinema Studio 28, which opened at 10, rue Tholozé in 1928, is the oldest cinema in Paris that is still in operation. The light fittings in the main cinema were designed by Jean Cocteau.

Ceramic decoration at 43bis, rue Damrémont ⑥

Building accessible Monday to Friday, 9am–6.30pm
Keypad-operated gate closed at weekends and public holidays

Built in 1910 by Coinchon, this has an entrance adorned with twelve wonderful faience panels separated by marble columns; these depict various children's games (skipping, snowballing, kite-flying, etc.) with the hill of Montmartre visible in the background. Mainly the work of Francisque Poulbot, these mosaics date from 1910 and are now listed as historic monuments.

NEARBY
Les fusains ⑦
22, rue de Tourlaque

Unfortunately – because of the theft of some statues from the interior garden – this has for some years been shut. Undoubtedly the most attractive of all the city's various housing/studio developments for artists, Les Fusains was constructed using material salvaged from the 1889 Universal Exhibition. Residents have included artists such as Renoir and Derain.

Saint Denis and street names in Montmartre

Halfway along rue Girardon a plaque recalls the legend that, after being decapitated upon the hill that would subsequently be known as Mont des Martyres (Hill of Martyrs), St Denis picked up his head and then walked to the spot where he would actually be buried, some 8 km away (the site of the basilica that bears his name). A little further up, not far from place du Tertre, rue Rustique and rue Saint-Éleuthère are named after the two deacons who preached Christianity alongside St Denis.

The real origin of the word "bistro"

The plaque on the façade of the restaurant *La Mère Catherine* in place du Tertre, Montmartre, gives an often-repeated explanation of the origin of the word "bistro": "On 30 March 1814 the Cossacks shouted their famous 'bistro', and thus on the hill of Montmartre was created a worthy ancestor to our own bistros. 180ᵗʰ Anniversary. The Old Montmartre Association". True, "bistro" does mean "quick, fast" in Russian, but the story of impatient Cossacks ordering their drinks appears to be nothing other than a pleasant anecdote; the real origin of the word seems to be local slang.

PISCINE DES AMIRAUX

A pyramid of subsidised housing, containing a swimming pool

6, rue Hermann-Lachapelle and 13, rue des Amiraux
Métro: Simplon or Marcadet-Poissonniers
Opening hours: Monday 5pm–8pm; Tuesday 7am–8.30am, 11.30am–1pm
and 4.30pm–6.30pm; Wednesday 7am–8.30am and 11.30am–6pm; Thursday
7am–8.30am and 11.30am–1.30pm; Friday 7am–8.30am, 11.30am–1.30pm
and 4.30pm–7pm; Saturday 7am–6pm; Sunday 8am–6pm • Admission: €3.00
(€1.70 for Parisians under 26; free for unemployed Paris residents)

The Amiraux swimming pool is a perfect example of the "hygienist" notions behind subsidised public housing at the beginning of the 20th century. Built as part of a public-housing scheme commissioned by the City Council's HBM (Office of Affordable Housing), the structure was designed by the architect Henri Sauvage. Seven storeys high, the building itself is a pyramid of stepped terraces, which means that each apartment enjoys natural light and has a garden balcony. The architect had initially intended that the centre of the pyramid be occupied by a cinema, but the city council opted instead for a swimming pool. Work began in 1922, and the first tenants began to move in in 1925; the swimming pool itself opened in 1930. The facility has been renovated several times and is now a listed building. The pool measures 33 m x 10 m and has two levels of walkways leading to the individual changing-rooms. Inside and outside, the walls are faced with the same white ceramic tiles as used in the métro, which adds to the "Old Paris" feel of the place; the slightly retro atmosphere here was exploited by the film maker Jean-Pierre Jeunet when he chose Amiraux swimming pool as the setting for a scene in his film *Le Fabuleux destin d'Amélie Poulain*.

In the 6th *arrondissement* (rue Vavin) is another building by Henri Sauvage which uses the same principle of tiered terraces (see page 113).

A mass in Aramaic, the language Christ spoke

Every Sunday at 11.00, the Chaldean Mission (13–15, rue Pajol) celebrates a Mass in Aramaic, the language Christ spoke. The Chaldean Catholic rite dates back to 16th-century Turkey.
For information: 01 42 09 55 07.

The Largest Community of Artists in Europe
Montmartre aux Artistes 187–189, rue Ordener

With its 184 studios, Montmartre aux Artistes is the largest community of artists in Europe. It dates back to the first half of the 20th century and was the idea of Louis Lejeune (1884–1969), winner of the *Prix de Rome* for sculpture in 1911. The first residents began to move in in 1933, when the project was far from completed. Access to the area is relatively easy, and you can stroll among the various structures. The studios themselves, however, are not open to the public.

NEARBY

◀ *Mosaics in the rue Ramey fishmonger's* ⑨

The fishmonger's at the corner of rue Ramey and rue du Baigneur is decorated with fine mosaics which, appropriately enough, depict a fishing scene.

An uncultivated garden at Saint-Vincent ⑩

17, rue Saint-Vincent
From 1 April to 20 October, open Saturday 10am–12.30pm and 1.30pm–6.30pm
(6pm in October) • Tel.: 01 71 28 50 56

For a long time this site of 1,500 m² was just wasteland, gradually becoming overgrown with weeds and shrubs that then attracted various kinds of wildlife. The landscape architects of Paris City Council saw this as a perfect opportunity to maintain rare examples of flora and fauna within the very heart of Montmartre. To preserve the biodiversity here, they simply consolidated the sloping terrain, created a small pond and laid out a path for strollers to visit the garden without causing any damage. The result is wonderful.

Ceramic decoration at 59, rue Caulaincourt ⑪

The entrance to this private building is decorated with fine ceramics of young female figures: one is shown at the seaside, another among vines, and yet others holding a watering-can or an umbrella. Beyond the entrance is an attractive little garden.

CALVAIRE CEMETERY

A cemetery that opens one day a year

2, rue Mont-Cenis
Métro: Abbesses
Open to the public on All Saints Day (1 November) and during the Journées du
Patrimoine *and the* Journées des Jardins
Apply to the Conservation du Cimetière Montmartre (01 53 42 36 30)

ocated alongside the Montmartre church of Saint-Pierre, this is the most unusual cemetery in Paris; it is only open on All Saints Day. The cemetery owes its name to the fact that it stands alongside a "Calvary" erected in 1833 around the church of Saint-Pierre which it served (see below). It was laid out in 1801 to replace an earlier cemetery that had been destroyed during the Revolution (taking the date of the creation of a cemetery to be that of the first individual tombs and not of unmarked graves on the site, that first cemetery dated from 1688). Though opened three years before Père-Lachaise, this is not – as many believe – the oldest cemetery in Paris; the cemetery of the Portuguese Jewish community in the 19ᵗʰ *arrondissement* dates from 1780 (see page 349).

Following the creation of the Saint-Vincent cemetery, the Calvaire cemetery was closed temporarily in 1823, then finally in 1831 (there were some burials here in 1828, 1830 and 1831). Now it contains a total of eighty-five very simple tombs, death apparently erasing all differences between the aristocrats of Bas-Montmartre (the present 11ᵗʰ *arrondissement*) and the humble families of Haut-Montmartre. One of the famous figures buried here is the navigator Bougainville. Contrary to legend, d'Artagnan is not buried here; Pigalle, the sculptor, was buried here but his tomb was another victim of the Revolution.

NEARBY

Montmartre Calvary ⑬

2, rue Mont-Cenis
Open on the parish feast day in June
Tel.: 01 46 06 57 63

Built in 1833 at the behest of the parish priest, Abbé Ottin, the Montmartre Calvary is a Via Crucis that commemorates Christ's Passion. It is one of the most unusual – and secret – places in the city and has a total of nine "Stations of the Cross" together with an artificial grotto that serves as the Holy Sepulchre (the tomb from which Christ emerged at his resurrection). Despite the indulgences granted by the pope, the Calvary did not attract many pilgrims and the abbé had to abandon religious services here. The construction of the Church of Sacré-Coeur later ate into the site, and two of the Stations of the Cross had to be moved.

Far from the Madding Crowd:
Strolling in Montmartre

While the summit itself can be unbearable when swarming with tourists, there is a more picturesque part of the hill which is still spared invasion by the crowds. Let us start at the charming métro station of Lamarck-Caulaincourt, from which steps lead up to avenue Junot, one of the finest in Paris.

At **No. 15** is the house that the Austrian architect Adolf Loos (1870–1933) built in 1926 for the Dadaist poet **Tristan Tzara**; it is a perfect expression of the architect's abhorrence of all forms of ornamental decoration. At No. 23, **Villa Léandre** is named after the local humorist, Charles Léandre; the low, Anglo-Norman-style brick houses are covered in climbing vines and the whole place is wonderfully charming. Note the door of No. 4 at the end, which is inspired by the sails of a windmill, once a common feature on the hill of Montmartre. At 21, avenue Junot, **passage Lepic-Junot** (sometimes referred to as passage de la Sorcière) cuts right through the heart of the *maquis de Montmartre* [the scrubland that once occupied this site]. A large stone still juts out right in the middle of the road; there is also a *petanque* court. This is reserved for members, but a polite request will get you something to drink at the bar, which you can then sip while enjoying the spectacle of a game of *boules*. From the passage, turn left into rue Lepic. Almost immediately on your left you will catch sight of La Gallette windmill, which is one of the last two in Paris.

Walking up the avenue on your left, you are back in avenue Junot, where No. 1 is one of the finest private residences in Paris. Untill a few years ago, the presence here of the *mire du Nord*, a listed monument (see page 275), meant that you could gain access to this fantastic place of climbing vines, where rabbits scurry around at the foot of La Galette windmill. The small theatre in front of the entrance to the house has two-seater sofas for couples ...

A little further on, at **11, avenue Junot**, you can peek into the **hameau des Artistes** that links the avenue to rue Lepic (No. 75); the keypad-operated gate is generally closed. Retracing your steps to the beginning of avenue Junot, you come to **place Marcel-Aymé**, which has an amusing statue of a man walking through a wall; this was placed here in homage to Aymé's novel *Le passe-muraille*, about a man who could do just that. Going down rue de l'Abreuvoir, on the right is a large uncultivated garden that serves as the setting for a few houses and artists' studios. This is a sort of Villa Medici within Paris itself: for very modest rents, foreign artists can have the use of studios of 60 m² to 100 m² for an entire year. The place is not open to the public. Slightly further down is **place Dalida**, with superb views towards Sacré-Coeur – probably the most picturesque views in Paris. If you want the statue of the famous *chanteuse* to acquire the smooth patina of Juliet's statue in Verona, then you are advised to briefly fondle her shapely breasts before turning right, up towards the vines. The métro station is close by.

The doors at 45, rue Lepic do not open into a building but onto a private road lined with studios for artists and craftworkers.

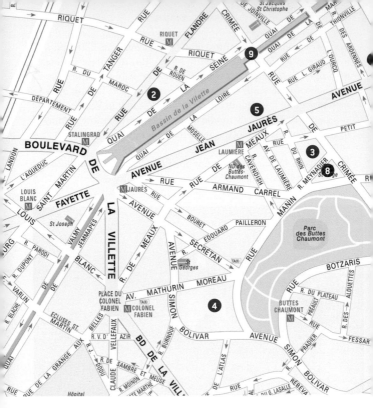

19th Arrondissement

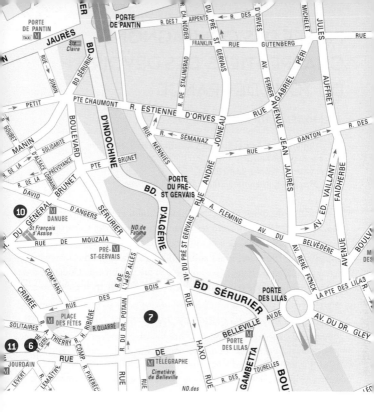

MUSÉE DES COMPAGNONS CHARPENTIERS DES DEVOIRS DU TOUR DE FRANCE

The journeymen's masterpieces

Entry through Aux Arts et Sciences Réunies *restaurant*
161, avenue Jean-Jaurès
Métro: Ourcq • Tel.: 01 42 40 53 18
Open by request, when the restaurant staff have time...

Located in the oldest journeymen's guild building in Europe, at the rear of *Aux Arts et Sciences Réunis* restaurant, the Musée des Compagnons notably possesses the collection of journeymen's masterpieces that were put on display at the 1900 Universal Exhibition held in Paris. Journeymen who undertake the Tour de France (see box below) are still provided lodgings today on the premises of the restaurant, which was originally their guild canteen.

The journeymen's guild: improvement throught work

According to oral tradition, the origins of journeymen's guilds date back to the era when Solomon's temple was being built in Jerusalem (10th century BC) and several accurate documents attest to the existence of journeymen's associations, more or less in their present form, during the Middle Ages. Contrary to common belief, the guilds still exist today. Only carefully selected craftsmen meeting rigorous professional and moral standards are admitted to the order. The candidate, sponsored by a member, must complete his apprenticeship (usually lasting three years). He then goes out on a Tour de France, staying at various "*cayennes*" (meeting halls offering hospitality to journeymen) for a period of five to seven years, while continuing his training before finally presenting a masterpiece, a work that demonstrates his acquired skills and mastery of his craft. This long journey, forming part of the guild's seven fundamental precepts (hospitality, journeying, craftsmanship, community, transmission, initiation and masterpiece), has only one aim: to provide training, in a fraternal spirit, to craftsmen whose ideal is to improve themselves through work. As proof of the quality of their labour, journeymen are called upon to restore some of the most beautiful buildings belonging to France's heritage, receive the award for "Best Worker in France", or are employed by the most prestigious firms. The journeymen have no connection with Freemasonry, despite the similarities of some of their symbols (in particular, the set square and compass). Freemasons simply took over and used certain symbols that had already been adopted by the journeymen's guilds.

PORTUGUESE JEWISH CEMETERY ②

A cemetery among the low-income housing blocks

44, avenue de Flandre
Métro: Stalingrad or Riquet
Consistoire Israélite de France
17, rue Saint-Georges • Métro: Notre-Dame-de-Lorette
Jacques B'Chiri: 01 40 82 26 90 – 06 09 21 15 04

If it was not for the discreet historical information sign, nothing would indicate that behind the imposing building at No. 44, avenue de Flandre is a cemetery measuring 35 m by 10 m. Surrounded by apartment buildings, this plot of land is home to a dozen tombstones and two sarcophagi, bearing some inscriptions that are still legible despite the ravages of time. The history of this cemetery bears witness to the ostracism suffered by the Jewish community under the Ancien Régime: along with Protestants, actors, and suicides, Jews were not allowed to be buried in cemeteries. But a certain Carnot, owner of the Étoile inn, located at the spot where No. 46, avenue de Flandre now stands, gave permission in 1691 for Jews to bury their dead here, on condition that they did so in secret and in return for payment: 50 francs for an adult, 20 francs for a child.

In 1780, the Sephardic Jewish community originating in Portugal bought two adjoining gardens and opened the Portuguese Jewish cemetery. This initiative was led by Jacob Rodriguez Pereire, agent for the Portuguese Jewish émigrés living in Paris, who had obtained a stipend from Louis XV for organising the education of the deaf and dumb. The burials were then allowed by the king, as long as they took place "nocturnally, without fuss or ceremony". The cemetery was finally abandoned in 1810, Napoleon having opened all the cemeteries to the Jewish community. Today listed as a historic monument, the cemetery is looked after by the Consistoire Israélite de France. To visit, arrange an appointment at the Consistoire, where the Hévra Kadicha (final duty) service will lend you the keys to the cemetery, to be returned afterwards.

La Villette rotunda, built in 1790, is one of four Parisian pavilions belonging to the city's former *barrière d'octroi* (tax barrier) that still remain standing. You can also see the barriers of Chartres (in parc Monceau), Le Trône (at Nation), and Enfer (place Denfert-Rochereau) (see page 321).

Masons at 97bis, rue de Crimée ③

An astonishing façade at No. 97bis, rue de Crimée, where the usual classical atlantes have been replaced by masons depicted at work on the building itself.

NEARBY

Butte Bergeyre: an island in the midst of the city

Rues Georges-Lardennois, Remy-de-Gourmont, Edgar-Poe, Philippe-Hecht,
Barrelet-de-Ricou

Built around 1927 on the former site of an amusement park ("Les Folles Buttes"), the Butte Bergeyre is like an island in the very midst of the city: almost invisible from the street, it is tucked away on a hill located between rues Simon-Bolivar, Manin, and Mathurin-Moreau. The presence of nearby quarries prevented dense urban development, and one finds pretty houses, some vine plantings, and a garden shared by residents who are well aware how lucky they are and anxious to preserve their tranquility 90 m above the surrounding chaos …

Jean-Jaurès Gymnasium ⑤

87, avenue Jean-Jaurès • Tel.: 01 42 08 57 11 • Open daily 7am–11pm

Take the time to ask at the reception for permission (readily granted) to have a look at this very beautiful gymnasium. This was built reusing a metal framework from the Galerie des Machines at the Universal Exhibition of 1878, like the famous Y hangar at Meudon (see our guide, *Banlieue de Paris insolite et secrète*). It was enlarged in 1913 by the architect Gautier and took the name of Gymnase Allemagne (German gymnasium), which it lost after the First World War, as did rue d'Allemagne, which became avenue Jean-Jaurès.

13, rue des Fêtes ⑥

Access usually restricted by a digital code panel

Nearby the concrete expanse of the place des Fêtes, rue des Fêtes conceals, at no. 13, a heavenly little garden-city built at the beginning of the 20ᵗʰ century on the grounds of a private townhouse that still stands at No. 11. Access is by a narrow passage that leads to a series of delightful detached dwellings surrounded by greenery. To be able to enjoy the arbour, the flower-filled terraces, the trees and the village-like atmosphere, it is probably best to visit during one of the "open workshop" days held in the Belleville neighbourhood: this place is now home to many artists. Otherwise, the gate is usually kept locked by a code panel.

Rues Émile-Desvaux and Paul-de-Kock

Rue Paul-de-Kock is closely connected to rue Émile-Desvaux as it starts at No. 4 of the latter and ends in a cul-de-sac at a flight of steps located at No. 30 on the same street… Together, they form a disparate grouping of houses dating from the 1920s by no means lacking in charm.

Shared Gardens

Promoted by the local Green Party, communal gardens have been adopted with extraordinary enthusiasm by Parisians. They not only satisfy residents' need for greenery, but also permit neighbours to develop ties with one another and even encourage the mixing of social classes. The 19th is the Paris *arrondissement* where such gardens have developed furthest, no doubt thanks to the dynamism of Espace 19, the association that manages the local social centres, but also looks after the many vacant lots that are widespread in this underprivileged corner of the city.

Existing shared gardens in the 19th *arrondissement*:
11, quai de l'Oise and 5, rue d'Argonne (P'tit Bol d'Air)
La Serre aux Légumes, 57, avenue de Flandre
La Butte Bergeyre
Le potager de Tanger-Maroc, 49ter, avenue de Flandre
La charmante petite campagne urbaine, rue de la Marne
18, rue Léon-Giraud
150, boulevard de la Villette
L'ilôt Lilas, 295, rue de Belleville
26, rue de Tanger.
In other arrondissements:
Potager des Oiseaux (3rd *arrondissement*, see page 60)
Jardin Catherine-Labouré (7th)
Jardin du passage Hébrard (10th)
Jardin nomade, 48, rue Trousseau (11th)
L'Aligresse, 41, impasse Druinot (12th, see page 229)
122, boulevard de l'Hôpital (13th)
Square Bédier-Boutroux (13th)
Square Auguste-Renoir (14th)
Square du Chanoine-Viollet (14th)
ZAC Alésia–Montsouris, rue Thomas-Francine (14th)
Rue de la Manutention (16th, see page 315)
Jardin CEFIA, 183, avenue de Clichy (17th, see page 325)
Jardins du Ruisseau, rue du Ruisseau/rue Bélliard (18th)
Eco Box, 22, rue Pajol (18th)
14–16, rue du Clos (20th)
3–5, rue Gasnier-Guy (20th)

How to create a shared garden

First you need to set up an association with your neighbours, and then contact the Cellule Main Verte within the Direction des Parcs, Jardins et Espaces Verts at your local *mairie d'arrondissement*.
For advice, contact Connaître et Protéger la Nature (CPN–Val de Seine): 01 42 22 43 46 or Gestion des Jardins Partagés Parisiens – Cellule Main Verte (Ville de Paris): 01 49 57 10 41.

CHURCH OF
SAINT-SERGE-DE-RADOGÈNE

An extraordinary Orthodox church hidden at the top of a mound

93, rue de Crimée
Métro: Laumière or Ourcq
Tel.: 09 51 32 01 66
Vespers Saturdays 6pm–8pm, Mass Sundays 10am–12pm

Concealed behind the gate at 93, rue de Crimée, perched at the top of a mound and screened by a row of trees at the end of a lane, the church of Saint-Serge-de-Radogène is perhaps one of the most charming churches in Paris.

Strange and exotic, the church has been through two histories under two different religions. Built in 1861 in the southern neighbourhood of Buttes-Chaumont at the initiative of the Lutheran pastor serving the émigré community of German workers in France, it was devoted to Protestantism until the declaration of war in 1914 forced German workers to return to their country. Confiscated by the French government, it remained abandoned until 1924, when it was bought by the Russian Orthodox Church and the Russian community that had fled the Bolshevik revolution. This change of use required some architectural modifications, as the Protestants did not indulge in much decoration or religious representations… A wooden stairway was added in order to allow direct access from the exterior to the storey where the church is situated. It was decorated with frescoes created by Dimitri Stelletsky portraying the holy fathers of the Orthodox faith. The doors on the ground floor as well as the upper storey were also painted with magnificent religious scenes, and the north side of the building received a carillon with a traditional Russian arcature.

The biggest surprise, however, occurs when you discover the interior of the church: submerged in the inevitable scent of wax and incense, you will behold, among the shadows of the walls entirely covered with more frescoes, a most remarkable iconostasis including more than a hundred icons, and a set of royal doors, authentic works made by the Moscow School from the 16th century. Magical.

NEARBY

Crimée bridge: the last drawbridge in Paris ⑨

End of La Villette basin, beginning of the Ourcq canal
Operates 24 hours per day, seven days per week

Built in 1885 by the same company that installed the lifts in the Eiffel Tower, the Crimée bridge, also called the pont de Flandres, is the last drawbridge in Paris: when boats are passing through, its articulated wheels mounted on Greek columns acting as racks literally lift up the roadbed. To view this spectacle of industrial history, pedestrians can use the nearby walkway, which is a convenient height.

LA MOUZAÏA

The American quarries

Neighbourhood within the loop on the 7bis métro line
Métro: Danube

If people in love with La Mouzaïa don't all share the same exact definition of the perimeter occupied by this very peculiar neighbourhood in the 19ᵗʰ *arrondissement*, they do agree on its extraordinary charms. More or less delimited by the Botzaris, Danube, Pré Saint-Gervais, and place des Fêtes métro stations, the neighbourhood has an exotic name that recalls Algeria, but its sights and scents are those of a provincial French village.

This very appealing belvedere was annexed by the city of Paris in 1860. The ground is as full of holes as Gruyère cheese, due to the presence of gypsum quarries that were mined until 1872. Some say that both the White House in Washington and the Statue of Liberty were built with gypsum extracted here (which would explain why the neighbourhood was for a time called "Les carrières d'Amérique", as one of the streets still reminds us). But it seems that this romantic story has no basis in fact.

On the other hand, the quarry does account for the fragility of the terrain that prevents any large-scale property development schemes from being carried out here: following an attempt to set up a horse-trading market, the area was finally given over to the building of detached individual dwellings with simple architectural plans (a ground floor topped by a single storey). Usually possessing both a front garden and a back yard, these dwellings are spread out on both sides of some twenty different lanes. The gradual completion of this project (which took nearly four decades) allowed a certain diversity of architectural styles to emerge in these houses. Originally intended for working-class families, today they are enjoyed by the privileged few.

NEARBY
Cité du Palais-Royal-de-Belleville ⑪
151, rue de Belleville
Hidden behind two successive courtyards, the cité du Palais-Royal-de-Belleville is a superb group of pretty low-rise houses standing on either side of a quiet tree-lined lane, once typical of the highly dispersed dwellings occupied by the working classes in Belleville. According to residents, the pompous name of this settlement comes from the fact that the sets for the Palais-Royal theatre used to be stored here.

Not far from here, at No. 13, rue de la Villette, the Villa de l'Adour, opened in 1817 under the name of Villa Barthélemy, is in another charming cul-de-sac.

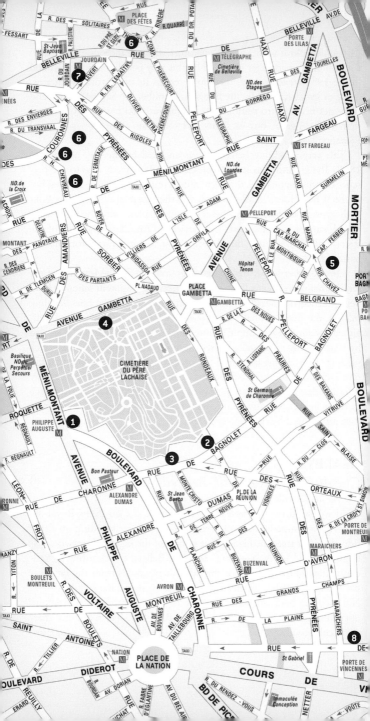

20th Arrondissement

KITCHEN GARDENS

A restful kitchen garden

8, rue du Repos

The residents at No. 8, rue du Repos have the incredible luck of possessing one of the most surprising green spaces in Paris. After crossing a first inner courtyard, a second opens onto a hallway that leads to an extraordinary kitchen garden lying at the foot of the wall of Père-Lachaise cemetery, which contains a dozen private plots. Everything needed is here, buckets for watering the plants, rakes, and even a scarecrow to ward off the crows from the cemetery on the other side of the wall.

Be tactful: this place is private and off limits to the general public. The only means of entering is to ask permission from one of the building's residents, as an exceptional favour.

Grapevines in Paris

The Paris region has an ancient winemaking tradition, which gradually declined in the face of the population increase, urban development, the phylloxera blight, and competition by wines from other regions. There are nevertheless traces of this past in street names: rue du Pressoir (winepress), rue des Vignes (grapevines), rue des Vignoles, rue Vineuse … The "Goutte d'Or" (golden drop) neighbourhood also owes its name to a wine produced there during the Middle Ages, while the "*guinguet*" of Belleville lent its name to the popular *guinguettes*, or open-air restaurants, on the banks of the Marne river. In addition to the famous clos Montmartre, today grapevines still grow in other parts of the French capital:

• Square Félix-Desruelles, 168bis, boulevard Saint-Germain (Saint-Germain-des-Prés church) – twelve vine stocks planted in 1993
• Garden of the presbytery of Saint-François-Xavier church (see page 147)
• In rue Blanche fire station (9th *arrondissement*, see page 185)
• In the cellar of Jacques Mélac wine bar (9th)
• At parc de Bercy (12th)
• At parc Georges-Brassens (15th)
• In the mairie of the 16th *arrondissement*
• Jardin du Trocadéro, beneath the Musée de l'Homme (16th)
• At parc de Bagatelle (16th)
• Rue Georges Lardennois (19th) – 200 vine stocks planted
• At jardin de Belleville (200 vine stocks)

THE NATURAL GARDEN

Wild weeds in the heart of Paris

120, rue de la Réunion
Métro: Alexandre-Dumas
Open from 8am until sunset on weekdays, from 9am until sunset on weekends and holidays
Information and bookings 01 43 28 47 63

At the very end of rue de La Réunion, at the foot of the Père-Lachaise cemetery, there is a small public garden unlike any other. Here, one does not find expert floral compositions or carefully mowed lawns: this na-

tural garden (like the jardin Saint-Vincent in Montmartre) is a free space where plants take root spontaneously, where both flora and fauna express themselves without human interference, and where both watering and mowing are banned. Since the garden was created, the people responsible for its upkeep have tended to observe the evolution of life therein rather than maintain it artificially. The garden pond is full of newts and tadpoles that swim peacefully among the irises and water mint. Information panels scattered through undergrowth, trellises and lawn offer details about the animal and plant species to be found in each part of the garden.

NEARBY

Villa Riberolle, Villa Godin and Cité Aubry ③

Just a few steps away from the natural garden there are other spaces to inspire souls in search of rural surroundings: Cité Aubry is a charming little passage following a curved path leading to an alternative cultural venue, the Goumen Bis. A little further on, at No. 35, rue de Bagnolet, Villa Riberolle is one of the most appealing sights in the neighbourhood (easy access on weekdays, but the gate is closed at weekends). It is also worth making a slight detour to see rue de Lesseps in order to take in its charms, without forgetting, nearby, the very pleasant Villa Godin with its maisonettes and gardens on either side of the paved lane.

Parisian heights

Montmartre: 130 m. The highest point in Paris
Belleville: 128.5 m. Highest point in east Paris at No. 40, rue du Télégraphe*
Ménilmontant: 108 m.
Buttes-Chaumont: 80 m.
Passy: 71 m.
Chaillot: 67 m.
Montparnasse: 66 m.
Buttes-aux-Cailles: 62 m.
Montagne Sainte-Geneviève: 61 m.

* Making use of the height of Belleville hill (as a plaque to the right of the entrance to the cemetery recalls), Claude Chappe experimented here with his telegraph system between 1792–1793. At first, the inhabitants of the neighbourhood thought that he was attempting to send secret messages to the French royal family, who were imprisoned in the Temple gaol at the time. Chappe owed his life to a quick flight, after destroying his installations in a fit of rage. The names of the street and the métro station nearby bear witness to his exploits.

LE MUR DES FÉDÉRÉS: GHOSTS OF THE PARIS COMMUNE

A ghostly wall

Square Samuel-Champlain
Métro: Gambetta

Alongside Père-Lachaise cemetery, square Samuel-Champlain has a wall that is both strange and striking in its realism: sculpted in the rock, ghostly faces struggle to emerge. One sees a worker, a priest, a *fédéré* (a member of the Communard militia), and a mother holding her child. Bullet holes surround these silhouettes.

Built in 1909 by Paul Moreau-Vautier (1871–1936), the wall is a monument dedicated to the victims of revolutions and was constructed using stones from the wall where the last Communards were shot.

That original wall is located within the grounds of the cemetery itself. A plaque recalls this bloody episode during which almost 2000 Communards were massacred.

The Paris Commune defined a revolutionary period in the French capital which lasted seventy-two days between March and May 1871. As was the case in many other cities in France (Marseille, Lyon, Saint-Étienne, Toulouse, Narbonne, Grenoble and Limoges), following the nation's defeat in the war against Prussia, insurgents rebelled against the government set up by Thiers at Versailles. They attempted to found workers' communes and proletarian rule.

Plaque in rue Stendhal

At Charonne, the plaque indicating rue Stendhal curiously calls the famous writer a "*littérateur*" (hack). Merely a question of taste on the part of the town councillors at the time?

NEARBY

La Campagne à Paris   ⑤

Rues Irénée-Blanc, Jules-Siegfried, Paul-Strauss and surroundings
Métro: Porte-de-Bagnolet

Located at an altitude of 100 m and just a short distance from the Périphérique motorway, "La Campagne à Paris" (The Countryside in Paris) is a small Parisian neighbourhood that fully deserves its name. Like La Mouzaïa in the 19th *arrondissement* (see page 357), the ground on which it lies is full of gypsum quarries and unstable, preventing the construction of buildings whose weight would overburden the fragile foundations. The streets bordering the dwellings bear the names of the community's founders: at the beginning of the 20th century, Jules Siegfried, Paul Strauss and Irénée Blanc (president) together decided to form a housing association and build small individual homes reserved for the poor. In all, eighty-five such houses were constructed, each with their own small garden. The official inauguration took place in 1926.

Water, source of many streets names

The history of water in the east of Paris has left numerous traces in the city's toponymy: the rues des Cascades, des Rigoles [brooks], de la Mare [pond], de la Duée [an ancient word for spring], des Savies [another word for spring] all derive their names directly from water usage.

Why does tap water taste different in different neighbourhoods?

Today, spring water still supplies half of the city's drinking water. These springs have differing mineral contents according to their geographical origin, so tap water inevitably varies in quality and taste depending on the neighbourhood.

What is a regard*?*

In order to preserve the purity of spring water until it reached its final destination, several dry stone structures were built, extending underground to the water reservoirs. These were located in buildings that were soon nicknamed "*regards*" [peepholes], because they permitted one to keep an eye on the state of the conduits carrying the city's water.

Belleville: an almost unique geographical feature

While presiding over a great burst of urban development in the 19th century, the prefect of Paris, Baron Haussmann, cut Belleville in two. It is for this reason that the borders of the 10th, 11th, 19th and 20th *arrondissements* all come together at a single point, just like the American states of New Mexico, Arizona, Colorado and Utah, or the French departments of Alpes-de-Haute-Provence, Vaucluse, Bouches-du-Rhône and Var (see our guide *Secret Provence*).

REGARDS IN EAST PARIS ⑥

Anachronistic regards

17, rue des Cascades (Regard des Messiers)
42, rue des Cascades (Regard Saint-Martin)
36–38, rue de la Mare (Regard de la Roquette)
213, rue de Belleville (Regard de la Lanterne – 16th century)

From the 12ᵗʰ century, in order to keep Paris supplied with drinking water, springs on the Belleville plateau were tapped. Although today these have dried up, four Parisian "*regards*" (peepholes – see opposite), anachronistic vestiges of a bygone era, still stand before time and the curiosity of Parisians. Some of them bear the names of the religious congregations that built them: the Regard Saint-Martin helped to supply water to the Saint-Martin-des-Champs abbey, while the Regard de la Roquette performed a similar role for both La Roquette convent and Saint-Antoine-des-Champs. The Regard de la Lanterne owes its name to the lantern turret that decorates its top and the Regard des Messiers is derived from the names of the guards who watched over the crops before harvest (see map). Another *regard* of the same type exists at Pré-Saint-Gervais (see our guide, *Banlieue de Paris insolite et secrète*).

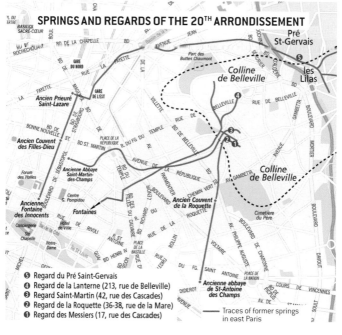

SPRINGS AND REGARDS OF THE 20ᵀᴴ ARRONDISSEMENT

⑤ Regard du Pré Saint-Gervais
④ Regard de la Lanterne (213, rue de Belleville)
③ Regard Saint-Martin (42, rue des Cascades)
② Regard de la Roquette (36-38, rue de la Mare)
① Regard des Messiers (17, rue des Cascades)

—— Traces of former springs in east Paris

SUPPLY OF DRINKING WATER TO PARIS

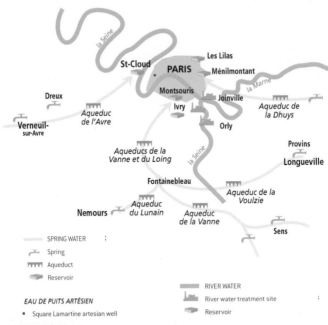

Les Lilas
St-Cloud
PARIS
Ménilmontant
la Seine
Dreux
Montsouris
Joinville
la Marne
Aqueduc de
la Dhuys
Ivry
Verneuil-
sur-Avre
Aqueduc
de l'Avre
Orly
Provins
Aqueducs de la
Vanne et du Loing
la Seine
Longueville
Fontainebleau
Aqueduc de la
Voulzie
Nemours
Aqueduc
du Lunain
Aqueduc
de la Vanne
Sens

SPRING WATER

Spring

Aqueduct

Reservoir

EAU DE PUITS ARTÉSIEN

- Square Lamartine artesian well

RIVER WATER

River water treatment site

Reservoir

Supplying Paris with water: a complex and varied network

The city of Paris is today supplied with drinking water in three different ways: from rivers and streams, from groundwater (artesian wells, see page 307), and spring water.

– **Rivers and streams** (Seine and Marne). This water is today treated by three plants located at Orly, Ivry, and Joinville. Before modern filtering methods were invented, river water was the simplest means for Parisians to find drinking water. This water, polluted by tanners, butchers and dyers, among others, was in fact not really suitable for human consumption. Under Napoleon I , the construction of the Ourcq canal and La Villette basin provided a new source of water for the northern part of the city. The water was then carried to the west by means of an aqueduct encircling Paris from La Villette to Monceau.

– **Wells** extracting groundwater provide water of a better quality. At the beginning, these wells were not very deep (4 m to 5 m), but since the streets were not always paved, pollution easily seeped in and also rendered this water unfit for consumption. In the 19ᵗʰ century, artesian wells tapped water at depths reaching 600 m, thus resolving the problem of surface pollution. But due to problems of flow (see page 307), only the Lamartine well still operates today.

– The third solution was to tap **spring water** and carry it to Paris by means of spectacular aqueducts. The first were the Gallo-Roman aqueducts: one of these collected water from Rungis (see page 265) and another from Belleville. Between the 12ᵗʰ and 14ᵗʰ centuries, the religious orders on the Right Bank tapped water from springs in eastern Paris (see map) and constructed underground aqueducts as well as the regards that can still be seen today (see page 367). A little later, Marie de Médicis ordered the building of the famous Médicis aqueduct (see page 265) in the south of Paris. As anachronistic as it must seem, these aqueducts are still being used in the 21ˢᵗ century. Today, five main aqueducts carry spring water towards Paris: La Vanne aqueduct (built on the same route as the former Médicis aqueduct that passes by Arcueil), Le Loing, Le Lunain and La Voulzie aqueducts which also run to the south, and L'Avre aqueduct to the west. To the northeast, a sixth aqueduct, La Dhuis, carries 20,000 m³ of water per day (about 5% of the total supply) over 131 km. The principle of the aqueduct is quite simple: means of the difference in levels between the point of origin and the point of arrival, to carry water wherever it is needed.

Today, almost half of Parisian water comes from springs. The city's drinking water, whether it comes from rivers and streams, or from springs, is held in five reservoirs: Les Lilas, Ménilmontant, Montsouris, Ivry and Saint Cloud. There are other reservoirs in Paris, but the water is not drinkable.

Country walks through the courtyards in the north of the 20th arrondissement

The northern part of the 20th *arrondissement* has managed to preserve a good part of its traditional habitat and is full of little-known corners of countryside and linked courtyards, most of which are totally invisible from the street.

18, rue de Belleville: after a courtyard and a hallway, you come across a row of workshops drowning in greenery.

23, rue Ramponeau (Forge de Belleville). A former key factory that was once illegally squatted by an artists' association (Arclefs) before being renovated by La Bellevilleuse association for use by artists (www.laforgedebelleville.fr)

38, rue de Belleville: a surprising series of four inner courtyards. Try following one of the residents inside.

Villa Castel, 16, rue du Transvaal: the provincial atmosphere of this site served as the setting for several scenes in the legendary film, *Jules et Jim*, directed by François Truffaut.

Cité Leroy, villa de l'Ermitage and cité de l'Ermitage: charming little streets bordered by pretty houses.

17, rue du Retrait: leave cité de l'Ermitage by the vaulted passage that comes out at No. 116, rue de Ménilmontant and go up this street to the crossing with rue de Retrait.

Cité du Palais-Royal-de-Belleville: 151, rue de Belleville. Officially, located in the 19th *arrondissement* (see page 357), but not to be missed.

Villa Olivier-Métra: 28, rue Olivier-Métra. A pretty private cul-de-sac accessible to discreet walkers, but closed at the far end by a mysterious iron gate.

Villa Georgina (from the name of an owner's daughter): a charming group of old detached houses and small gardens.

Villa du Borrégo: 33, rue du Borrégo. Pretty crooked houses surrounded by greenery alongside the Belleville reservoir.

NEARBY

African plants at No. 10, rue Du Jourdain ⑦

Dating from 1885, several buildings look out over a stretch of greenery which is in fact composed of African plants and grasses brought to Belleville by Senegalese riflemen who settled here after the end of the First World War.

The only level crossing in Paris ⑧

In a somewhat gloomy street in the 20th arrondissement, rue de Lagny, is the only level crossing in Paris, which lets trains from line 2 of the métro pass through on their way to be repaired or parked nearby.

NOTES

NOTES

NOTES

. . . .

. . . .

. . . .

. . . .

. . . .

. . . .

. . . .

. . . .

. . . .

. . . .

. . . .

. . . .

. . . .

. . . .

. . . .

. . . .

. . . .

. . . .

. . . .

. . . .